The History of
FRANCE

SIR WALTER SCOTT

TALES *of a* GRANDFATHER

The History of
FRANCE

(Second Series)

Edited by

William Baker and J. H. Alexander

NORTHERN ILLINOIS UNIVERSITY PRESS

DeKalb 1996

© 1996 by Northern Illinois University Press

Published by the Northern Illinois University Press, DeKalb, Illinois   60115

Manufactured in the United States using acid-free paper

Design by Julia Fauci

Scott, Walter, Sir, 1771–1832.

Tales of a grandfather : the history of France (second series) /
Walter Scott ; edited by William Baker and J. H. Alexander.

p.   cm.

Includes bibliographical references and index.

ISBN 0-87580-208-7 (alk. paper)

1. France—History. 2. France—Kings and rulers—History.

I. Baker, William, 1944—   . II. Alexander, J. H. (John H.)

III. Title.

DC61.S43   1996

944—dc20   95-47959

CIP

Contents

Acknowledgments   vii
Introduction   ix
Note on the Text   xxxi

Acknowledgments

The editors gratefully acknowledge the permissions of Patricia Maxwell-Scott and of the King's School, Canterbury, to publish this edited version of the manuscript of *Tales of a Grandfather; Being Stories Taken from the History of France—Second Series*. They are indebted for many kindnesses to David Goodes, formerly keeper of the Hugh Walpole Collection at the school, and they thank the librarian of Canterbury Cathedral, Sheila Hingley, and her staff for providing facilities for consulting the manuscript.

The editors further gratefully acknowledge grants-in-aid toward publication from the Carnegie Trust for the Universities of Scotland and from the University Studies Committee of the University of Aberdeen (Michael C. Meston), and a matching grant from the Deans' Fund for the Humanities Research of Northern Illinois University (Jerrold H. Zar, associate provost for graduate studies and research and dean of the Graduate School; and James D. Norris, former dean of the College of Liberal Arts and Sciences).

The editors thank the following for help in preparing the edition, in particular with the deciphering of exceptionally difficult passages in the manuscript: W. E. K. Anderson, P. D. Garside, Frank Jordan, Claire Lamont, D. S. Mack, Jane Millgate, Mark A. Weinstein, and G. A. M. Wood. For help and encouragement, thanks are also due to Mary Lincoln, director of the Northern Illinois University Press, and to the interlibrary loan department, Founders Memorial Library, Northern Illinois University (Toby Miller and her colleagues).

Introduction

WILLIAM BAKER *and* J. H. ALEXANDER

Here, published for the first time, is the fifth and final series of historical accounts (three of Scotland and two of France) that Sir Walter Scott
wrote in the final years of his life for his grandson Johnnie Lockhart. The
three Scottish *Grandfather* series were dated 1928, 1829, and 1830 (in each
case actually appearing in the preceding December), and the first French
series followed in 1831. The final series, dealing with the history of France
from Agincourt until the invasion of Italy by Louis XII a century later,
was left incomplete by Scott at his death in 1832 and never published.

In the spring of 1827, near to completing his massive *Life of Napoleon
Buonaparte,* Scott conceived the idea of writing a history of Scotland that
would match J. W. Croker's popular *Stories from the History of England for
Children* published a decade earlier. He would, however, adopt a signifi-
cantly different approach, as he explained to his friend and printer, James
Ballantyne:

> I will do something greatly better than Croker. It is a mistake to suppose you
> should be childish because you write to children. The language should be
> simple and being simple may be as energetic as if you were addressing a sen-
> ate. . . . I should wish it to be work written for children but [at] which if a
> man look he should be induced to read. I am not even sure that children do
> not like and are improved by something that is not so immediately compre-
> hended but finds exercize for their thoughts. To interest them is the point.[1]

On the day he wrote the last pages of *Napoleon* he entered into an agreement with the publisher Robert Cadell for a first edition of ten thousand
copies of *Tales of a Grandfather,* for which he would receive 750 guineas,
with a possible second edition on the same terms.[2] (The money would be
a welcome addition to his own funds rather than a contribution toward
paying off his creditors after his financial failure in 1826.)[3] Scott thought
of himself as creating the *Tales of a Grandfather* for his beloved, sickly six-
year-old grandson John Hugh Lockhart ("Hugh Littlejohn, Esq."). Writing
went ahead rapidly during the summer and early autumn, and by November 1827 the work in three volumes, terminating respectively with Bannockburn, Flodden, and the Union of the Crowns, was finished. It was
published in December and was immediately so successful that in January
1828 Scott was called on to furnish additional matter to bring the first

two volumes up to the length of the third for a revised edition (he insisted that the carefully calculated termination points of each volume should remain unchanged, "[h]appy points of pause which I cannot think of disturbing").[4] He followed up the success of the 1827 *Tales* with a second series—which appeared in November 1828, carrying the story more amply down to the Union of 1707—and a third series, marketed in December 1829, terminating on a still more ample scale with the events of 1745.[5] To avoid confusion, in this edition (apart from the title page) the plain terms "first," "second," and "third" series are reserved for the Scottish *Tales.* The first series of French *Tales,* and the incomplete second series presented here to the public for the first time, are referred to as the "fourth" and "fifth" series.

At the beginning of 1828 the idea had entered Scott's head that he might give up fiction and devote himself entirely to the writing of history for children:

> Nay—I will hash History with anybody, be he who he will. I do not know but it would be wise to let romantic composition rest and turn my mind to the History of England, France and Ireland to be *da capo rota'd* as well as that of Scotland. They would laugh at me as an author for Mr. Newberry's shop in Paul's Church Yard. I should care little for that. *Virginibus puerisque.* I would as soon compose histories for boys and girls which may be useful, as fictions for Children of a larger growth which can at best be only idle folk's entertainment.[6]

Scott was not to write histories of England or Ireland,[7] and he never gave up romantic fiction (in 1827 and 1828 he finished the two series of *Chronicles of the Canongate,* and in 1828–1829 *Anne of Geierstein*), but in 1830 he composed and published a fourth series of *Tales of a Grandfather,* covering the history of France from the earliest times to the end of the fourteenth century. The reading required for this series also fed into his work during that year on *Count Robert of Paris.*

Scott was widely encouraged to continue his *Tales,* as the reviews were almost entirely favorable for each of the first four series.[8] He himself had ended the fourth series with a promise: "I shall here close my Tales for the present, not unwilling to continue them, if they shall be thought as useful as those from the History of Scotland."[9] Immediately after publication of the fourth series Cadell referred to its "favourable reception" and went on: "You may most certainly put down a *Second Series* for Xmas 1831—I observe more than one response to your hint as to this at the Conclusion of the *First* Series."[10] Scott replied on 30 December with a commitment to the fifth (the second French) series:

> The Second series you shall certainly have if it will cover £200 or £300 at the term which however do not press. I think I will set to work to them unless Robert of Paris comes more readily than just now but I will try him first after the 6th.[11]

Cadell was genuinely enthusiastic about the proposal, which he included in his anticipatory list of projects for 1831 at the beginning of his diary for that year,[12] and on 3 January he offered what amounted to a contract for the new series:

> I beg of you, with reference to your letter of 30th. Decr. to act on the French Tales *Second Series* so as to suit your own comfort and convenience. . . . I do now offer you Eight Hundred pounds for the right to print Five thousand of a Second Series on French History to appear at Xmas 1831 &c. 3 Vols—with a right, as in the former Series to print ten thousand additional paying you at the same rate for the number printed. . . . The French Tales continue to move off very well, and are in every respect well received[.][13]

Twice during the year (apart from what he may have said to Scott when they were together) Cadell emphasized that Scott was not to overtax himself in his weak condition and that the French tales were to be regarded as almost a relaxation from his main work on *Count Robert of Paris* and *Castle Dangerous*. On 13 February he wrote:

> . . . it is presumptuous in me to lay down the law to you, but above all things do not over exert the mind when the body is under regimen, there is no call for your over-doing—Count Robert will do right well in April— then there is an occasional hour now and then to the Notes for the Magnum—or the next French Tales—*but all with slaving in noway*. We cannot have you long if you load yourself with work.[14]

And on 16 May he communicated in the same vein:

> By means of the Tales of a Grandfather and the notes to the Novels I have no doubt the Summer and Autumn will glide on very pleasantly for you so far as regards work. Pray think of it only as light work[.][15]

Scott evidently entered into the sprit of Cadell's plan, writing in his journal for 21 May: "As for my *Tales* they go on well and are amusing to myself at least. The history of France is very entertaining."[16] By 25 May he had completed the first volume, Cadell advising him "I would most decidedly say to you, continue at your own time and at your own leisure to finish the French Tales by adding Volume Second to the Volume you have already done."[17] On 12 June Scott wrote that "[t]he first & second volume of the Grandfathers tales will be ready to go to press when you like."[18] The first volume is indeed complete in the manuscript, but the second is only approximately half so, breaking off during Louis XII's Italian campaign in the second decade of the sixteenth century. What plans Scott had for the remainder of the second volume and the third are not known. He must have suspended his work on the fifth series to complete *Castle Dangerous* and *Count Robert of Paris* during July and August. In September he left

Scotland for the Malta voyage and returned only to die the following year. On 17 September 1831 Cadell noted at the end of his account of his conversations with Scott that "he . . . gave me a considerable portion of Tales of a Grandfather French History Second Series,"[19] but there is no reason to think that it was more than the one and a half volumes that we have today.

The fifth (second French) series of *Tales of a Grandfather* is one of the most substantial manuscripts by a major Romantic writer to survive unpublished. It has at least three claims on the attention of modern readers. It is, first of all, the final part of a significant contribution to the debate about and practice of writing for children. Second, although obviously imperfect and incomplete, it is a notable example of Scott's ability to organize complex material on a broad scale. And third, it is an important exhibit in the evidence for the interrelatedness of history and fiction in Scott's work, and, more generally, it exemplifies a powerful narrative vision informing the presentation of material largely derived from written historical sources. These three facets are interconnected, yet they may be commented on one by one to suggest the manner in which the three series making up the Scottish *Tales of a Grandfather* established the basic procedures and patterns Scott was to follow in the fourth and fifth series.

In his dedication of the first series to "Hugh Littlejohn, Esq." Scott openly confronted in print the issue we have seen him articulating in his letter of spring 1827 to James Ballantyne, that of the appropriate intellectual and stylistic level in writing for children. Alluding to Croker's 1817 collection he writes:

> I have in this little book imitated one with which you are well acquainted,—I mean the collection of Stories taken from the History of England, and which has been so deservedly popular.
>
> As you, however, happen to be a person of quick study, and great penetration, it is my purpose to write a little work, which may not only be useful to you at the age of five or six years, which I think may be about your worship's present period of life, but which may not be beneath your attention, either for style or matter, at the graver term of eight, or even ten years old. When, therefore, you find any thing a little too hard for you to understand at this moment, you must consider that you will be better able to make out the sense a year or two afterwards; or perhaps you may make a great exertion, and get at the meaning, just as you might contrive to reach something placed upon a high shelf, by standing on your tiptoes, instead of waiting till you grow a little taller. Or who knows but papa will give you some assistance, and that will be the same as if he set you upon a stool that you might reach down what you wanted.[20]

The first volume of the first series shows Scott experimenting until he believed he had found the right level. He explains this in a preface, dated February 1828, to the second edition of that series:

The Compiler may here mention, that, after commencing his task in a manner obvious to the most limited capacity, of which the Tale of Macbeth is an example, he was led to take a different view of the subject, by finding that a style considerably more elevated was more interesting to his juvenile reader. There is no harm, but on the contrary there is benefit, in presenting a child with ideas somewhat beyond his easy and immediate comprehension. The difficulties thus offered, if not too great or too frequent, stimulate curiosity and encourage exertion.[21]

Scott believed that it was better to puzzle children a little rather than write down to them and that he could both satisfy children of different ages and attract adult readers by adopting a plain but not simplistic style and by combining historical anecdote with a measure of "philosophical" criticism. This approach J. G. Lockhart saw as the secret of the initial and subsequent popularity of the *Tales*,[22] and several of the first reviewers commented favorably on this aspect, among them the *Athenaeum,* which welcomed the new publication as an important contribution to the campaign for improving writing for children:

It is true, that the work of improvement in this department has already commenced, and the examples of Miss Edgeworth and Mrs. Hoffland, have been followed by a host of successors. But even here the ground has been but badly occupied, and in the volumes of numerous well-intentioned but powerless imitators, children continue to be treated as "pretty dears," and not as reasoning beings—as amusing idiots and not as embryo men.[23]

The *New Monthly Magazine*'s short notice of the first series struck a dissentient note, contrasting Scott's volumes unfavorably in this respect with Alexander Stewart's single-volume publication that had appeared a few months earlier, *Stories from the History of Scotland:*

Mr S. makes his personages unfold their own characters in their own language, as far as chronicles and tradition allowed him; and he has thus given an air at once dramatic and real to his portraits, which must be very attractive to juvenile readers, and in this Sir Walter Scott has followed him. However amusing Sir Walter's longer tales may be to readers of a more advanced age, we think Mr. Stewart's better calculated, from their conciseness, to amuse younger students, who are uninfluenced by the magic of a name.[24]

After the uncertain opening chapters of the first series, where there is some "writing down," Scott settled into his preferred plain style, avoiding both self-conscious simplicity and the Johnsonian periods of the *Life of Napoleon Buonaparte* and eschewing for the most part the vivid imagery that characterizes most of his other writing (what little imagery there is in the *Tales* tends to be conventional). This plain style was also generally welcomed. In the fourth series the *Athenaeum* found a "style, familiar without meanness, and perspicuous without being too bare, . . . skilfully adapted to the purpose for which the book is intended," and the *Monthly Review* "an easy, clear, and lively style, very little partaking indeed of that garrulousness, which might be expected in a Grandfather."[25]

The French *Tales* have a more consistently adult feel to them than their predecessors. They were written, no longer for the six- to eight-year-old dedicatee "Hugh Littlejohn Esq.," but for Master John Hugh Lockhart in propria persona, who in all the dignity of ten years must no longer be treated "as a child." [26] The foreign subject means that the personal references to the grandfather's experience are no longer appropriate, and only occasionally does a "you must remember" or similar phrase remind adult readers that they are present by invitation.

In spite of the *New Monthly*'s doubts, the popularity of the *Tales* would seem to have justified Scott's method. The six-year-old dedicatee of the first series certainly seems to have found his grandfather's approach to his liking, reveling in the battles and not at all put off by the philosophical elements. On 27 February 1828 the boy's mother wrote to Scott:

> I do not know what to do with Johny he has gone quite mad about knights and bravery and war and when he gets into a passion talks of dirking the offender he has been in terrible disgrace for wounding poor Watt with a pair of scissors in short you must write *an antidote* to your book which he studies constantly.[27]

Sophia Lockhart is writing lightheartedly, but the same issue (essentially the question of Scott's ideological weighting) is raised more seriously by more than one reviewer. It was accepted that Scott had tried very hard to be evenhanded in his treatment of different political groups,[28] but a generally favorable review of the second series in the *Westminster Review,* probably by Andrew Bisset,[29] takes Scott somewhat to task for a failure to provide moral guidance. This is no crude attack by a radical publication on a well-known Tory;[30] nor is it a simple demand that Scott should give more of his own opinions, such as one finds elsewhere in the reviews,[31] or a request for straightforward overt moral instruction, although at first sight it might seem to be just that:

> An historical work composed for the instruction of youth, should, above all things, be careful to point out what is commendable, and what reprehensible, in the actions recorded.—The work, in this respect, falls far short of the character of a good instrument of education. Censure and commendation are often not dealt out at all, or are not adequately explicit; and sympathy is wanting with the interests, the characters, and the principles, with which it is for the good of mankind that every man should sympathize.[32]

Bisset does go on to provide a searching deconstructive analysis of Scott's apparently objective and unbiased rhetoric. His first example will indicate the quality of the criticism:

"The three kingdoms formed by the Britannic Islands came into the *possession of* one sovereign." In a work designed for the edification of a very tender age, it is not hypercritical to object to the use of certain archaisms calculated to convey erroneous notions. There is not the remotest analogy between the case of an heir entering into possession of his estate, and that of a prince succeeding to the first magistracy of a nation. The misconceptions of former ages on this subject have been long rectified; and the forms of speech flowing from them should likewise be exploded.[33]

Bisset suggests that there is a pervasive "contrast between the leniency of the language and the heinousness of the fact" in Scott's careful historical balancing act and that there are hidden limits to his toleration.[34]

Before considering the remaining two topics—Scott's organization and his vision—some attention must be paid to the extent and nature of his reliance on previous written sources.

His principal source for the fifth series was Claude Bernard Petitot's fifty-two-volume *Collection complète des mémoires relatifs à l'histoire de France, depuis le règne de Philippe Auguste jusqu'au commencement du dix-septième siècle,* published in Paris by Foucault in 1819–1826,[35] which includes inter alia the chronicles of Pierre de Fenin, Philippe de Commynes, and Jean de Troyes. Scott draws freely on these for his narrative and on Petitot's long essays on the reigns of each of the French kings of the period (though there is none for Louis XI). When he appears to be drawing on a range of sources, these are often to be found brought together in Nicolas or Petitot.[36] For most of the series Scott supplements Petitot by reference to the relevant volumes (edited by Smollett) of *The Modern Part of an Universal History, from the Earliest Account of Time.*[37] In the opening chapters especially, Raphael Holinshed is an important witness,[38] and Scott makes much use there of Nicholas Harris Nicolas's *History of the Battle of Agincourt.*[39] From the fifth chapter of the second volume onward, Nathaniel Wraxall's *Memoirs of the Kings of France, of the Race of Valois* was an invaluable guide.[40] For the concluding Italian chapters Scott made some use of Francesco Guicciardini's *Della istoria d'Italia,* of which he owned the 1738 edition, though he is here still relying heavily on Petitot and the *Universal History.*[41] He was also able to draw, in his concluding pages, on William Robertson's *History of Charles V.*[42]

Approximately three-quarters of the existing text of the fifth series is drawn from the sources just mentioned. Perhaps one of those three quarters is directly translated from the French, or directly transcribed from the English of the *Universal History* or from Wraxall. Something like half of the whole text is adapted to a greater or lesser extent from the sources.

Scott's adaptation of his sources involves the application of several techniques, any or all of which may be present in a single passage. There is a general tendency to summarize, both on a large scale (the *Tales* are a fraction of the length of the sources) and in recounting individual episodes. The fourth paragraph of the first chapter typically compresses two folio pages in the 1808 Holinshed (3:65–66), omitting much arcane archiepiscopal lore and increasing the dramatic effect leading up to the concluding exclamation of "War! War! France! France!"—an exciting moment that Holinshed throws away in the middle of a paragraph. The stark and impressive narrative of the trial and execution of St. Pol (pp. 152–53) is similarly abridged from Jean de Troyes's more detailed narrative.[43] Scott's narrative skill in the alteration of details can be observed more closely in his account of the death of Henry V (pp. 38–39). Petitot's account, in his "Tableau du règne de Charles VI," runs thus:

> Ayant appelé les princes de son sang, et Hue de Lannoy, envoyé du duc de Bourgogne, il leur dicta ses dernières volontés. Après leur avoir recommandé son épouse et son fils, il donna aux ducs de Bourgogne et de Bedford la régence de la France, au duc de Glocester la régence de l'Angleterre, et au duc de Warwick la surintendance de l'éducation du jeune Roi. Il les conjura de vivre unis, et insista fortement pour qu'ils ne délivrassent pas, avant la majorité de son fils, les princes français prisonniers en Angleterre depuis la bataille d'Azincourt. Henri reçut ensuite les secours de la religion: tandis qu'on lui lisoit le psaume *Miserere,* où se trouvent ces mots: *ut ædificentur muri Jerusalem,* il sortit d'une profonde rêverie, et dit qu'il avoit en le projet, après avoir pacifié la France, d'aller délivrer la Terre Sainte.

> Having summoned the princes of his blood, and Hugh of Lannoy, sent by the duke of Burgundy, he made known to them his last wishes. After commending his wife and son to them, he gave to the dukes of Burgundy and Bedford the regency of France, to the duke of Gloucester that of England, and to the duke of Warwick the supervision of the young king's education. He entreated them to live in harmony, and strongly insisted that they should not release, before his son attained his majority, the French princes who had been prisoners in England since the battle of Agincourt. Henry finally received the sacraments; when the *Miserere* psalm was read to him, at the place where these words occur "that the walls of Jerusalem may be built up," he came out of a profound reverie, and said that he intended, after having pacified France, to go to liberate the Holy Land.[44]

Petitot is already brief, so that no summarizing is needed. Scott transfers Henry's concern for his wife and son to form part of a crescendo of intensity and typically converts Petitot's concluding indirect speech to a more telling direct utterance: "'It was my purpose,' he said, 'had I lived to settle France in quiet, to have gone to the conquest of the Holy Land.'"

Even when Scott is following a source fairly closely, he will often interpret the events he is describing with interpolated phrases or in a more pervasive manner. The account given by Commynes of Louis's reception of Edward IV's herald (compare p. 138) runs as follows:

Le Roy leut la lettre seul: et puis se retira en une garde-robbe tout fin seul: et fit appeler ce heraut: et luy dit qu'il sçavoit bien que le roy d'Angleterre ne venoit point à sa requeste, mais y estoit contrainct, tant par le duc de Bourgogne, que par les communes d'Angleterre: et qu'il pouvoit bien voir que ja la saison estoit presque passée: et que le duc de Bourgogne s'en revenoit de Nuz, comme homme déconfit, et pauvre en toutes choses: et qu'au regard du connestable, il sçavoit bien qu'il avoit quelques intelligences avec le roy d'Angleterre, pour ce qu'il avoit espousé sa niece: mais qu'il le tromperoit: et luy conta les biens qu'il avoit de luy, disant: *Il ne veut sinon vivre en ses dissimulations, et en entretenir chacun, et faire son profit:* et dit audit heraut plusieurs autres belles raisons, pour admonester ledit roy d'Angleterre de prendre appointement avec luy. Et donna audit heraut trois cens ecus, de sa main, comptant: et luy en promit mille, si l'appointment se faisoit: et en public luy fit donner une belle piece de veloux cramoisy, contenant trente aunes.

The king read the letter to himself; and then he retired into a closet entirely alone; and had this herald summoned; and said to him that he knew well that the king of England had not come on his own initiative, but that he was constrained as much by the duke of Burgundy as by the Commons of England; and that he could see that already the season was almost over; and that the duke of Burgundy was returning from Neuss, like a defeated man, poor in everything; and that as to the constable, he [Louis] knew well that he had some understanding with the king of England, because he [Edward] had married his [the constable's] niece; but that he would deceive him; and recounted the favors that he had received from him, saying, *He only wishes to live in dissimulation, deal with everybody, and make his advantage;* and gave the herald many other good reasons to advise the king of England to make peace with him. And he gave the herald three hundred crowns counted with his own hand; and promised a thousand, if the affair were settled; and in public had him given a fine piece of crimson velvet thirty ells long.[45]

Scott interpolates Louis's good-humored smile at this first receipt of the message, and in the rest of the passage he concentrates on an interpretative retelling of the story, placing it in the context of Louis's manipulative patterns of behavior: on this occasion the interpretative bent leads him to drop Commynes's gesture toward direct speech.

The quarter, more or less, of the text that is wholly Scott's can for the most part be readily identified by the reader. Any extended interpretative passage, and in particular any of the numerous character analyses, will almost certainly be his, and these passages usually include telltale indicators such as "It is probable that," "You will recall that," or "We must recollect that." The third paragraph from the end of the first chapter is a good test case (p. 8). The first three sentences and a little more (up to "wages in advance") are based on Nicolas; the remainder of the paragraph, with its interpretation of the feelings and motives of the actors and its remark on chivalry, are almost entirely Scott's. The most extensive analysis of this sort is that relating to Joan of Arc (pp. 59–62).

The Scottish *Tales of a Grandfather* established a basic pattern of anec-
dotal narrative linked and pointed by "philosophical" comment and generalizing overviews.[46] In 1827 Scott wrote in his journal:

> If I have a knack for anything it is for selecting the striking and interesting
> points out of dull details, and hence I myself receive so much pleasure and
> instruction from volumes which are generally reputed dull and uninterest-
> ing. Give me facts I will find fancy for myself.[47]

The "striking and interesting points" often take the form of anecdotes.
From a wealth of available material Scott selects stories that will be interesting in their own right, and also representative. The typical movement is
represented by a sentence from the second series: "And here I may interrupt the course of public events, to tell you an anecdote not generally
known, but curious as illustrating the character of Cromwell."[48] Anecdotes
are often enlivened by noteworthy utterances attributed by history to individuals, sometimes reaching their climax in such memorable *mots*.

In the French *Tales* this basic narrative structure is maintained, and one
can also observe Scott's organizational ability on a broader scale, as he uses
chapters and volumes to block out the main stages of the historical narrative. The incomplete fifth series did not undergo the normal editorial
tidying up by intermediaries or indeed by Scott himself. If it had been
completed and edited, the very short chapters would almost certainly have
been incorporated into neighboring ones, but as it happens this process
would have obscured some of the play of Scott's mind over his material.
Occasional details may be confusing in the manuscript as it stands, but the
broad outline of the narrative is clear and satisfying.

The first three chapters center on Henry V's activity in France, leading
up to the battle of Agincourt.[49] Chapters 4 and 5 both reach their climaxes
in disastrous events arising from the renewal of the Orleans-Burgundian
rivalry that had temporarily been suspended at the end of the fourth series: the sack of Paris and the murder of John the Fearless on the bridge at
Montereau. The sixth chapter ends with the contrasting deaths of Henry V
and Charles VI—the latter's idiocy having formed a melancholy ground
bass during the opening chapters; the old actors leave the way clear for
Charles VII to take the stage in chapter 7, where his weakness dominates
the events. The short eighth chapter gives the first hint that fortune is
turning against the English: it acts as a "false start" or prelude to the story
of Joan of Arc, who in the ninth chapter raises the siege of Orleans. In
chapter 8 it had seemed possible that the death of Salisbury might have
terminated this siege. Joan's achievements are fulfilled after her death with
Charles's expulsion of the English from all of France except Calais in
chapter 10. The personal problem of Louis the dauphin's rebellious nature
counterpointing Charles's public triumphs in the tenth chapter comes to
the fore in chapter 11, which ends with Charles's death.

Louis XI is the central figure of this fifth series as it stands, dominating the movement from chapter 12 to the fifth chapter of volume 2. Chapters 12 to 14 tell of his vindictive early years, leading to the war for the public good and its termination with the peace of Conflans. The last two chapters of the first volume concentrate on Louis's duplicity, especially as exemplified in the appalling story of the sack of Liège. The second volume neatly begins[50] as the first had done, with three chapters narrating the return of the English to the Continent, now under Edward IV and culminating not this time with a battle but with the treaty ratified at Picquigny. The grim fourth chapter covers the collaboration of Louis and Charles of Burgundy in the execution of St. Pol and the end of the Burgundian line with the death of Burgundy after his invasion of Switzerland to relieve the boredom of the new peace. Chapter 5 shows Louis at his most cruel and despotic and details his bizarre last months. The sixth chapter covers the regency of Anne of Beaujeu, and the seventh Charles VIII's invasion of Italy and his death. The eighth chapter and the fragmentary ninth are concerned with Louis XII's resumption of this ill-advised invasion. Only in these last chapters are there any signs that Scott's impressive architectural control is beginning to weaken.

In his *Westminster Review* critique Andrew Bisset recognized what is now widely accepted: that the writing of history is a creative act paralleling that of fiction.[51] The Scottish *Tales* for the most part tell stories with apparent objectivity interspersed with the occasional generalizing gnomic remarks. But Scott was never in a simple sense "only the amanuensis of truth and history."[52]

Scott instinctively accepts a number of limitations in his source material of which a modern reader will be aware. The Scottish and French tales consequently share certain omissions. They are very much a history of nobility and of battles. The "lower orders" are referred to only occasionally, with a general recognition of their suffering or a fearful awareness of their potential for making mischief.[53] The arts are hardly mentioned; there is no recognition that the court of Burgundy was one of the greatest centers of artistic excellence the world has ever known. (This situation had been mentioned in *Anne of Geierstein* [1829], but almost incidentally, to contrast the Burgundian court with the enfeebled Provençal Court of Love.) Scott's history is of course predominantly patriarchal, but the creator (or part creator, part transmitter) of Meg Merrilees, Di Vernon, and Jeanie Deans, of Mary Queen of Scots in *The Abbot* and of Queen Elizabeth in *Kenilworth,* is fascinated by the feminine assumption of authority in Isabelle of Bavaria, Anne of Beaujeu, Agnes Sorel, and above all Joan of Arc.

In his choice and presentation of material from his sources, as much as in the passages of overt comment, Scott presents the reader with a vision of history. Johnnie Lockhart may have been boyishly captivated by the martial excitements in that first Scottish series, but the adult reader is likely to be struck rather by the darkness of Scott's historical vision. Scott himself recognized this when he refused to allow Cadell to disturb those "[h]appy points of pause" at Bannockburn and Flodden in the first series: "the first in particular for surely we ought to close one volume at least of Scottish history at a point which leaves the Kingdom triumphant and happy, and alas! where do her annals present us with such an aera excepting after Bannockburn?"[54] The story of Scotland in the first three series involves a constant alternation between brief periods of peace and prosperity and long wars, and although the concept of Providence is invoked on several occasions, it carries little more force than a generalized fate or fortune, whose dealings of good and evil are as puzzling as human inconsistencies. Scott's narrative position may be summed up as "Stoic Enlightenment Protestant." Bisset was probably right to detect legitimist leanings in Scott's rhetoric, but no reader can be in any doubt as to his revulsion against inhumanity as he narrates the seemingly unending series of appalling cruelties that make up his story. He openly celebrates the Enlightenment concept of the progress of human society and the virtues of modern civilization, which in one sense might be thought of as a posthistorical age.[55] There are, of course, limits to his disapproval of cruelty,[56] and the posthistorical concept was probably no more valid in the 1830s than in the 1990s. Scott's nagging awareness of this possibility is evident in his dismayed recognition that the horrors Paris experienced in 1417 had been repeated in his own lifetime (p. 28).

Scott's dark vision of history is painted on a different type of canvas in the French *Tales*.[57] His imagination in later life was repeatedly drawn to fifteenth-century France and the disintegration of the feudal and chivalric ground rules of medieval society. In *Quentin Durward,* and even more so in *Anne of Geierstein,* the consciously contrived happy endings of the romance plots reinforce rather than diminish the dark vision of the period. The *Tales* again characterize France as a deeply disturbed country,[58] and frequently Scott casts a gloomy eye forward anticipating the results of human folly and wickedness (e.g., p. 100). Acts of appalling cruelty are narrated and found intolerable even where they conform to the accepted standards of less-civilized periods (pp. 18–19). There are of course tributes to individual heroism, generosity, and integrity, and recognition of generally admirable characters such as Charles the Good of Burgundy. But the overwhelming effect is profoundly melancholy. In counterpoint to the clear progression of the main narrative outlined above, other movements reinforce the sense of fatality: the succession of royal deaths, somberly detailed,[59] and the pattern centering on the murder of John the Fearless on the bridge at Montereau. This fatal interview is anticipated by several unfortunate meetings in the fourth series (as well as by the murder of the duke of Orleans in 1407, which was its ultimate cause), and it echoes on in the fifth series in specific references to its disastrous effects and in the emphasis on subsequent encounters at Saint-Omer, Péronne, Cheron, and Picquigny.[60] Montereau embodies all that is self-destructive in France and ultimately much that is self-destructive in human nature.

Readers coming to this second series of the French tales from *Quentin Durward* will find that Scott's sources are the same for the fictional and factual works. Thus, material for the Péronne and Liège episodes is often common to both *Quentin Durward* and the fifth series, though sometimes the historical context is different to that familiar from the novel. For example, Louis's witticism about St. Pol's head is addressed in the history to Contay and Howard, whereas in the novel it is a joke between Louis and Charles.[61] That sort of transposition is not unexpected, but is effectively and skillfully managed, as is the inventive and bleakly atmospheric fictional development of the Nancy episode in the final pages of *Anne of Geierstein,* which can now be easily compared with the historical account in chapter 11 of the first part of the fifth series. Scott's view of the contrasting personalities of Louis XI and Charles the Bold, or the Rash, has not changed between the two novels, but as historian he fills in details of their careers (especially their early careers) and their characters. One may cite Louis's replacing "all the exhausted machinery of a feudal government" during his residence in Dauphiné,[62] his belated recognition of his mistake in dismissing so many able officials at the beginning of his reign,[63] the commencement of Charles's delusions of grandeur at Montlhéry,[64] and the early manifestation and late consummation of Louis's long cat-and-mouse game with his rival.[65] Significant additional judgments of Louis in particular testify to the fascination his deeply ambiguous character held for Scott; Louis's treatment of his father can be accounted for only by "a strain of insanity which can sometimes be traced in the actions of very able men . . . when from some inward feeling they are apt to prefer the gratification of their humour to their direct and solid interest,"[66] and the episode of the mock herald referred to in a note in the Magnum edition is subjected to further detailed analysis so as to throw additional light on Louis's complex motivation.[67] The central chapters of this series of tales may be regarded as a further expansion of the historical matrix provided by the introduction and notes which Scott as self-editor produced for this edition at the end of 1830 *(Quentin Durward)* and in early 1832 *(Anne of Geierstein).* Like the Magnum material, they enrich the 1823 and 1829 texts of the two novels by providing for the reader matter that was in some sense part of the novelist's vision of his fiction, and they stimulate further thought on the relationship between novelist and historian and (more intriguingly) between the historian as novelist and the novelist as historian.

The early editions of the four series published in Scott's lifetime provided his readers with helpful summaries of the main events described in each chapter. Using this model, the present editors offer the following summary of the fifth series.

VOLUME 1

Chapter 1 The rivalry of the Orleanists (Armagnacs) and Burgundians (Cabochians) is temporarily in abeyance—Henry V plans war in France—a conspiracy against him in England is defeated.

Chapter 2 Siege of Harfleur—Henry V, withdrawing toward Calais, crosses the Somme—the French decide to join battle.

Chapter 3 The battle of Agincourt.

Chapter 4 The dauphin (Louis of Guienne), forced to incline to the Armagnacs, appoints Fizenval (Bernard), earl of Armagnac, constable of France, and comes under his influence—John the Fearless, duke of Burgundy, behaves ambiguously—successive dauphins Louis of Guienne and John of Touraine die, and the future Charles VII becomes dauphin—Tanneguy du Chastel frustrates a Burgundian plot to seize power and executes Queen Isabelle's favorite—Burgundy liberates Isabelle and is reputed to be her lover—Perrinet Le Clerc betrays Paris to the Burgundians—Tanneguy du Chastel rescues the dauphin—the Paris mob (led by the executioner Capeluche) rise in support of the Burgundians and massacre the Orleanists.

Chapter 5 Burgundy, alarmed at Isabelle's trafficking with the English, seeks a reconciliation with the dauphin—Tanneguy, with the assistance of the Lady of Giac, arranges for Burgundy to meet the dauphin at Montereau, where Burgundy is murdered—his successor Philip the Good forms an alliance with Henry V of England.

Chapter 6 Montereau makes the Burgundian cause popular—Treaty of Arras between Henry V and Philip of Burgundy and Isabelle by which Henry is to marry Catherine and succeed to the French throne—Henry takes Melun and enters Paris—the dauphin is banished—Henry takes Catherine to England for her coronation—the dauphin, assisted by Scottish forces, defeats the English at Baugé and makes earl of Buchan constable—deaths of Henry V and Charles VI.

Chapter 7 The duke of Bedford as regent is inhibited by decline in the English army in France—Scots are involved in French defeats at Cravant and Verneuil, where Earl Douglas is killed—weaknesses of Charles VII—Charles appoints Arthur count of Richmond constable—Richmond insists that Tanneguy du Chastel and other favorites should leave the court—he is defeated by the English at Beuvron—he rashly introduces La Trémoille to be Charles's companion.

Chapter 8 Quarrel between the dukes of Gloucester and Burgundy—the earl of Salisbury is killed at Orleans, but the English maintain the siege with the help of the Fight of the Herrings.

Chapter 9 The story of Joan of Arc—she raises the siege of Orleans and conducts Charles to his coronation at Rheims—she is betrayed to the English—her character analyzed—she is burned at Rouen.

Chapter 10 Character of Charles VII—character and influence of Agnes Sorel and Queen Mary—the French are successful against the English—internal divisions over La Trémoille are patched up—dissension between Bedford and Burgundy—Burgundy and France agree pacification at Arras after English withdrawal from negotiations—deaths of Queen Isabelle and Bedford—the English leave Paris and Charles enters in triumph after taking Montereau—rights of French church increased by the Pragmatic Sanction—dauphin Louis opposes king in the *Praguerie* but is reconciled—Charles captures Pontoise—his moderate conduct and establishment of a standing army, reducing power of nobles—decline of English forces during truce—Somerset is appointed regent—Charles reconquers all of France except Calais—bravery of Shrewsbury, killed at Castillon.

Chapter 11 Charges against the dauphin Louis, who retreats to Dauphiné—accusation and acquittal of Peter de Brézé—Louis's independent conduct—Dammartin expels Louis from Dauphiné—Burgundy allots Louis Genappe—treachery of Alençon—death of Charles and retirement of Tanneguy du Chastel.

Chapter 12 Burgundy's moderate conduct at Louis's coronation—Louis takes revenge on his enemies at court—he introduces high taxation—Burgundy forms an alliance with the duke of Brittany—Louis mediates between kings of Aragon and Castile—Dammartin banished—Charolais vows to avenge Louis's insults.

Chapter 13 Francis II of Brittany strengthens alliance with Burgundy—Louis renounces the Pragmatic Sanction—assembly of nobles at Tours generally supports Louis against Francis—Charolais instigates the war for the public good against Louis—indecisive battle of Montlhéry—disunity of the nobles—overtures toward a settlement.

Chapter 14 Incidents illustrative of simplicity of times—Louis is reconciled with Dammartin and negotiates a general peace—Louis cedes Normandy to Charles duke of Berry—Charolais is rebuked for placing himself in Louis's power—treaty of Conflans is finalized at Vincennes.

Chapter 15 Louis expels his brother Charles from Normandy—his designs on Britanny—he supports the Liégeois against Charles of Burgundy—Liégeois are defeated at Brustem—Burgundy enters Liège—Burgundy is angry to learn that Brittany and Normandy have submitted to Louis—Louis's agents stir up the Liégeois to sacrilegious mutiny while he is visiting Burgundy at Péronne—Louis agrees to give his brother Charles Champagne and Brie instead of Normandy and to help Burgundy punish the Liégeois.

is established against France—French appointments in Italy are inadequately backed up at Charles's withdrawal—loyalty of duke of Orleans—Charles survives attack by Gonzaga at Fornovo and retreats to France—Ferdinand II of Naples dies during his restoration by Gonsalo de Cordova—Charles renounces a second Italian campaign—his death.

Chapter 8 Recapitulation of Louis XII's early misfortunes—he divorces Princess Joan and marries Anne of Brittany, widow of Charles VIII—supported by Pope Alexander, he conquers Milan—Ludovico Sforza is imprisoned—Ferdinand of Aragon and Louis agree to divide southern Italy—Frederick of Naples is pensioned off in France and his son imprisoned in Spain—French and Spanish quarrel—Spanish break treaty arranged by Archduke Philip of Austria—renewed efforts at conquest of Italy by Louis frustrated by Gonsalo of Cordova and Pope Julius II—fearing that Louis may die, Queen Anne tries to remove her valuables to Brittany but is frustrated by Maréchal Gié upon whom she takes her revenge—deaths of Isabella of Castile and Aragon and of Archduke Philip—Ferdinand secures regency of Castile and marries Germaine de Foix—he dies and is succeeded by Charles V—Charles's upbringing and character—the Reformation and invention of printing—developments in warfare—Henry VIII of England is unsure whether to support Charles V or Francis I.

Chapter 9 The Italian campaign continues.

Three types of superscript in the text refer to different sorts of notes. The most frequent (°) is placed at the end of a word or passage emended and refers to the corresponding entry in the "Emendations to the Base Text" (pp. 207–29). Superscript numbers refer to the "Explanatory Notes" (pp. 231–37). Footnotes by Scott himself are found at the bottom of the relevant page of text and are keyed in the text by an asterisk (*).

NOTES

1. *The Letters of Sir Walter Scott,* ed. H. J. C. Grierson et al., 12 vols. (London: Constable, 1932–1937), 10:218, 25 May (1827). Croker's *Stories* were published in 1817 by John Murray, London (anonymously, but with a preface signed J. W. C.).

2. *Letters,* 10:217–18n, letter from Cadell to Scott, 7 June 1827; cf. *The Journal of Sir Walter Scott,* ed. W. E. K. Anderson (Oxford: Clarendon Press, 1972), 312.

3. *Journal,* 312n.

4. *Journal,* 405 (28 December 1827).

5. The third series was an expansion of what Scott had originally intended for the final part of the second series. See *Journal,* 501; *Letters,* 10:462.

6. *Journal,* 411–12 (7 January 1828). John Newberry (1713–1767) was

publisher and originator of books for children. Compare Scott's letter of the following day to Cadell: "Various proposals have been made to me for Tales of the History of England etc but all these will keep cold. We have eggs enough on the spit for one while" (*Letters,* 10:356).

7. In the dedication to the fourth (first French) series (1:6–7) Scott writes: "It would have been natural that I should next have adopted English history as my theme; but there are so many excellent abridgements, that I willingly leave you to acquire a knowledge of that important subject from other sources. The History of England, in Letters, said to be from a nobleman to his son, and sometimes called Lord Lyttleton's Letters, but in reality written or compiled by Dr Oliver Goldsmith, gives the liveliest and best views of it; to this you must, in due time, add the perusal of the many and interesting volumes which give a fuller account of the history of the more important part of our island of Britain."

8. The literary reviews in periodicals for the relevant years have not been fully cataloged, still less those in newspapers. James Clarkson Corson listed the reviews of which he was aware in *A Bibliography of Sir Walter Scott . . . 1797–1940* (Edinburgh and London: Oliver and Boyd, 1943).

9. *Tales of a Grandfather; Being Stories Taken from the History of France, Inscribed to Hugh Littlejohn, Esq.,* 3 vols. (Edinburgh: Robert Cadell, 1831), (hereafter *Tales—Fourth Series*), 3:360.

10. *Letters,* 11:448n (27 December 1830).

11. *Letters,* 11:452.

12. National Library of Scotland (hereafter NLS) MS 21021, f. 1r.

13. NLS MS 3916, f. 14r.

14. NLS MS 3916, f. 147v.

15. NLS MS 3918, f. 45r.

16. *Journal,* 657.

17. NLS MS 3918, f. 73r.

18. *Letters,* 12:21. J. G. Lockhart (*Memoirs of the Life of Sir Walter Scott, Bart.,* 2d ed., 10 vols. [Edinburgh: Robert Cadell and London: John Murray, and Whittaker, 1838], 10:70) says that the fifth series was begun as late as May, but he gives no definite evidence to support his assertion.

19. NLS MS 21043, f. 120r.

20. *Tales of a Grandfather; Being Stories Taken from Scottish History, Humbly Inscribed to Hugh Littlejohn, Esq.,* 3 vols. (Edinburgh: Robert Cadell, 1828), 1:4–5.

21. Preface, ii. Lockhart records (9:123) that in the summer of 1827 Scott "rode daily among the woods with his 'Hugh Littlejohn,' and told the tale, and ascertained that it suited the comprehension of boyhood, before he reduced it to writing."

22. Lockhart, 9:186–87.

23. *Athenaeum,* 22 February 1828, 134.

24. *New Monthly Magazine,* 24 (1 June 1828): 244. The *Edinburgh Literary Journal* (29 November 1818, 31) doubts if the second series could "be read with advantage by either a boy or girl under fourteen or fifteen."

25. *Athenaeum,* 25 December 1830, 808; *Monthly Review* (new [fourth] series), 1 (February 1831): 316.

26. *Tales—Fourth Series,* 1:3.

27. *Letters,* 10:385n.

28. Not, however, without reservations. Thus the *Monthly Review* (new

[third] series, 10 [March 1829]: 333) writes: "We suspect strongly that the candour of our author is rather of an equivocal kind, being more characterised by a studied forbearance towards the adversaries of the political party to which he is known to be attached, than by a straight-forward and independent anxiety after truth." The reviewer then provides a detailed critique of Scott's cavalier attitude to detailed historical accuracy. The *Edinburgh Literary Journal* (29 November 1828, 30–31) stated the wish that Scott had been more willing to express his own views on the events narrated.

29. *Westminster Review,* 10 (April 1829): 257–83. The attribution is given in *The Wellesley Index to Victorian Periodicals: 1824–1900,* ed. Walter E. Houghton et al., 5 vols. (Toronto and Buffalo: University of Toronto Press, 1966–1988), 3:567.

30. Only the *London Weekly Review* (29 November 1828, 757–59) mounts a straightforward radical attack.

31. *Edinburgh Literary Journal,* 29 November 1828, 31.

32. *Westminster Review,* 10 (April 1829): 257–83, at 262.

33. Ibid.

34. Ibid., 271. For a deconstructive investigation of these limits see Beth Dickson, "Sir Walter Scott and the Limits of Toleration," *Scottish Literary Journal,* 18/2 (November 1991): 46–62.

35. In his *Letters* (11:470) Scott refers to "those very interesting & useful publications the Memoirs of France," meaning Petitot's 52-volume collection, supplemented by a 78-volume series coming up to 1763, together with Jean Alexandre Buchon's *Collection des chroniques nationales françaises, écrites en langue vulgaire, du treizième au seizième siècle,* 47 vols. (Paris: Verdière, 1824–1828). Buchon was of less value for the series than the original Petitot collection. A separate edition of the principal witness for the period included in Buchon, Enguerrand de Monstrelet, was published in 1595; it is in the Abbotsford library, though one does not know when Scott acquired it. Scott had cause to refer to the French historians collected by Petitot toward the end of 1830 in preparing the notes for the Magnum edition of the Waverley novels (the collected edition, with textual revisions and extensive editorial material by Scott, published by Cadell at Edinburgh in 43 vols., 1829–1834). Robert Cadell was revising *Quentin Durward* for the Magnum in the light of Scott's notes and textual emendations between 3 and 15 January 1831 (NLS MS 21021, f. 3v).

36. See, for example, notes 16, 46, and 103.

37. In 44 vols. (London: S. Richardson, 1759–1766).

38. Originally published in 1577, *Holinshed's Chronicles of England, Scotland, and Ireland* were reprinted in 6 vols. (London: J. Johnson, 1807–1808).

39. London: Johnson, 1827. The eccentric roman pagination one finds in the first edition of Nicolas's work results from his having greatly expanded the original introduction.

40. In 2 vols. (London: Edward and Charles Dilly, 1777). Very occasionally Scott also drew on [Charles Pinot] Duclos, *Histoire de Louis XI,* 2 vols. (Amsterdam: Aux depens de la compagnie, 1746).

41. Scott warns his son Charles that though Guicciardini and E. C. Davila are "very good historians . . . their stile is verbose and languid owing to its prolixity. There is an accuracy of detail which I think makes amends for this" (*Letters,* 11:320, 1 April 1830).

42. William Robertson, *The History of the Reign of the Emperor Charles V,* 3

vols. (London: W. Strachan, 1769). Although Scott had used [Amable Guillaume Prosper Brugière, baron] de Barante's *Histoire des ducs de Bourgogne de la maison de Valois, 1364–1477,* 8 vols. (Paris: Chez Ladvocat, 1824–1825), in writing *Anne of Geierstein,* there are no significant debts to that work in the fifth series of the *Tales.*

43. Petitot, 14:21–25. Duclos's account (2:172–74) is briefer than Petitot's, and Scott's is shorter still.

44. Petitot, 6:360.

45. Petitot, 12:126–27. Scott may have been influenced by Duclos's version of the beginning of this episode ("Le Roi reçut ce défi avec plus de sang froid que de mépris marqué," 2:147—The king accepted this challenge with more coolness than marked scorn), but he is basically following Commynes here.

46. In the late spring of 1829 Scott wrote a one-volume *History of Scotland* up to 1603 for Lardner's *Cabinet Cyclopaedia* where he adopted different principles, designed for adult readers: "a history may be written of the same country on a different plan, general where the other is detaild and philosophical where it is popular" (*Journal,* 547–48, 16 April 1829).

47. *Journal,* 405 (28 December 1827). Compare 18 July 1827: "Enterd this morning on the history of Sir William Wallace. I wish I may be able to find my way between what the child can comprehend and what shall not yet be absolutely uninteresting to the grown reader. Uncommon facts I should think the best receipt" (329).

48. *Tales of a Grandfather; Being Stories Taken from Scottish History, Humbly Inscribed to Hugh Littlejohn, Esq., Second Series,* 3 vols. (Edinburgh: Robert Cadell, 1829), 2:71 (chap. 46).

49. Scott wrote that the first French series "is intended to convey some general idea of French history, especially as it bears upon, and is connected with, that of Britain" (*Tales—Fourth Series,* 3:4 [chap. 17]).

50. Scott's volume division may have been influenced by Commynes's ending his second book at this point, as did Petitot his eleventh volume. He would also have calculated that he had completed enough material to fill one printed volume.

51. See Hayden White, *Metahistory: The Historical Imagination in Nineteenth-Century Europe* (Baltimore: Johns Hopkins University Press, 1973); and H. B. de Groot, "History and Fiction: The Case of *Redgauntlet,*" *Scott in Carnival: Selected Papers from the Fourth International Scott Conference, Edinburgh, 1991,* ed. J. H. Alexander and David Hewitt (Aberdeen: Association for Scottish Literary Studies, 1993), 358–69.

52. William Hazlitt, "Sir Walter Scott," in his *The Spirit of the Age; or, Contemporary Portraits,* ed. E. D. Mackerness (London and Glasgow: Collins, 1969), 104.

53. There is an unusually vivid description of general suffering in the fourth series, *Tales—Fourth Series,* 1:20 [chap. 8]); in the fifth series Scott's fear and hatred of demagoguery are apparent at the sack of Paris (pp. 25–28).

54. *Journal,* 405 (28 December 1827).

55. The first chapter of the second series is called "Progress of Civilisation in Society," and this comment in the first French series is typical (*Tales—Fourth Series,* 1:184 [chap. 7]): "The ruling character of the agents, in the extraordinary efforts which I am about to relate to you, requires now to be stated. It was in

many respects different from the principles by which mere barbarians are guided, but varyied no less from those views and notions which direct civilized nations" (the text is substantially varied in Scott's *Prose Works*, 28 vols. [Edinburgh: Cadell, 1834–1836], 27:123).

56. The gruesome procedures involved in execution for treason are a "cruel custom of the time," but as Bruce Beiderwell has carefully shown Scott was a strong supporter of only slightly less nasty forms of capital punishment; see *Power and Punishment in Scott's Novels* (Athens and London: University of Georgia Press, 1992).

57. For a fuller account of this vision, see William Baker, "Sir Walter Scott's 'Tales of a Grandfather—France. Second Series'," in *Scott and His Influence: The Papers of the Aberdeen Scott Conference, 1982,* ed. J. H. Alexander and David Hewitt (Aberdeen: Association for Scottish Literary Studies, 1983), 199–207.

58. *Tales—Fourth Series,* 1:183 (chap. 7).

59. In the fourth series, Philip the Fair dies of melancholy, like several of his predecessors (2:239 [chap. 15]); in the fifth series there are notably the deaths of Charles VI and Henry V, of Charles VII and Louis XI.

60. See "Montereau" in the Index of Places.

61. Compare p. 151 (Commynes in Petitot, 12:163) and *Quentin Durward,* 3 vols. (Edinburgh: Archibald Constable, 1823), 3:60.

62. See p. 82 (compare Petitot, 11:193).

63. See p. 104 (compare *Universal History,* 24:56).

64. See p. 100 (compare Commynes in Petitot, 11:372–73).

65. See pp. 106–7 and 152 (Scott's own analyses).

66. See p. 83 (Scott's own analysis).

67. See p. 142. The Magnum note can be found in vol. 32 (1831): 334–36.

Note on the Text

The hitherto unpublished manuscript of *Tales of a Grandfather; History of France—Second Series*, which forms the base text for the present edition, is preserved in the Hugh Walpole Collection at the King's School, Canterbury. It contains 422 main leaves, numbered (slightly erratically) from 1 to 244 for the first volume and from 1′ to 176 for the second. The paper was produced by A. Cowan & Son, Penicuik, and includes batches dated 1825 and 1829. Sheets have been folded in the normal Scott fashion, to form sets of quarto bifolios with leaves measuring approximately 26.5 cm by 20.5 cm. The main text is written on the rectos, with the opposing versos left blank for the insertion of extra material.

Most of the manuscript, of approximately 100,000 words, is in the hand of Scott's factor and amanuensis, William Laidlaw. Scott has written several pages himself, however, and revised all except chapters 7 to 9 of the second volume, often making substantial additions. As a result, approximately 17,000 words are in Scott's hand. Laidlaw's hand is clear, but he capitalizes initial letters in an eccentric manner. It is indeed often impossible to tell whether initial letters (especially *c*) are intended to be upper- or lowercase. Laidlaw's spelling of French names is irregular, and he has several unusual spelling practices that may arise from an old-fashioned Border upbringing. Scott's hand at the end of his life presents some difficulties. Throughout his career he was capable of writing the wrong word, and this tendency increased toward the end of his life; frequently words are very approximately formed or lack one or more letters. The editors have sometimes had to make informed guesses as to the identity of particular words, and inevitably there will be a handful of misreadings and mistakes. It has been possible, however, to decipher almost all of Scott's portions with reasonable certainty. A very small number of phrases or sentences that have defied all attempts by the editors and colleagues have been omitted: they will be found in the list of emendations following the base text. Both Laidlaw and Scott provide only the most minimal of punctuation, usually no more than an indication of sentence and paragraph divisions. The normal practice at this time was for punctuation to be supplied in the printing house.

The manuscript appears never to have been set in type, so that we do not have a version of the text that has been regularized and supplemented with respect to punctuation or consistency, a process normally provided in the printing stage of production. We are left with a document in which chapters and paragraphs differ greatly in length; obvious orthographical and factual errors abound, and some passages do not make sense as they stand. The modern editor is thus faced with an unusual challenge, and more than one approach could legitimately be employed.

It would be possible to adopt either of two extreme approaches. A literal transcript of the manuscript could be printed. The result would be a faithful representation of what survives, but it would be very difficult to read (as a glance at some of the longer items in the emendation list will demonstrate), and the specialist scholar would in some respects be better served by a photograph of the original. We have, however, prepared such a verbatim transcript: copies have been deposited in the National Library of Scotland, Aberdeen University Library, the Hugh Walpole Collection at the King's School Canterbury, the British Library, the Library of Congress, and the library of Northern Illinois University.

A second possibility would be to edit the manuscript as if one were a publisher of Scott's time, tidying up all of the defects mentioned above, even when this involved extensive rewriting of sentences, equalizing roughly the lengths of chapters, combining very short paragraphs and dividing very long ones, and inserting period punctuation to match that in the First Series of the French Tales. The result would be readable, but it would be open to the charge of pastiche and would involve very extensive conjectural emendation. If one were to attempt to punctuate the text in period style while omitting the other regularizing normally provided in the printing house, the result would be inconsistent.

The present editors have adopted a middle way that we believe will result in an approachable and usable text, one that clearly signals itself as the work of modern intermediaries as well as a faithful response to the manuscript.

We have followed the manuscript closely but always with the aim of providing a readable text. Since much of the orthographic detail of the text is Laidlaw's rather than Scott's, and since the manuscript was never prepared for publication, it has seemed sensible to correct obvious errors of presentation and factual mistakes when this can be done simply (supplying an obvious missing word, correcting a name, title, or date). The few confusions that cannot be rectified simply and the factual errors clearly derived by Scott from one of his sources (unless another of his sources gives the correct version) have been allowed to stand, with an explanatory note where appropriate. The modern forms of words are preferred, providing that they were in common use in Scott's time, and modern forms of proper names are similarly adopted. The manuscript's anglicization of first names is followed except when this would seem eccentric (as, most notably, in the frequent use of "Lewis" for "Louis.") All emendations (indicated by ° in the text), except those outlined in the following paragraph, are noted in the list following the base text.

Certain changes have been made silently, to avoid swelling the emendation notes to daunting proportions. The minimal punctuation of the manuscript has been supplemented according to modern grammatical usage, but the handful of changes to the manuscript sentence and paragraph structure are noted. First letters of words have been interpreted or rendered as lowercase except where capitals are clearly required, in accordance with modern practice in works of history. Ampersands have been spelled out, as have abbreviations such as *wh* and *shd,* accents have been supplied, and Scott's final -*d*s have been expanded to -*ed* (in words such as "amassed"). Obvious misspellings and malformations have been corrected, as have inadvertent repetitions of words or phrases; but spellings supported by the *Oxford English Dictionary* as possible conservative period usages are noted. Scott's *u* has been rendered as *w* in words such as "crown." The following frequently recurring manuscript spellings (and their grammatical variants) are silently changed: alledge, antient, Arma(g)niac (emended to Armagnac), Arrogon (Aragon), atchieve, attatch, Beaugé (Baugé), Berri (Berry), Bourdeaux (Bordeaux), campain(e), carreer, Charlerois/Charolois and so forth (Charolais), Chatharine (Catherine), Com(m)ines (Commynes), controul, Cressy (Crécy), Dammertin (Dammartin), Dauphiny (Dauphiné), desease, dissappoint, dutchy, expence, emisaries, forreign, Franch(e)mont (Franchimont), freind, Glocester, Gonsalez/Gonsalvo (Gonsalo), Gonzego (Gonzaga), heroin (heroine), D' Hymbercourt and so forth (De Humbercourt), Katharine (Catherine), Lewis (Louis), Leige (Liège), Montl'heri and so forth (Montlhéry), negociate, opertunity, Phillip (Philip), Poictiers (Poitiers), poision, Pontois (Pontoise), possest, Rhiems (Rheims), risque, rout (route), St/Saint Paul (the person: St Pol), shew, seige, sieze, sovreign, Ta(i)nqui du Chatel (Tanneguy du Chastel), Tremouil(le)/Tremeuille (Trémoille), Vaucoulour and so forth (Vaucouleurs), vengence, yeild. Laidlaw and occasionally Scott tend to double the "l" in words such as "powerfull" and "untill": these words have been silently shortened. Letters and words deleted in the manuscript have been ignored, as have catch words at the ends of pages or at the ends of insertions. The styles of chapter headings, dates, and royal titles have been standardized on modern practice. Errors arising from faulty assimilations of insertions made into the initial text have been silently rectified.

Apart from these exceptions, all changes to the manuscript text are included in the emendation list, with an explanation for the change where necessary.

The History of
FRANCE

Volume I

Chapter 1

Our first collection of these Tales concluded at a period (1412) when France appeared shaken to the very centre° by the inveterate civil disunion between the houses of Orleans and of Burgundy, two kindred branches of the royal family of France, or, according to the popular designation, between the Armagnacs and the Cabochians.° What was very remarkable amidst these bloody feuds was that none of the party on either side seemed to have nourished any intention of assailing the tottering authority of the lunatic king, although naturally so liable to attack. Whether it was the natural loyalty of the French of that period, or the fear of putting the crown upon the head of one of the pretending branches, and thereby giving too much authority to the party with which he was connected, it would be perhaps difficult to ascertain, but° certain it is that the power of the crown was respected though in such hands as those of Charles VI,° his profligate wife Queen Isabelle of Bavaria, and latterly the dauphin Louis, a young man of early debauched habits and no very promising talents.

In our last Tales taken from the History of France we had noticed the temporary truce which had been established between the duke of Burgundy and the Armagnacs, and which it was hoped might put an end to this envenomed civil war. Meantime a third party, more powerful perhaps than either, began to show a strong desire to interfere° with the affairs of France. A great revolution, the bloody presage of a century of civil war, had taken place in England, where Richard II had° been dethroned and murdered, and his cousin Henry IV of the line of Lancaster had been irregularly elevated to the throne in his stead. He had an embarrassed and precarious enjoyment for about thirteen years of the power which he had usurped, while on the other hand his predecessor Richard's memory was dear to the Gascon° vassals of England, who for his sake were very much disposed to transfer their allegiance to the crown of France upon the dethronement of their lawful prince.[1] Henry IV therefore, sensible of his unpopularity amidst the few partisans which England retained oversea, and more than sufficiently occupied by repeated rebellions at home, does not appear to have retained any purpose of agitating those pretensions which were so strongly urged by Edward III. It° is therefore probable that while Henry IV existed, if his life had been prolonged, the memory of Edward's claims and the pretensions of the English monarchs to the French crown would have been gradually suffered to fall into oblivion; but it was the will *A.D.* of Providence that they should be the cause of still more blood. When the° *1413* fifth King Henry had ascended the throne of England, France, weakened by her internal divisions, was matched with an antagonist bold, popular, fond of fame, and ambitious to follow the same course which had been chalked out by Edward III and his son the Black Prince.

At first the young King Henry V only took some steps for a general pacification between France and England, with the purpose undoubtedly of obtaining the most full information which he could concerning the state of his claims and the fitness of the occasion for presenting them. In the meantime he nourished certain ambitious hopes of carrying into effect the purposes of Edward III,° following up the war which that monarch had raised against France, with little available effect perhaps, yet with great temporary success and with enduring glory won in his own person.

The expense was perhaps the principal objection to so huge an undertaking, and that was unexpectedly removed. The reign of an usurper is seldom favourable to great exactions on the subject.° Besides, Henry IV's reign was short, nor had he in the course of it amassed much treasure. Indeed the attention of this monarch and his great national council had been solicited to the great wealth of the church, which begins to be hinted at as a fund from which the wants of the state might be supplied. Thus it chanced that in the last year of Henry IV's reign[2] the House of Commons attracted the king's attention by an allegation that the lands belonging to the spiritual estate were° sufficient to maintain for the honour of the king and defence of the realm fifteen earls, fifteen hundred knights, upwards of six thousand esquires, upwards of a hundred almshouses also for relief of the poor, impotent, and needy, and besides all this an annual payment to the king's privy purse of twenty thousand pounds sterling. This bill was very much dreaded among the clergy, who liked not to see the exorbitant° wealth of the church set forth in contrast with the efficient service which if applied otherwise it might do to the crown and nation both in war and peace. They resolved therefore to venture on some bold
A.D. expedient to° turn the king's intention from the bill and engage him in
1413 other projects of a nature to engross° his attention and find him abundance of occupation. Chicheley archbishop° of Canterbury undertook to his brethren to make a bold oration in which, flattering the king with his high military talents, he remonstrated that it was inconsistent with his glory to permit the French king peaceably to enjoy Normandy, Anjou, Touraine, Maine, and part of Guienne, all those provinces having been taken away from the kings of England by mere force and upon frivolous pretences. The prelate endeavoured to demonstrate that the sovereign had not only an incontestible right to these countries, but might even justly pretend a good right to the whole kingdom of France in quality of heir and successor of Edward III. The archbishop then took the Salic° law[3] into his consideration as the only rule which could be quoted against the king of England's, and argued that that celebrated law exclusive of female succession did not extend to the kingdom of France, and that° it was inconsistent with the directions of the Book of Numbers laying down: "When a

man dieth without a son let the inheritance descend to his daughter."[4] Having thus to willing and partial ears proved the lawful pretensions° to the crown of France descended to King Henry, the prelate with great address as well as eloquence exhorted the king to spread his banner to conquer his inheritance and to spare neither blood, sword, nor fire since the war was just, his cause good, and his claim true. The earl of Westmorland° replied to this artful speech, the tendency of which was to draw the king from the dazzling view of the great wealth of the church to engage him in an expensive war with France. He exhorted the king if he was determined upon war to begin first with Scotland and unite by conquest the whole island of Britain under one king, which would greatly further, as he alleged, the final purpose of subduing the Frenchmen. This proposal was answered by the duke of Exeter, who pleaded that the war in Scotland was entirely owing to the encouragement of France, and that kingdom being once conquered Scotland could not long resist. This last speech obtained the assent of the meeting, who raised an exclamation° of "War! War! France! France!"

Ambassadors accordingly were sent in the month of July 1414, who being admitted to the presence of the French king required him to deliver up to their master the realm and crown of France with the duchies of Aquitaine, Normandy, and Anjou, and the counties of Poitou° and Maine. They° expressed their master's readiness to take in marriage the Lady Catherine, daughter of the king of France, providing that she was endowed with the crown, duchies, and counties above mentioned. To this embassy no immediate answer was returned, excepting that the French councillors refused to enter into any negotiation whatever which affected the right of Charles VI to the crown although touching the proposed° match, but it was promised that an embassy should be sent with the French king's reply.

It presently afterwards arrived composed of persons of distinction the chief of whom was the archbishop° of Bourges,[5] a prelate of great ability and talent with power to consent to the proposed match under such conditions as he thought might satisfy the king of England. Meantime King Henry V with his natural desire of fame and thirst of enterprise, obedient also to the dying instructions of his father who had instructed him on his deathbed never to let England remain long at peace lest it should leave the nation at leisure to enquire into his right to the throne, seized upon the opportunity which the offers of his parliament had presented to him, and made° great means of gathering money with which he raised numerous forces and increased his navy by hiring vessels in the Low Countries. In the meantime the archbishop of Bourges° and other ambassadors offered° to agree to the match taking place between the king and the Lady Catherine, to whom they proposed to grant a large sum of money and even considerable landed property, but bearing no proportion to the demands of England nor in the least admitting any challenge of the crown. It is generally said that the dauphin, in ridicule of Henry's demand of the crown and upbraiding° him with the dissolute habits of his early youth, sent him over a box of tennis-balls as fitter for his amusement than the agitation of so great and dangerous a conquest as the kingdom of France.* This insult, imprudent at least while a hope of amicable accommodation remained, was resented by Henry as a personal insult.

In the meantime Henry's preparations went forward. One resource which Henry had recourse to was the generosity of his subjects, and the° trading towns in particular who furnished considerable sums to help forward an expedition so honourable to the country.° Another was the pawning or pledging the articles of royal treasure, many of which were taken to pieces and the fragments° pawned to different persons in security for such sums of money as individuals were able to advance. Thus we learn that a crown royal called the *Great Henry Crown*[6] was broken to pieces and the fragments divided among four knights who advanced considerable sums thereon. By this means Henry was with much difficulty enabled to raise° a sum of money sufficient to pay his army one quarter's wages in advance, which was his stipulation with them and appears not to have been made good but with great difficulty—enough certainly to have made the king pause to reflect how he could possibly carry on to its effectual close a purpose which it seemed so difficult even to commence. But it was a part of the spirit of chivalry rather to consider the importance of the object than the adequacy of the means by which it was to be accomplished. The war was popular, the monarch was beloved, the more so as his character had turned out greatly better than was expected from some excesses of his youth, and the terms were fulfilled° readily, as it does not appear that the French ambassadors were alarmed or became more serious in their desire to dispel the storm by negotiation. It° is not improbable that they founded their hopes of peace upon their having some private knowledge of a conspiracy among the English nobility, adherents° of the late Richard II, who were resolved to kill or surprise Henry V before success° in his undertaking should render him yet more popular, and that the French ambassadors trusted the success of that conspiracy. The earl of Cambridge, Lord Scrope of Masham, and Sir Thomas Gray° a knight of Northumberland were the chiefs of this conspiracy, of which the king appears to have had° private information.

Meantime the archbishop of Bourges,° who saw his proposals neglected and the expedition against France like to proceed, made an angry remonstrance to the king and demanded his permission to depart to his own country. Henry V answered publicly° that it should not be within less than three months he would himself follow him with banner displayed, where

---

* This anecdote is mentioned[7] in a very curious contemporary account of Agincourt of which the publication has been superintended by that excellent antiquary Nicholas Harris Nicolas° Esquire, from which we have not failed to borrow some curious particulars not to be found elsewhere.

he trusted to vindicate his right to the king not with brags of words but with deeds of men, and, assuring the ambassadors of safe conduct to France, promised he himself would visit that kingdom sooner than they should have cause to bid him welcome.° The archbishop of Bourges° therefore returned with his companions to carry to the dauphin the bad success of his negotiation.°

The king had proposed to embark at Southampton and was travelling hither when the conspiracy against him suddenly broke forth. We do not precisely know its purpose or extent, but it is certain that the earl of Cambridge, Lord Scrope° of Masham, and Sir Thomas Gray were beheaded on account of their accession° to it.

Chapter 2

14 AUGUST 1415° After this act of justice and policy the king embarked his whole army prepared for the invasion of France and landed after a favourable passage at Normandy near the mouth of the Seine where he found the siege of Harfleur, a town of consequence situated° on both sides of the Seine river.[8] King Henry pressed the siege on both sides of the river and by his ships prevented them obtaining relief by sea. The French defended themselves with much bravery. They dammed° up the course of the river through the town and thereby compelled it to run on the English camp. The dauphin on the other hand was not ready for battle but dispatched for the relief of Harfleur a body of troops under D'Albret,° then constable of France, Boucicaut, a valiant knight, then marshal,° and other leaders of experience. They did not however judge it safe with the numbers of men they had to venture a battle in relief of the town, which after a month's siege was reduced to capitulation. The terms granted were by no means favourable, for both the goods and persons of the citizens were to be at the king's pleasure, and in fact Harfleur was sacked so soon as surrendered on the day on which the victors were admitted into the place, but Henry followed the policy which his grandfather had done with regard to Calais,[9] expelling the original inhabitants from the town and establishing English in their room.

Henry vindicated his severity towards the citizens by alleging that on the day they had promised to surrender they endeavoured to elude[10] their promise which rendered it necessary to carry the place by storm, which was followed with its usual consequences to the vanquished.

Having attained this considerable advantage, the English king perceived the winter to approach and had the misfortune also to observe that his army suffered much from contagious diseases from the ground which they had occupied during the siege, of which fifteen hundred men at least had died. Prudence therefore recommended that the campaign should be closed with the gaining of Harfleur and that the army should be led back to England. But to have done so by sea as he came Henry found would subject him to the reproach of flying from the French army, which was still in the field daily increasing and had at its head many noble and experienced commanders. The English monarch therefore resolved to proceed by land from Harfleur to Calais so as to afford the French an opportunity of battle and accomplish his retreat in the way of a conqueror, not a fugitive. It occurred° to some of the English leaders that this was in some degree incurring a gratuitous risk, as the efforts of the French of every condition were° daily augmenting the army which the constable D'Albret° had in the field. But Henry no doubt calculated on the terrors impressed by the recollection of Crécy and Poitiers, and was loth to diminish in the opinion of the soldiers he commanded the idea of superiority which had been impressed by these victories, both in the minds of the victor and vanquished nation. No doubt Henry expected that he would meet with no more forcible opposition than he had hitherto encountered.

But the national bravery of the French nobility continued to assemble their troops and strengthen the superiority of the army under D'Albret and Boucicaut,° both of whom were officers of great fame, until° betwixt the difference in muniment strength in the state and condition of the two armies and confidence in the experience of their leaders, who were in comparison opposed to a mere boy, it seemed to the French that they could not fail to intercept Henry and annihilate his army on his proposed march to Calais.

In pursuance of their separate plans the English continued marching forwards towards Calais, although suffering greatly by the progress of the malady already raging in their army and by the difficulty of obtaining quarters and provisions where they were closely watched by the French army, nearly six times the number of their own, rendering it° difficult for them to send out parties either for collecting refreshments or any of the usual purposes of a hostile army in a strange land.

{The river of Somme° was betwixt the English and Calais at which Henry to accomplish his purpose meditated to arrive, but he was in nearly the same situation with his grandfather Edward III previous to the battle of Crécy.[11] The ford of Blanchetaque° was now defended by stakes placed at the bottom so as to render passage impossible. Henry therefore marched on and got possession of St Maxence° [12] from whence he might espy° the constable's full forces, which amounted to 30,000 men. Here he waited two days expecting battle. At length he moved forward and was assailed with skirmishers as° before. But the French not stirring themselves, Henry resolved to gain a passage over the Somme by marching up its course, so that the English began to fear that they would be unable with an enfeebled° and diminished army to retreat sixty miles into a country° of the enemy while they were watched at every turn by an army so very superior, and unable to avoid battle whenever it was the enemy's° choice to bring it on. This position struck terror into the most resolute, who deeply regretted that their boastful resolution to march through France from Harfleur to Paris should have ever involved them in such risks.

Accordingly wherever the English approached the Somme they found all° bridges and modes of communication destroyed, while the French on the opposite side showed themselves in battle array to defend passage.}

The garrison of Corbie in particular made a desperate attack upon a part of the English forces. At° the first attack the French, who were numerous and chosen men, obtained great advantage and took the standard of their adversary. A noble esquire of Staffordshire named John Bromley of

Bromley was so fired at witnessing this that he desperately charged the French men-at-arms, slew one or two, and recovering the standard displayed the same over his countrymen and led them to the charge once more, in which the garrison of Corbie was routed with considerable loss.

Thus daily weakened by skirmishes the English army made their way reduced to about two thousand men-at-arms and fifteen thousand archers[13] and infantry of every other description. Provisions were scarce, for they had been driven off or destroyed by the French army wherever they were likely to be useful to their enemies. Daily° it rained and nightly it freezed, to the great increase of the disorders which wasted the camp. Yet they conducted themselves with such discipline to the French peasantry that they° brought what provisions they possessed to the English camp and received liberal payment. King Henry also showed a high sense of religion in punishing° all plunder of churches and sacred buildings and in treating the peasantry with humanity, which ensured° their obtaining some supplies of provisions.*

The French king, now in one of his lucid intervals, was in the meantime lying at Rouen and heard° that the army of English were passed the Somme. This important manoeuvre had been achieved near the town of Nesle° where the Somme is joined from the left side of the river by the waters of a morass. The English having crossed this were for some time slowed up in the crook° formed by the junction of the morass with the river. But before the enemy were aware of this advantage Henry pushed forward° a body of cavalry, crossed the Somme by a ford,° and established a position of troops on the left side strong enough to cover their whole army, which now passed the river without difficulty.

The French king and his son called his council together, thirty-five in number, of whom thirty gave it as their opinion that battle should be avoided,° and five only gave it their opinion that the present opportunity of striking a signal blow and obliterating the scorns° and disgrace of Crécy and Poitiers was, since the rashness of the English king offered it, not to be neglected.° [14] Notwithstanding the great majority on the part of those who voted for postponing the combat, the contrary opinion after some debate prevailed,° every counsellor fearing that to give his final opinion in that manner might subject him to unworthy misconstruction. Finally Montjoie, the principal herald of France, was deputed to the camp of King Henry to defy that monarch in the name of the king of France and to assure him of instant battle. In one thing alone they profited by former experience,° for they resolved that it was not expedient that the king and dauphin should be in person at the proposed battle and thus avoided a fatal mistake like° that of King John, which might have a second time

---

* On this subject the following extract from the orders of march is illustrative of the disposition of a monarch so long the darling of English tradition as they are given by Shakespeare°: "We give express charge that in our marches through the country there be nothing compelled from the villagers, nothing taken but paid for, none of the Frenchmen upbraided or abused with disdainful language. For when lenity and cruelty play for a kingdom the gentler gamester is the sooner winner."[15]

thrown the king of France into the hands of his national enemies.[16] Henry, who had seen the great numbers of the French host which almost sur-rounded him, answered coldly and firmly "That he himself and his army were in the hands of God° and ready to submit to his decision. That he sought not to encounter the king of France at this moment, neither did he shun it. If any attempt to stop me on the road to Calais whither I am now marching I will," he said,° "colour their tawny soil with their red blood."

Chapter 3

The answer received from Henry, and the desire to avenge former national defeats, excited amid the French the utmost ardour for battle, and with universal consent they° assembled the whole nobility of the kingdom, forgetting for a while their private quarrels of Orleanist and Armagnast as men° universally taking arms in the general cause.

The king of France, notwithstanding his calamitous state of health, was with difficulty prevented by the reasoning of his counsellors from joining the army of the kingdom. The duke of Berry persuaded the unfortunate monarch to retire to Paris and thereby contrived to prevent° the fatal battle which was about to follow from being yet more calamitous than in effect it was. The nobles of the first consequence contended which should repair to the army, and D'Albret° and Boucicaut had instructions to bring the English to battle without delay.

On 24 October° Henry, perceiving there lay in his road to Calais another bridge, forced forwards a body of troops who found the French about to destroy it and preserved it until the king had crossed.

From a hill on the opposite side of this bridge the vanguard of the English might discover the immense army of the French who seemed to be moving towards them. Henry, advancing with caution and duly reconnoitring the ground, came to a small village[17] which they had the good fortune to find better supplied with provisions than those they had lately passed through.° Here the king resolved to pass the night and make his arrangements° for tomorrow. The army, inspired by the king's own disposition, passed the night cheerfully in despite of the privations which they suffered and the inequal battle that lay before them. They° adopted that stern resolution of conquest or death which has so often atoned for every disadvantage. The French on the other hand, proud of their immense superiority of numbers, spent the night in feasting and jollity which ought in prudence to have been° deferred till the battle was won.° Nor does it appear that their generals,° the constable and marshal° of France, took the necessary duty of assigning their forces with so much precaution as the importance of the occasion might have recommended.

In this respect Henry set his more experienced enemies D'Albret and Boucicaut° the perfect example of a general. Having surveyed the country accurately, he fixed on an open piece of ground in front of the ground where he had supped for drawing up the main body of his army. A space of low meadow ground which commanded the post of the French vanguard afforded an excellent spot to an ambush of five hundred archers who were placed there with directions not to stir or show themselves until

Sir Thomas Erpingham, an old knight of much experience, should give the signal, and then to do their utmost. Henry then placed the main body of his army in front of the village. It consisted chiefly of archers, the same terrible bowmen to whom the praise of Crécy and Poitiers chiefly attached. The vanguard was commanded by the duke of York, a valiant nobleman who had solicited that task° with his cousin° the duke of Gloucester,[18] and the duke of Exeter led° the rear in which the archers were mingled with billmen.° The few horse which the king had were disposed as was his usage, one on° each side for protection of his infantry, especially the archers, against such men-at-arms as should endeavour to attack them on the flanks.

The archers were select men both in point of skill and strength of body. They were clothed in loose and easy jackets to which their hose, that is to say the lower part of their dress, was attached not by a number of ligatures as the usual fashion but by a single stout strap. By this means their limbs were totally unconfined, either by the tightness° of their dress or the cramping effect of the knots° with which it was fastened together, and the archers were thus left at liberty to use the bows which they carried, though much above the common size, and to draw to the ear the shafts of a cloth-yard long which it was then the fashion° to use. With° these they had orders to furnish themselves on the two last days' march. Their° side-arms were in most cases swords and battle axes, but reaping hooks, mauls or club, dagger or large knives are also mentioned. They had steel caps but in many cases fought bareheaded. Others wore defensible hats made of boiled leather, others a sort of headpiece° made of wicker and defended with rings of iron, while others in face were absolutely bareheaded. It is also remarked that some of them went° barefooted while others wore boots on their feet.[19] In a word, they seem to have been very irregularly accoutred, but alike disposed to fight bravely, and alike expert at the use of their favourite weapon the longbow. They carried with them a stake six feet in length shod with sharpened iron at both ends, which when they were in order they stuck down° before them as a protection against the charge of the cavalry. Their constant practice with their weapon and their familiarity with the danger of battle rendered them the best disciplined troops of any nation during the middle ages.

On the other hand the French divided their large army into three partitions, or, as they then called them, battles. The lord D'Albret° constable of France, having with him the dukes of Orleans and Bourbon, Philip° count of Charolais (afterwards Philip the Good,° duke of Burgundy, son of John° the present duke) the counts of Richmond and Eu, and the marshal Boucicaut,° the count° of Vendôme Sir Louis Bourbon, and other men of quality, led the wings which flanked this vanguard.[20] A central body then followed of equal strength with that which went first, and as the chivalry of the kingdom were all drawn up under their respective banners nothing could be more glorious than the appearance which they made as the armies stood in array opposite to each other. This first line, a mass of men-at-arms, were all dismounted and had cut their spears to six feet that they might be manageable in their conflict with° the English bowmen, the° country being all woody and marshy both by the nature of° the ground and through the long tract of rainy weather. Besides this great battalion of infantry, consisting all of dismounted men-at-arms with a very large proportion of nobles and knights, the constable and marshal° had arrayed upwards of a thousand or twelve hundred mounted men-at-arms which were designed to ride round the English wings and attack the archers in flank and rear, which manoeuvre failed as we shall hereafter see.

It is said[21] that the French made so secure of victory that they went to dice for the ransoms of the English and framed a magnificent chariot in which they expected to convey King Henry captive through the city of Paris. It must not be forgotten that in their humour of insult they had a second time sent a herald to King Henry to treat concerning his ransom.° To this he made the well-known reply that a few hours would show which army would have to treat for ransom,° averring° that for his own part his dead carcase should rather be a prize to the French than his living body the subject of ransom.° The hosts had hitherto stood ranged opposite to each other, stimulating their mutual resentment by shouts and cries of opprobrium, and now at the return of the herald the French knights began° to assume their helmets and cause their trumpets to blow to battle. It is also stated by the French historians[22] that Henry entered upon some treaty for yielding up his conquest of Harfleur if permitted to march to Calais without fighting. If so, it was the ill genius of France counselled° her generals to refuse so fair an offer.

It is mentioned[23] as an instance of the imprudent haste of the French that all the young nobility, without or contrary to orders, pressed forwards to place themselves in the first line, which alone it was expected would be engaged. It is mentioned as an instance of their precipitance that they neglected° their usual attendance and marks of distinction, so that the duke of Brabant, finding that his banner was not come up, snatched a cloth bearing his arms from a trumpet to which it was attached, as the military fashion still is, and tying it to a lance ordered it that day to be borne° before him instead of his banner which he had outridden. No doubt if this° precipitance on the part of Brabant° and others had been followed by the expected victory it would have been accounted a sign of courage and of the noble desire of battle; but as the case happened it only argued unfounded presumption and rash precipitation. When the armies approached within three bowshots of each other King Henry on his side advanced his main body slowly towards the French, who on their part led onward their vanguard till its flank was nearly opposite to the ambuscade of English archers hid in the little meadow and formed in modern military phrase *en potence*[24] with respect to King Henry's front.

Old Sir Thomas Erpingham, laden as an historian says with years and honour,[25] rode considerably the foremost of King Henry's host with a warder in his hand, and, watching the moment when the enemy's° vanguard were exposed both to the discharge from the English main body and that from the ambuscade on the flank, he tossed up his warder as a signal for the conflict to commence, using the English phrase *Now strike.* The main body of the English immediately began to shoot *wholly together,* as the phrase went, at the great body of dismounted chivalry which was approaching them. The French were less astonished by this discharge, which° they had expected, than by the flight of arrows which suddenly were shot from the ambuscade in the meadow and which fell upon their undefended flank and even their rear. When they perceived this body of chosen archers they gained also the melancholy certainty that they could not charge them with their lances, though according to French custom they were shortened for the purpose of fighting on foot, as well on account of a large ditch which divided the meadow from the rest of the ground as because the archers were defended by the sharp stakes with which they had fenced themselves. They had no resource but to endeavour to rush forwards and come to close battle with the English vanguard, but the effect of the unsparing discharge of arrows wounded the horses of such men-at-arms as had remained mounted and should have advanced from the wings. Their intended operation was rendered° difficult or incapable of being executed by the state of the ground, which was quite swampy, and the heaviness of their own armour° and the greatness of their numbers, which rendered them incapable° of moving with precision or alertness° and galled the men-at-arms so cruelly that they broke their array,° rushed upon each other, and rode down the infantry, and thus at the first joining the English were highly encouraged and the French put to great loss. One great cause of their confusion was the want of ground to draw up their numerous forces so that they could have been brought in regular divisions to each others' support; and certainly D'Albret and Boucicaut° for two officers of so much experience seem in that particular strangely to have neglected an obvious part of military duty. The vanguard of King Henry, advancing without interruption, laid aside their bows, and, betaking themselves to swords, bills, axes, malls, and other close weapons, made an almost unresisted slaughter among the French vanguard, who were thrown into such pitiable confusion that they could not offer any effectual or combined resistance to the efforts of an enemy made with union and precision. The second division of the French advanced to the support of the first, but as it proved they were only able to share their comrades' disorder. The battle was for some time doubtful and perilous, continuing undecided for three long hours, for the numerous battalions of the French had not for a long time even space to fly, which rendered the slaughter more grievous.

Henry himself behaved like a valiant° knight as well as an excellent general. He pressed forwards in person on the vanguard of the French at the head of his guards and fought for a fame which should be entirely personal. He engaged the duke of Alençon hand to hand, and although he was struck down by his antagonist he not only recovered himself but cut down Alençon in his turn and slew two of his principal followers. The duke d'Alençon, though he named himself and requested quarter, was unhappily slain in the confusion by some of the men-at-arms who rallied round Henry. The king himself, perceiving that this battle might long endure, considering the great numbers of the defeated party, and that if any spirit of resistance should revive among them they might yet rally and recover the day against such slender odds, resolved to make an effort to bring the strife to a conclusion. He placed himself at the head therefore of the small body of men-at-arms and, extricating them from the tumult of the fight, he fetched a compass° round the battle, cutting his way through such fugitives as were flying in every direction, and charged the rear of the French whose numbers still maintained the conflict. Surprised at being assailed from behind when their enemies, as they supposed, were all in front of them, this part of the French army was also thrown into total disorder and fled with great precipitation. There never was so much noble blood spilled perhaps in any one action. The number indeed of the French who fell was not past sixteen hundred of the meaner sort, but of knights, esquires, and gentlemen eight thousand four hundred fell, and of those of the nobility that died Charles d'Albret high constable, James° of Châtillon (lord of Dampierre,° admiral of France), John de Rambures° master of the crossbows, Sir Guichard Dauphin° great master of France, John duke of Alençon, Anthony duke of Brabant brother to the duke of Burgundy, Edward duke of Bar, the count° of Nevers another brother to the duke of Burgundy, with Marle,° Vaudémont,° Beaumont, Grandprée, Roussi, Fauquemberg, Foix,° and Lestrake, beside a great number of lords and barons of name; nor must we omit to mention Boucicaut° marshal of France, who being early wounded and taken died in England.

Of the English there fell at this battle Edward duke of York, the earl of Suffolk whose father had died before the town of Harfleur, Sir Richard Kighley,° and David Gam a Welshman of great gallantry. About five or six hundred persons of less credit were slain.[26] An unhappy accident sullied the English victory. Two or three French knights, either fugitives from the battle or leaders of independent companies, fell upon the little village called Maisoncelles° in King Henry's rear, where the English had left their baggage while the battle was fighting, and plundered it. They met with little resistance, as King Henry had found it necessary to carry all his forces into the combat, and a small party of men-at-arms were left° to protect the priests who were engaged in religious offices. Hearing this fresh alarm Henry had no doubt that the French had rallied, and ordered his prisoners to be put to death excepting the princes and men of high rank. This barbarous order, hastily and imprudently given, was executed with the same rapidity and considerably sullied the renown of his victory. Apparently it was justified by the manners of that time, for the knights who commanded the attack upon the baggage were considered by their own leaders as having acted improperly and as being deserving of punishment. It is said that the order at first was that each Englishman should kill his prisoner, but finding it difficult to obtain obedience to this mandate the task was committed to an officer with three hundred cavalry.[27] Such was the fatal issue of the battle of Agincourt fought on the 25th day of October 1415.

We° cannot help separating one of the French prisoners from his companions. This° was the duke of Orleans, son of that duke who was murdered, as you have already been informed,[28] by the faction of Burgundy. Hitherto° the course of his life had been singularly unfortunate; but what is still more uncommon his captivity seemed to prepare for him a happier lot. Removed from the factions of his own country and furnished with every leisure and accommodation during his imprisonment, he became a poet of no mean celebrity, and probably lived more happily as such than when the turbulent chief of an envenomed faction in his own country of France.*

The despair which the battle of Agincourt spread in France is more easily conceived than it can be described. It could be little comfort that the king of England, who had scarce found himself equal to engaging in the battle, should with such imperfect force avoid pressing the advantage which he had obtained and satisfied himself with pursuing his march to Calais, on which route° he had been interrupted, and from that city returned to England to recruit his army and enjoy his triumph. Pageants and solemn festivities were exhibited in the wonted style° of the age to congratulate the victor on his most unlooked-for triumph.°

---

* This poetical prince was Charles duke of Orleans, eldest son of Louis duke of Orleans.° He was born on 26 May 1394 and made° prisoner at Agincourt in 1415. He remained in captivity in England, principally in the Tower of London, for twenty-five years, having been at length ransomed by Philip the Good, duke of Burgundy, for three hundred thousand crowns.

He composed poems both French and English,° the last of which are preserved in the British Museum. An elegant edition of the last has been printed for the Roxburghe Club by George Watson Taylor Esq., A.D. 1827.[29]

Chapter 4

Meanwhile the French court still resided for the present at Rouen and the° dauphin endeavoured to modify it so as to meet the coming tempest. He had no great choice whom to employ in the public service. The° only persons out of whom he could raise forces for the service of the estate were the vassals° of princes holding great fiefs of the crown, most of whom were prisoners in England while the rule of their vassals° devolved upon the king and government. Almost all of these were Armagnacs in party principles° and had with their masters a hearty hatred at the faction of Burgundy. Whether willing or not the dauphin Louis was therefore obliged to throw himself into the arms of that of Orleans, and to show how entire was his confidence in them he called to court Fizenval count° of Armagnac, from whom the Orleanists took their popular name of Armagnacs, and entrusting° him with the baton° of constable placed him at the head of his administration.

In some respects he could not make a better choice. The new constable was a man of first-rate military talent, and most likely of any person in France to repair the disaster of Agincourt. He was also a man of good morals, or at least less licentious than° the times seem to have authorized. But with these° advantages, and that of possessing great courage and enterprize, he was not a person to heal the discords of France which were° then of so envenomed and rankling a character. Notwithstanding also his warm professions of attachment to the party of Orleans, the count° of Armagnac secretly piqued himself on a real or fancied descent from the ancient King Clovis, from which he had persuaded himself that he had in his own person the legitimate right to the crown. He was besides of a fierce, relentless, unforgiving temper° which pushed him always to abuse his successes by party violence, and to prolong the remembrance of wrongs which if it had not been for his° own eagerness of temper would have sunk into oblivion. He was therefore an useful but most dangerous minister, and to have made use of him it would have been necessary to pass his infirmities over.

On the other hand the resentment of the duke of Burgundy, that great independent house, when° he saw his personal enemy thus raised to the highest power in the estate rendered his own conduct extremely dubious, and his own conduct showed itself equally ambiguous. On the one hand he sent a defiance to King Henry of England alleging as the cause the death of his brother the duke of Brabant at Agincourt. On the other hand he parted from Dijon at the head of a considerable party with which he seemed to threaten Paris, in which city he always maintained a party. The intentions therefore of this powerful prince were doubtful, nor could it be guessed whether he was about to join in the common defence of France against the English or had a design to play a game of his own which could not but augment the disorders of the kingdom. The dauphin augmented this risk by treating the envoys of Burgundy with a haughty contempt, charging them to command their master in the name of the king of France to disband his forces; but this prince, who was now at least° ostensibly the regent of the kingdom, was before the Burgundian ambassadors' departure seized with a dysentery which terminated in death, not without suspicion of poison.

In the meantime the count° of Armagnac came to Paris and was confirmed by the king, then in a lucid interval, in his military office of constable and at the same time created superintendent° of the finances which united in his person every species of civil authority. He set about the exercise of his high privileges with such quick penetration, and disposed the military power of the kingdom to such advantage, that the duke of Burgundy retreated from Paris in despair, while the constable executed several° of the duke's° retainers and emissaries in the city, turned others out of the university, and new modelled° the state, and the municipality in particular, after the fashion of his own faction. What chiefly embarrassed the count° of Armagnac in his administration was the conduct of John duke of Touraine, who had become dauphin by succession upon the death of his elder brother Louis. He had formed a marriage in Flanders with Jacqueline,° daughter and heiress of the count of Hainault, by whose persuasion, or owing perhaps to being overawed by him, the young prince entered France with Brabant his father-in-law. But on his arrival he expressed himself so keen a partizan of Burgundy that he refused to come to Paris unless that prince was also invited to the capital.

The constable therefore, to have at least a name which might be opposed to the influence of the dauphin, created the young count of ° Ponthieu, the fourth° son of the king, duke of Touraine and governor° of Paris, and so far fixed himself in authority that the duke of Burgundy quitted° France, which he had entered, and retreated to Flanders in submission real or pretended to the orders of the dauphin.

The different fate of these two princes, successive dauphins of Charles° of France, rendered the promotion of the count° of Ponthieu, the fourth son of Charles VI,° more important than the constable himself had apprehended. Upon 5 April[30] 1417 the dauphin suddenly was taken ill and died of an imposthume in the ear, which was as usual ascribed to poison. The young prince, now the only surviving son of the reigning monarch, and destined by heaven to succeed him on the throne, being in the hands of the count° of Armagnac partook of his passions, saw through his eyes, and was taught in particular to regard his mother's authority with contempt and her conduct with undisguised suspicion.

At the same time the duke of Burgundy renewed° his conspiracies for possession of the capital. The plan was to massacre the Armagnac party, to shut up the king and queen in a castle or distant fortress, and to call the young dauphin who still lived, though in weak and infirm health, to the ministration of public affairs under the direction of the duke of Burgundy. The explosion of the conspiracy was fixed for Easter 1416, but one of the persons concerned[31] could not conceal the secret from his wife, who, alarmed at the blood which was about to flow, carried her discovery to the queen Isabelle. This person lost no time in instructing the princes of their danger; for although rather a Burgundian than an Armagnac, that princess was sufficiently alarmed at the imprisonment with which she was threatened to feel alarmed at a conspiracy contrived for the sole elevation of the duke of Burgundy, and comprehending such results to herself.

Tanneguy du Chastel, provost of Paris under the Armagnac administration, was one of the most intrepid men of the time and was employed by the constable in baffling this Burgundian conspiracy.° He boldly seized upon the principal conspirators and delivered them up to the vengeance of the constable, who returned from a short tour not distant from the city full of fury against the rebels and desirous to stifle° the spirit of revolt by multiplying punishments; he even destroyed the grand butchery, which is described as a stately building, where the factious spirit of the Cabochians induced° them to hold frequent meetings. All these violent steps rather irritated than suppressed the disaffection of the rabble° of Paris amongst whom the strength of the Burgundian faction chiefly consisted. In the meantime Queen Isabelle, though a person arrived at a certain age, endeavoured to maintain a considerable rank by keeping an expensive court, and which as was more than suspected was extremely immoral and ill regulated.

The severe eyes of the constable, who, as was said, was a man of austere manners, were shocked with this frivolity and licence, and he resolved° to check it in the rudest and most effectual manner. He° seized without scruple° upon the treasure which Queen Isabelle had accumulated to maintain her discreditable expenses, and he also made prisoner Bois-Bourdon her maître d'hôtel,° who as scandal affirmed was also her personal favourite.

The unfortunate steward was put to the torture and compelled to avow the things alleged against him; being then sewed up in a sack of leather inscribed with these words, "Let the justice of the king have a free passage," he was plunged into the Seine. So violent a temper as that of Queen Isabelle was dreadfully incensed at so cruel an insult, to which her son the dauphin had given a free consent. She and her daughter were banished to Tours, where she spent her time in devising revenge with the Armagnac° faction by whom she was entirely guided.

Meantime the dauphin, being a very young man, saw only with the eyes and heard but with the ears of the count° of Armagnac, conformed in every respect to the wishes of his constable Armagnac, and seemed himself to partake in° the furious party quarrel, of which imprudence he should have been the moderator, not a party; and thus both factions went on extending the bloodshed between the parties, serving° only like oil upon a flame, and the total perdition of the country seemed every day more inevitable. Notwithstanding the great success of Henry V, the honours with which his country° had loaded him, and the willingness with which his subjects had submitted to great taxations, the expense of the French war proved greater than the sums which he had provided; and it was not without pawning his crown and his jewels, after breaking them to pieces as° we have already described, that he was at length able to fit out another army for the conquest of France, and which after all was greatly inadequate to the gigantic object which he proposed to himself. A second time he crossed the sea and with five-and-twenty thousand men resumed his attack upon Normandy where he retained little of his former conquests, although made at a time so favourable for England.

Henry however had endeavoured by negotiation to obtain the same point in which he was listened to by such of the French princes of the blood who were prisoners in England. It is plain from the documents referred to in Rymer's *Fœdera*³² that these unfortunate princes, eager to receive parole, had listened to the English monarch and had° agreed on certain terms to acknowledge the right of the king of England to the French crown, although with the insincerity which was almost proper to that guilty age they afterwards refused to fulfil their agreement. Henry had however still the hope of an ally who was more powerful by far than these captive princes and was more likely besides to be serious in any treaty in which he might choose to engage. This was the duke of Burgundy who, feeling his implacable enemy Armagnac fixed in power and not to be shaken by any ordinary force, determined to make such a one as, either with the assistance of the king of England or that of Queen Isabelle with whom it could not be difficult to form an alliance, could not be easily resisted. Burgundy might obtain security for such of his friends as survived, and revenge for the death of such as were slain. With this view the powerful duke undertook a march from Flanders towards Paris at the head of no less than sixty thousand men, and sent a herald to the dauphin who announced to that° young prince that he had not the free exercise of his inclination, and that his master the duke of Burgundy willingly offered his services to rescue him from the captivity under which he was at present detained. The young prince replied with great spirit: "Herald, your master the duke of Burgundy is not animated by such sentiments as you have intimated; if he would have my father and me believe him an affectionate relation and a faithful vassal, let him give battle to the English, the common enemies of our country. As for me, I am subjected to no restraint; I am at full liberty."

On receiving this answer which implied the resolution of the dauphin to stand or fall by his minister, the duke of Burgundy immediately revived anew his ancient intrigues among the lower part of Parisian citizens, and upon the one hand drew his army nearer the city to take advantage of

such opportunities as might occur, while on the other hand he opened a
negotiation with Queen Isabelle, being sensible that, however odious to
her at one time on account of his share in the assassination° of her supposed lover the duke of Orleans, that feeling had been long since overcome by a stronger resentment against the constable Armagnac and her°
own only remaining son the dauphin, owing to their share in the seizure
of her treasures and the death of Bois-Bourdon her steward and her own
imprisonment and exile, together with such gross reflections thrown by a
son° and a subject on a mother and a queen claiming the dignity of regent.

Burgundy's view of the incensed queen's temper did not deceive him.
Having received a favourable answer from Isabelle he went in person to
the neighbourhood of Tours.

The queen had obtained permission to hear mass attended by three
magistrates under whose charge° she was placed. One of these gentlemen
having expressed his anxiety at seeing some soldiers about the church, Isabelle silenced him by praying him not to interrupt her devotions. A gentleman named Saveuse, whom she knew to belong to the court of Burgundy, at this moment appeared at the entrance of the church. The queen
went to him and asked in a low voice, "Where is your master?" "Not° far
off," answered Saveuse. "In that case arrest," said Isabelle, "the traitors who
guard me." The duke of Burgundy then appeared at the head of the cavaliers of his guard, carried off the queen, by whom he was joyfully received,
and fixed her residence at the town of Chartres under the protection of
the Burgundian party.

The service which the duke of Burgundy had rendered on this occasion recommended him so strongly to Isabelle that she was universally
supposed to have admitted him to the same intimate share of her favour
which she had granted not only to the deceased duke of Orleans but to
Bois-Bourdon and other favourites.° This criminal intrigue, which received every credit from Isabelle's general° character, had the most unfavourable effect upon° that of the duke of Burgundy.

He had been hitherto accounted a man of severe morals, and his being
supposed to fall into this guilty commerce with a faithless woman caused
it to be said of him that he had become licentious and profligate, which
was not his wont, without being either less cruel or less ambitious than
formerly. And this was the rather believed when he also engaged in a similar commerce with the Dame de Giac, an unprincipled female of Isabelle's°
court, and who was afterwards the means of having this unfortunate
prince to his death. As for Queen Isabelle, she again assumed the quality
and dignity of queen regent to which she claimed a right by the nomina-
tion of her husband.

In the meantime the army of the duke of Burgundy continued to
blockade Paris, and the citizens became daily more inimical to the constable Armagnac, whom they considered as the chief obstacle to peace. They
alleged that it was part of his intention to maintain his power by a general

massacre of his enemies, and that he was making preparation for such an event by distributing medals made of lead among those citizens whom he meant to reserve in the general slaughter.

It is no wonder that with such belief concerning the intentions of the count° of Armagnac the° Parisians should be desirous to yield up the city to his enemies, and it is rather remarkable that the duke of Burgundy should so long have failed in effecting the revolution which he meditated. The displeasure of an obscure youth decided the fate of Paris.

Perrinet Le Clerc,° an obscure citizen who had sustained some blows from Tanneguy du Chastel, provost of the city, could obtain no satisfaction from that officer or his superiors. He entered out of revenge into a negotiation with an officer named Lisle-Adam who commanded a body of Burgundian troops occupying the left bank of the Seine.° Perrinet stole the keys of the gate of St Germain from beneath the head of his father, who commanded in that quarter of the town on behalf of the constable, and admitted the Burgundians, in number sixteen hundred men-at-arms, who *28/29* marched on in silence as far as the Châtelet until they were joined by *MAY*° many thousands of the lowest inhabitants who waked the startled city *1418* with the shouts of "Peace! peace! Burgundy! Burgundy!"

They could not probably have succeeded if the Armagnacs had had their whole forces in the capital, but the opportunity was taken when a large detachment had been made to take the neighbouring villages of Montlhéry and Marcoussis,° in which they succeeded, but left their chief the constable without troops at his greatest need.

One Lambert, a tinsmith and violent member of the Burgundian or popular party, put himself at the head of a body of the insurgents who went with horrible shouts to the hotel of St Paul where the king and the dauphin resided for the time; but the dauphin had already been rescued by the dauntless fidelity of Tanneguy du Chastel. This faithful partizan had been waked by the cries of the opposite faction, and without considering that he himself was a principal object of the popular hatred he resolved to save the dauphin or perish. He had assumed a disguise under which he penetrated unknown into the palace of St Paul,° found the young prince wrapped° in peaceful slumber, took him in his arms, wrapped° him up in his mantle, and carried him through the midst of a thousand dangers till he lodged him in the Bastille, still occupied by the soldiers of his party and under his own command, from which on the ensuing night he conducted him to Melun where he left him in comparative safety.

Most of the ministers of the late ruling faction, being arrested in their beds, were sent to the Châtelet. This, the principal prison of Paris, was soon occupied, and several private houses were turned to the same purpose according as they were thought adapted for the security of such prisoners as were lodged there. The constable himself took refuge with a mason whom he believed faithful, but in two days he was delivered up to the insurgents by the man whom he trusted. Lambert the tinsmith, finding that he was deprived of half his booty in the person of the dauphin, seized on that which was still within his grasp. He caused the unfortunate monarch Charles VI° in person to dress himself at that undue hour and mount on horseback, and forced him to give his ostensible countenance to the violences which were acted in this popular insurrection. Lambert did not suffer his royal prisoner to return to his palace, alarmed for his security by a second daring attempt of Tanneguy du Chastel.

This dauntless individual, having reinforced himself with the garrison of Melun, formed the daring project of recovering Paris by a *coup de main*. He rushed boldly into the city at the head of about sixteen hundred men-at-arms and made his way to the hotel of St Paul where he had left the king and where he expected to find him. Disappointed by the precautions of Lambert, and assailed both by the Burgundian soldiers under Lisle-Adam and the insurgent citizens of Paris, he effected his retreat after again displaying his courage in a bloody engagement fought in the suburbs of St Antoine, in which notwithstanding every effort to cut him off he made his way through every obstacle and effected a safe retreat.

The daring audacity of this attempt struck alarm into the insurgent Parisians, besides which a rabble, if not always cruel during their success, are certain to be so if that success be mingled with fear. The behaviour of Queen Isabelle° aggravated the resentment of the insurgents against the constable and other prisoners taken in the late revolution. When she received the news of Lisle-Adam's success she is said to have expressed herself in° terms which implied that she would not enter Paris so long as the constable and so many of his soldiers existed.° This was spread among the multitude as a reason for massacring all whom they had in° their possession.

With this humane purpose these warriors of the rabble went first to the private houses which had been set apart as prisons after the Châtelet° had been filled with captives. They summoned forth by one at a time the unfortunate prisoners and put them to death in the streets. They then proceeded to the Châtelet,° the inhabitants of which were the constable himself, the chancellor, several prelates of high rank, and other respectable characters. The prisoners, suspecting their lives to be aimed at, had at the instigation of the constable resolved to defend themselves as well as they could, and for that purpose indicated some signs of resistance. They° adopted the war-cry of "Long life to the dauphin" and arranged themselves on the towers and battlements of the prison in an attitude of defiance. But the rabble, alarmed at these tokens of resistance and by a report that Tannneguy du Chastel was coming upon them, as cowardly too as sanguinary, prevented the last hope of brave men, and by setting the house on fire consigned the inmates to certain death, receiving such as threw themselves from the balcony upon the pikes which were the principal weapons of the mob. The bodies of the constable and of the chancellor De Marle° were exposed upon the marble table used for such purposes, and those of lower persons were dragged through the streets, and the people of Paris were completely engrossed with that spirit of carnage which seems like the frenzy which seizes upon cattle at the sight of a slaughterhouse.

The duke of Burgundy with the queen soon after entered the city, and the poor king, who could not be said to possess a clear mind at any time, received them with a show of kindness. Indeed it is humane to hope that repeated attacks° of his recurring malady had rendered him incapable of judging of what he saw or of recalling the scene which passed around him, and he seems to have sunk into an apathy not far removed from idiocy in which° he seemed to witness without disapprobation.

Meantime the duke of Burgundy found that the spirit of popular insubordination which he had excited by his own machinations was become far too furious for him to check. Amidst such scenes of blood and slaughter the principal executioner of the city, hateful for his office upon ordinary occasions, became then the admiration and even the hero and leader of the populace. This man, whose name was Capeluche, headed the mob upon all occasions, and if it was said such a man was called an Armagnac he did his office upon him without further sentence or conviction. The sons of the sentenced were often slaughtered with their parents. This odious functionary, dressed in the livery of his detestable office, had the impudence to go to the Hôtel d'Artois where the duke of Burgundy had taken up his residence. Capeluche caused himself to be introduced to that proud prince by office and name, thrust his bloody hand into that of the duke, and accused in the name of the people certain prisoners spared till then because lodged out of Paris in the castle of Vincennes° of having formed a conspiracy and demanded that they should be transferred to the Châtelet.° The duke, in his nature so proud, was obliged to receive this villain with courtesy, granted his demand, charged him with the execution of it, and in a few hours the prisoners were massacred on the road to the Châtelet.° Shortly after this the duke of Burgundy had the dexterity to engage a part of the insurgents in the task of besieging Montlhéry while he called into Paris a strong body of his own troops; he took this opportunity, or rather he made it, for the purpose of hanging Capeluche the executioner, whose insolence he had never brought himself to forgive. A sum of money distributed in good time among the populace reconciled them to the execution of their friend the hangman.

It was also a sign of the times worthy of noting that Perrinet Le Clerc,° whose merit towards the popular party consisted in having robbed his father and betrayed the public trust to the enemy, became by these virtues a hero of the people. His statue was set up in public, and for a considerable time he experienced a respect which might have been well bestowed on one who had actually served his country. He was guilty of the meanest acts of vengeance and most atrocious cruelty.°

Ere the Burgundian generals gave orders that their authorised massacres should cease it is said that three thousand five hundred citizens, many of them of the highest rank, had fallen victims to popular fury. During this frightful period the mob proceeded with the same vehemence, breaking down and burning houses and massacring respectable citizens. A historian, Juvénal des Ursins,[33] describes in the most melancholy terms the condition of the wives and daughters of those who had perished. They were the objects of popular hatred, despoiled of their goods, chased from their houses, and though accustomed to every species of indulgence forced to the meanest disguises in order to escape from the city into a country which was miserably laid waste, and where they found themselves exposed to the insults of the licentious° soldiers of every party without the least security either for their° property or for their lives.

These scenes of misery shown amidst burning houses and streets flowing with blood were shockingly contrasted with the display of extravagance and pomp exhibited at the reception of Queen Isabelle into Paris.

We would not have been so particular in detailing these odious cruelties if they had only been known to the Parisians in this barbarous age; but alas, in these massacres of the fifteenth century we are only tracing the exact outline of what was performed in the end of the eighteenth and must be well remembered by most of my elder readers. In the meantime it is instructive to remark that the duke of Burgundy was continually tormented by the recollection of the murder of the duke of Orleans, of which he had been the principal machinator. He published, you will remember,[34] a defence of that crime of which the doctrines were formally condemned by decrees of the parliament and of the Sorbonne while under the influence of the Armagnacs; he insisted therefore that the present parliament convoked under his authority should publish a declaration acknowledging that the defence of the doctor Jean Le Petit concerning the death of the duke of Orleans contained the just principles° which should be acted upon, whether between two equal princes or between sovereigns and their subjects.

He little knew that his own blood shed within a few months was to confirm the principles thus proclaimed with so much solemnity.

Chapter 5

France stood now in a singular situation: it was divided into three parts who fought relentlessly against each other. The first of these was the party of the duke of Burgundy who affected to protect the insurgent city of Paris, although in effect as much displeased with the cruelties° of the wretched inhabitants as if they had not been committed in his own name. Rouen and other considerable towns were favourable to this prince, who with Queen Isabelle's concurrence convoked a parliament at Troyes where she created a new chancellor, new constable, and other ministers, reserving however the chief power for the duke of Burgundy.

On° the other hand the dauphin° headed a second party composed not only of all the remaining Armagnacs who hastened to arrange themselves under his banner. He also convoked a parliament composed of those statesmen who had been banished by the duke of Burgundy, and its place of sitting was fixed for Poitiers. Above all, under the eye and in the army of the young prince arose a crowd of youthful heroes: le maréchal de Rieux, Vignolles de La Hire, Poton de Xaintrailles, La Trémoille, and Barbazan;° names which distinguished young men who were afterwards to make a brilliant figure in the restoration of French independence. Thus seconded in his own person, seventeen° years of age, and affording room for the most brilliant hopes, Charles under the title of dauphin regent° had an authority generally recognised through the whole south of France. This was the second party which divided the kingdom.

The third party was that of the king of England, who with a small but formidable army made war in Normandy under pretence of asserting his title to the crown of France, still however averring his willingness to treat for the precise period when it should be delivered to him. Queen Isabelle, always malevolent to the interests of her son Charles, showed herself bent to exercise her full influence in favour of an agreement with the king of England by which he was to be married with her favourite daughter Catherine, having the kingdom of France for her dowry. This unnatural mother managed the conferences with Henry himself, and to make Henry more eager for the match carried her daughter thither herself that her personal charms, which were very remarkable, might have their effects in the treaty. In this she was mistaken,° for, being more a warrior and statesman than a courtier, every proposal which was made proved inefficient for the time.

The duke of Burgundy saw the progress of this treaty with apprehension. He was by no means° seriously desirous of placing a prince such° as Henry V upon the throne of France in the character of his own suzerain, and he began to feel that he could not do so without losing generally the interest he hitherto possessed in the hearts of the French people at large. In this dilemma he cast in his thoughts the possibility, notwithstanding his accession to the duke of Orleans' murder, again° to make his peace with the party which called themselves by their prince's name.° But the path by which he proposed to extricate himself from his dilemma had already been stained with blood, and his own was to be the second or retributive sacrifice.

John duke of Burgundy in the meantime began to repent in the share he had had in the invasion and success of the English. Henry, it is said, was aware° of this vacillation in his purpose, and let him know his sense of it by saying to him at their last interview what° he supposed to be the hindrances of his match with the princess Catherine and his coming to agreement with Queen Isabelle:° "Fair cousin, we will have° your king's daughter to wife, and all that we desire to her dowry,° and moreover we will drive° both your king and you out of the country." The duke of Burgundy felt the sarcasm and answered in the same tone. "Well," said the duke, "before you drive the king and me out of France you shall be a prisoner, and that I do° assure you." Being on such indifferent terms with Henry, it was natural that Burgundy should look for means of reconciliation with the dauphin and his adherents. The prince indeed was no less anxious at° seeing the management of a treaty with England in the hands of his unnatural mother, and became desirous either that the duke of Burgundy should return to his allegiance or that he should be put to death. Whatever° were the dauphin's intentions, those of his emissary Tanneguy du Chastel were fixed upon revenging the murder of the duke of Orleans killed at Paris in 1407.° Tanneguy du Chastel was a man of the most resolute bravery, but deeply tinged with the vices of the time, perfidy and cruelty. He also retained the deepest° resentment of the duke of Orleans' memory, for it was in his household that he was bred up. Having° great influence with the dauphin, it seems likely that he communicated to the young prince some feelings of the vengeful passions by which he was himself actuated.

Certain it is that Du Chastel was sent by the dauphin to the camp of the duke of Burgundy, where he lost no time in finding a fit engine to work with, without whom he would not probably have effected his purpose. This was the faithless Lady of Giac, mistress of the duke of Burgundy and possessing a boundless influence over him. By her persuasions the duke was prevailed upon to meet the dauphin at a village between Melun and Corbeil.[35] Burgundy came there with a very small suite, and it seems that the dauphin and he parted on the most friendly terms. The duke, to testify his respect for the heir of the crown, held the stirrup of the dauphin at parting. Good Frenchmen saw no doubt of the reconciliation, and as little that, if it was sincere, their united power would soon expel the English from the kingdom. When these princes were about to part, another meeting had been fixed upon to be held at the bridge of Montereau upon the Yonne. An unexpected exploit of Henry revived the dauphin's° distrust of the duke, though without any very good cause. The king of England sent a strong detachment of his forces to surprise the city of Pontoise. The commander Lisle-Adam and six thousand Burgundian troops escaped over the walls in their shirts, and their treasure of two millions, much of it the property of the duke of Burgundy, became the prize of the English, to whom their want of money rendered it highly acceptable. The dauphin revenged this in some degree by falling upon and cutting off about four hundred Irishmen, part of Henry's followers. Not satisfied with this, and continuing to think that the loss of Pontoise was to be ascribed to the duke of Burgundy, the young prince seems to have listened to the suggestions of Tanneguy du Chastel his favourite,° who insinuated into his mind a plot as bloody and perfidious as the murder of Orleans which it was intended to revenge. At least circumstances make it plain that what followed, if it did not take place by the dauphin's° express command, must yet be° allowed to have been acted by his connivance.

Montereau upon the river Yonne has a bridge uniting the town and castle. This, when put in order for the proposed meeting with° all those signs of suspicion which used to be expressed on such occasions, was defended at each end by strong palisades and a space railed off in the middle where the two princes were to meet. The castle, void of provisions and ammunition,° was delivered up in that untenable condition to the duke of Burgundy's troops, who did not pay attention to its defenceless state. In° the meantime the duke of Burgundy was seized with apprehensions which it required all the art of the Lady of Giac and the affected frank assurances of Tanneguy du Chastel to remove; in so much that the dauphin° remained at Montereau fifteen days waiting for the expected conference. **10 SEPTEMBER 1419°**

Repeated proposals on the part of the duke of Burgundy were sent by him while on the route to have the place of meeting changed. All were removed by new protestations and by the influence of the faithless paramour, and, dragged on as it were contrary to his own intentions, the duke of Burgundy by a sort of fatality came to the place of meeting at Montereau. Here they met in the salon appointed in the centre° of the bridge. The duke kneeled to the dauphin,° who was looking over the central arch which he had not yet crossed, and in doing so it is said threw his sword too far behind him; for this or for some other reason he put his hand on the hilt of his weapon, upon which Tanneguy du Chastel called out with a stern voice, "It is time!" and throwing himself on the duke cut off his chin and with the second blow dashed out his brains. Only one of his attendants, Navailles,° brother of the count de Foix, endeavoured° to save his master and died in his defence. The rest fled, while such as were of consequence among them were made prisoners. The senseless body, having sustained some brutal insults from those of the dauphin's suite,° remained unburied during great part of the day, until the dauphin at length commanded it to be removed and interred. A priest of mean rank performed the ceremony with so little mark of respect that the clothes of the deceased were not removed when he was hurried to the grave in the boots and doublet which he wore when he was slain. As if, however, he had fallen into the hands of ordinary robbers, the slain prince was stripped of his rings, chains, and personal ornaments of value. Montagu, one of his retinue, by extraordinary exertion of activity, contrived to return back over the barricades,° which was thought impossible. Burgundy's° eight remaining friends° were executed by the dauphin and his party.

Thus fell John the Fearless by an act of treason as foul as that against the duke of Orleans to which he had long since given occasion. His death in this cruel and treacherous manner awakened the recollection of his good qualities among his countrymen in general, and far from serving the cause of the dauphin had very near reduced it to total annihilation.

John duke of Burgundy, called the Fearless from his tried intrepidity, was succeeded in his large estates and his great wealth by his son Philip count of Charolais, who was of a temper so very moderate that he was distinguished among the princes of his house by the name of the *Good*. He assembled his principal vassals and the chief citizens of Flanders, and required their advice and assistance how to revenge his father's foul murder committed under the eyes, and probably by the command, of the dauphin° of France.

The great council had no hesitation in a case so extraordinary to recommend to their young lord to renounce his allegiance to the dauphin in consequence of this foul injury and breach of faith and form an alliance with the king of England, by which he could not fail to obtain the deepest revenge by the forfeiture of the royal inheritance of his enemy Charles the dauphin.

Chapter 6

It is a remarkable instance of an overruling providence that bloody crimes similar to the murder perpetrated at Montereau often are attended with consequences the very reverse of those expected. We have seen that the slaughter of John duke of Burgundy, instead of crushing for ever that party which called him their head, on° the contrary in a manner compelled his successor to become the ally of England, with this apology, that what was in his father's case accounted an act of treasonable rebellion, was in his almost justifiable as the only manner in which he could fully revenge the perfidious death of so near a relation. The league against the dauphin then was so far justified in public opinion that a legal cause with which everybody would sympathise was alleged for its continuance. Queen Isabelle, acting also in the name of her insane husband, brought all her wrongs and all her sorrows to augment the charge against her son the dauphin, and publicly lamented the death of the duke of Burgundy as if she had never entertained sentiments° respecting him except those of approbation of his politeness, and kindness to his person.

It is no less worth remark that the character of a person suddenly removed by a treacherous and bloody death is apt to be wonderfully cleared of such accusations as may have been received against him on grounds however strong during his lifetime, and this was also the case with the deceased John of Burgundy. He had originally raised himself to the popularity which he had enjoyed in Paris by assuming a mask which will fit almost any demagogue, a great tenderness namely for the lower classes and the ready disguise of a violent patriot having the interest of the subjects eternally uppermost in his thoughts. But any man of common sense had begun to doubt these zealous pretences of the duke of Burgundy when they tried to reconcile them with the severe measures in which he governed his own subjects, and more especially with his suffering his name to be used as a sanction to the frightful massacres of Paris, and when they heard it urged that the league he had formed with Isabelle of Bavaria had engaged the duke of Burgundy in a guilty intrigue with the false wife of the unfortunate king, and in a negotiation with Henry of England, the national enemy of France. But upon the bloody deed of Montereau all recollection of the deceased duke's failings seemed to be obliterated with his life, and every attempt by which the dauphin endeavoured to show that the duke had fallen in an attempt against his person was treated as totally impossible and incompatible with the facts of the case.

Paris was plunged in the deepest sorrow; the people seemed to have lost a father and expressed their grief° by the most frightful menaces against the unfortunate dauphin. The young count of St Pol, governor of the city, caused honours to be rendered to the memory of the duke which awakened all the passions. His funeral oration was pronounced by L'Archer, rector of the university, a man powerful in eloquence according to the ideas of the time, at whose discourse the whole audience melted into tears and swore revenge for his death.

The other good towns of France, especially those in the north and east of the kingdom, were so worn out and exhausted by war, and so bound by recollection of the popular opinions patronised by the deceased duke, that they sent representatives to a congress appointed to be held by the queen and the new duke of Burgundy, together with the English monarch, for the settlement of their various interests.

The English monarch, who had previously found himself in a very embarrassing position, and who could not trust the overtures either of Isabelle or of the Burgundian faction, now beheld them both obliged without a possibility of pursuing a different course to consent to all measures which favoured his interest, and owed his advantages less to the victory of Agincourt and his own great military talents than to the ill-advised crime which the dauphin had either planned or permitted with the hope of a very different result.

The negotiation at Arras was so extremely short that in little° more than five months the queen and young Philip of Burgundy had subscribed along with Henry preliminaries of peace which overset the Salic law so long acknowledged by France, and dictated to that kingdom a new order of succession. This important treaty bore as its general tenor,° first that Henry should take in marriage the Princess Catherine, second that Charles VI should bear the name of king during his lifetime, but that the government should be administered by Henry of England under the title of regent, who upon the demise of Charles should succeed to the throne of France; a° truce between the contracting parties from which the dauphin and his party were excluded. It is not known whether the unfortunate Charles ever had an interval sufficiently lucid to make him sensible that a king of England already stood on his throne and wielded his sceptre, watching the moment of his death to enter upon his kingdoms with the full right of his successor.

Nor was it the least extraordinary feature of this singular treaty that even if the Salic° law had never existed the succession of the kingdom could not be in the person of Henry V but in that of the next heir of the unfortunate Richard II whom Henry IV, the present king's father, had deposed and it is generally believed murdered. But though Henry V was in no legal sense possessed° of the right of succession to the crown of France, yet he was possessed of many of those advantages which have in history sometimes induced a people to prefer a usurper to their vacant throne instead of a legitimate heir. He was a conqueror at the head of the army which had fought the battle of Agincourt, a prince of great popularity as well as high accomplishment, and likely to possess that power among his vassals° which the French monarchs had long forfeited by intermingling in their feuds.

It was no doubt a strange and sad sight for Frenchmen to regard the English monarch as heir to their ancient kingdom, and they liked the prospect the less that the ancient monarchs, though possessing less despotic authority over their subjects than the kings of France, nevertheless exercised greater form and process than was the custom of French princes, who lived on freer and more easy terms, contenting themselves with the reality of authority and neglecting the visible signs of it as something inconsistent with the liveliness and antiquity of their national character.

Thus the French were shocked at their future monarch very soon after the settlement of the treaty because he manifested in the maréchal de Lisle-Adam,° a Burgundian officer, what Henry conceived to be an unusual degree of boldness, looking Henry straight in the face instead of keeping his eyes lowered as was the fashion of the English nobility. When it was remarked to Lisle-Adam that his boldness gave offence he justified it by saying that this manner of looking to those whom you addressed was the manner of France, and that if any dared not look upon the person to whom he spoke such a man was held an evil-disposed person and a traitor, "And such," said he, "I have never been." King Henry was supposed to nourish ill will against this baron, and some time° afterwards laid him under arrest, from which he was not dismissed without the personal intercession of Philip of Burgundy, to whom he had rendered many services.

But it must be remarked that the story is not fairly told unless we add that Lisle-Adam, a Frenchman, had not only betrayed his own country to the Burgundians by delivering up his own town of Lisle-Adam for passage of their army, but° had been the express agent to whom Paris had been surrendered by Perrinet Le Clerc, and that he was not arrested on account of his boldness in looking upon the king of England but on other and very important public charges.*

In another respect it appears that King Henry resembled more the idea of him which survives in England as the merry Prince Hal° than the stiff punctilious person with whom the French historians are willing to identify him.

In the month of May 1420 the high contracting parties of the treaty of Arras, having met together at Troyes, proceeded to confirm the articles of that treaty, and upon the second of June following the king of England was married to Catherine of France, the archbishop of Sens performing the ceremony. This active monarch did not allow the pleasures of his marriage to suspend the march of his enterprising disposition. Before entering triumphantly into the city of Paris he resolved to dispossess the dauphin of the towns of Sens, Montereau,° and Melun, which were still occupied by

---

* See Memoirs of Pierre de Fenin.° [36]

that party in the vicinity of the capital. When at Sens he experienced little opposition, and going to the cathedral church said kindly to the archbishop by whom he was accompanied, "It was but yesterday that you bestowed on me a wife: I now return the compliment by restoring your own to your reverence." This good-humoured jest had the effect of showing to what degree Henry possessed the winning qualities necessary to gain the attachment of his new subjects.

Montereau, being equally ill defended as Sens, fell into the hands of the English, and the duke of Burgundy caused disinter the corpse° of his father, who had been huddled into a mean and bloody grave, making him to be wrapped in more royal cerements, and transported° his remains to the church of Charlereuse in his capital of Dijon.

Melun stood a short siege when it was considerably battered with firearms, then instruments of late invention; a mine was also driven by King Henry beneath the walls of the fortress. The Frenchmen within the town ran a countermine so as to cut the subterranean works of the English, so that both parties might meet in combat in these underground excavations. Henry commanded his troops to prepare for the attack, for in these times the plan of blowing up the mines by gunpowder was not yet understood. Two English lords entered into a dispute between themselves which should command the attacking party. King Henry upon this resuming the command threw himself into the mine, and engaged in personal conflict with the sieur de Barbazan,° one of the bravest lords of the besieged party. After an equal combat they agreed to pause and tell each other their names, and the combat was for a time put an end to, Barbazan° expressing himself sufficiently honoured by meeting so great a monarch in single fight.

Melun, reduced to the extremity of famine, surrendered to the English, and no obstacle now remained betwixt King Henry and the possession of Paris. He entered in company of his unhappy father-in-law, yielding him the upper hand as they rode through the city gaily adorned and hung with tapestry between the gate of St Denis° and the cathedral of Notre Dame. The next day witnessed the triumphal entry of the two queens, who were received with honours similar to those of their husbands. The estates of France were convoked, or at least a large assembly of judges was° held upon the suit of the duke of Burgundy against the dauphin for the murder of his father. The prince of France was only termed in these proceedings the self-entitled or *soi disant* dauphin. In this extraordinary process the young prince was condemned as guilty of contumacy, and judgement having been passed against him as° convicted of murder he was declared to be banished France for ever, and to be incapable and unworthy of succession to the crown. This sentence was authenticated by the signature of John Le Clerc who acted as chancellor of France.

At the same time a heavy subsidy was laid on by the estates, in which every man was to pay in one-eighth of his substance. An edict was made debasing the coin to the amount of one-eighth, and the subjects paying in their proportions at the exchequer in heavy° money were acquitted of the tax by receiving as much in the same.

Henry of England assumed in the meantime the powers of sovereignty, making such alterations in offices and office-bearers as seemed most favourable to his own interest, and new modelling in many respects the laws of France. How far he might have been successful in reconciling the kingdom to the government of an English monarch time was not allowed to afford him a fair trial.° He was compelled to leave Paris on 6 January 1421[37] and retired to England by way of Rouen, being desirous° both that his young wife should be crowned in his native kingdom, and also because it concerned him deeply to obtain the assent of an English parliament to the important treaties which he had made whilst in France.

During his halt at Rouen he received homage of many of the French nobles in Normandy and bestowed the lieutenancy° of France with full regal power upon his brother Thomas duke of Clarence, and that of Normandy upon the earl of Salisbury.

It would be but a waste of time to declare with what joy and triumph this victorious young monarch, who in so short a time had added to his own crown one which was at least equally valuable, was received in° his hereditary dominions. The queen was crowned in the cathedral at Westminster,[38] and with most stately and magnificent ceremony. The festival or banquet was entirely composed of fish, as appropriate to the season of Lent, interspersed with various emblematic representations in which St Catherine the patron saint and namesake of the queen appeared.°

After these solemnities Henry V and his queen made a solemn progress as well in fashion of pilgrimage as for the purpose of remedying abuses.

While they were thus employed the king received news of the unfortunate battle of Baugé, of which we shall speak, and° which was fought on Easter Even in the year 1421.

Having convoked a meeting of his parliament upon hearing the state of affairs in France, the Commons gladly granted a fifteenth, and the clergy offered a double tenth, of which the wealthy bishop of Winchester advanced to the king twenty thousand pounds that his affair might not stop from the delay of money. With these supplies he levied an army consisting (some authors say) of four thousand men-at-arms and twenty thousand archers; others say that the whole army, counting forces of every description, did not exceed twelve thousand men.[39] With these apparently small forces he hastened over to France, leaving his wife about to be confined, who was shortly after delivered of a son, the ill-fated Henry VI. He confided in his own talents as well as in the courage and discipline of his troops, and quickly began to appear in the field to repel the force of his rival the dauphin.

This young prince was in the meanwhile at the head of all the nobles in the south of France and endeavoured to fill his ranks, far too small for the occasion, by applying for foreign assistance. Already in 1419 he had sent an embassy to the duke of Albany, regent of Scotland, requiring the support of Scotland. In consequence the Scottish nation, little disposed to see their old allies fall under the crown of their ambitious neighbours, sent an auxiliary force of nearly seven thousand men led by John Stewart,° earl of Buchan, son of the regent, and the dauphin instantly united them with his own little army in order to defend the province of Anjou against the attacks of the English duke of Clarence, whom Henry V had detached for its reduction. The English general upon 22 March 1421 obtained information that the whole Scottish auxiliary force and some French troops were lying at the town of Baugé in Anjou. Clarence was at dinner when he received the news, but eagerly sprung from table exclaiming, "Upon them, they are ours! but let no one follow me except the men-at-arms."

After a quick and exhausting march Clarence came to Baugé, where the few French defended the church on the right of the river and gained time for the earl of Buchan to place his troops in order at the farther end of the bridge for its defence. This interrupted the English attack upon the church, and leaving it untaken in their rear the English cavalry pressed° forwards to the attack of Buchan along the long and narrow bridge. Their leader Clarence led the band, being distinguished by a coronet of gold richly decked with jewels. Sir John Swinton of Swinton, a Scottish man of great strength, rode upon the English prince with his lance and bore him to the ground, while the earl of Buchan slew him with a battle-axe as he endeavoured to rise. The count of Kent,° Lords Grey and Ross, and about fourteen or fifteen hundred English men-at-arms fell on the same occasion,[40] and the French and their adherents rejoiced over the first victory which they had for a long time attained over their enemies of England.

The dauphin rewarded Buchan by the dignity of constable of France which he bestowed on him, and employed him to engage his countrymen to send him further assistance. In the meantime, whatever was the success of the battle of Baugé it would probably have been soon balanced° by the experience and valour of Henry V, but heaven had set an unexpected bound to his progress, without which it is perhaps possible that he might have established his family on the throne of France. The° dauphin having advanced as far as Chartres, the English monarch, almost always victorious, not only repulsed him but made himself master of the town of Meaux after a gallant defence.[41] The dauphin in the meantime resolved to harass° the duke of Burgundy, and entering his dominions laid siege to the town of Cosne. King Henry prepared to march to the relief of his ally, but he found himself assailed on his march by an invisible enemy. This was a severe attack of a disease which can now be cured by a surgical operation but was then believed to be beyond the power of healing art.[41] Being obliged to stop at the castle of Vincennes, and feeling the approaches of death though in the prime of manhood, he summoned around his bed the princes of his blood and Heu de Lannoy, envoy of Burgundy, and dictated

to them his last will. By this he bequeathed the regency of France jointly
to the dukes of Burgundy and Bedford, the regency of England to the
duke of Gloucester, and the superintendance of the education of his infant
son to the earl° of Warwick. He conjured the assembled princes to live in
union together, and cautioned them against setting at freedom any of the
French princes of the blood who remained prisoners in England since the
battle of Agincourt. Finally he earnestly recommended to their faithful
charge his queen, soon to be an early widow, and his infant son, afterwards
the unfortunate Henry VI. He then received the consolations of religion,
and it is remarked that while they read in his dying ear the Psalm called
miserere° [43] he awaked as out of a profound trance at hearing the words of
scripture concerning the rebuilding the walls of Jerusalem. "It was my
purpose," he said, "had I lived to settle France in quiet, to have gone to the
conquest of the Holy Land."

Thus died Henry V of England on 31 August° 1422. He had seemingly
raised his son to the noble inheritance of France as well as of England, to
neither of which he had a legitimate right, but having exhausted his realm
by gigantic efforts and enterprizes which could only be supported by talents equal to his own he in fact paved the way for the total ruin of his
own family. Three weeks after the death of a prince who was, or seemed
to be, the very favourite of fortune Henry V was followed to the tomb by
his unfortunate father-in-law Charles VI,° a prince in some sort marked
out as a special butt° for the arrows of misfortune. This unhappy prince
had been long considered as a mere cypher, and his queen Isabelle, though
inhabiting the same house, did not even appear by his dying bed during
his last illness. No prince of the blood, no high officer of the household,
was present at his parting scene, and the people with a mixture of public
sorrow and private shame saw the duke of Bedford, an Englishman, regent
of France, conduct without assistant the obsequies of the unfortunate king
of France. When his coffin was lowered into the tomb at St Denis° a herald
pronounced these words: "Pray for the soul of Charles VI,° king of France,
and long life to Henry of Lancaster, king of France and of England."

By this funeral orison the mortal life of Charles VI° was not only declared to be ended, but the accession of a new race was proclaimed over
his coffin: but heaven had decreed otherwise in its own time and by its
own means.

Chapter 7

The deaths of Henry V and of his father-in-law Charles removed the old actors from the field, and a new course of events seemed about to take place. The late English monarch had left the ministration of his power in France to the joint charge of his brother the duke of Bedford and his ally the duke of Burgundy, while Queen Isabelle set up in her own right the same title which she had before pretended to a share in the government of France; but her conduct and character had gained no respect with either party, and from the time of her husband's death she appears to have been maintained and protected by the English out° of decency and propriety as the mother-in-law of their deceased monarch, but in no respect either to her character or her office. The French writers say[44] that the English upbraided her with her irregular life, but though such instances might occur among the low and illiterate, yet to the period of her death in 1435 she always termed the duke of Bedford her son, which was a proof of his uniform kindness towards her. The duke of Burgundy had a better right to claim a share in the regency, but he probably foresaw° that he would only be permitted to exercize it for the sake of England and for no advantage of his own or that° of France herself, and besides he probably held himself sufficiently bound by the treaty of Arras, which bound him as we have already said to sacrifice the interest of his own house to that of° England, while it assured him of no advantage for the sacrifice excepting revenge for his father's death. He therefore declined acting as joint regent, and the duke of Bedford exercised the authority of that great office without a partner and without control. He was a prince of abilities scarcely inferior to those of Henry V, and if his long efforts in favour of his nephew's authority were less successful than his warlike brother's° they appear to have been neither better planned nor more sincere. He then it was who held up the banner of England within the realm of France. The provinces peculiarly subject to him were those of the north, the east, and the extreme western provinces, the counties adjacent to Flanders indeed being determined by the continued adherence of the duke of Burgundy to the English interest. On the other side were the° whole south provinces of France, namely Dauphiné, Languedoc, Bourbonnais, Auvergne,° Berry, Poitou, Saintonge, Touraine, and Orleans; and the dauphin's sway was even interrupted in these provinces by the intrigues of great lords who thought the time favourable for setting up for independence and were many of them privately in league with the public enemy. His principal allies were the poor natives of Scotland, who could afford him no assistance except those auxiliaries of whom Douglas brought over to France a second army in 1424. Charles VI° had endeavoured to render the service acceptable to these auxiliaries by liberal rewards to their commanders. The earl of Buchan had been created count d'Aubigny as well as constable of France.[45] He besieged the town of Cravant° in the same year, but having the misfortune to be surprized his army was defeated with the loss of a thousand men. The constable himself and his relation Stewart of Darnley° were made prisoners.

In point of character the dauphin appears to have had that gentleness and affability which always render a prince popular, but it was some time° ere he displayed that judgement which observes quickly the time for action and instantly seizes upon it; and for some time he appears to have been unfit for the hardy and resolute character which fate had designed him to exhibit. Meanwhile the adherents on both sides continued a petty warfare of no great consequence, unless in teaching the partizans of the dauphin the° qualities necessary to secure success in the long run in a struggle of this nature.

Towns, castles, and villages were taken on each side and sometimes retaken in an incredibly short time. Skirmishes were fought without much result except inuring the combatants to the use of arms and the habits of a martial life. It was easy to observe the reason why in such continued warfare the party defending their own country must have obtained gradual advantages over the invaders. They became accustomed to the terrors of the English archery, and although they could not form a rival force of the same kind yet by means of pavoises or large targets, by the frequent use of their men-at-arms, and other warlike evolutions they learned to elude, if not to oppose, the fatal arrows of the English. The mere habit of war of itself forms soldiers, and the custom of meeting an enemy armed in a particular manner creates in time the habits of resisting them. On the other hand the English troops in France were never very numerous and began to grow thin in prosecution of a constant and wasting, though an unimportant warfare. The officers of Henry V became in time desirous of ease, sensible of the advance of old age, and less fit for active war than when they first followed the banners of that victorious monarch. Still° however among a long tract of uninteresting hostilities we may notice some events which had a more important effect either on the one side or on the other. The first actions were greatly to the disadvantage of the French, and in fact deprived them of the sole body of auxiliaries which adhered to them in their misfortunes. We have said that the celebrated earl of Douglas had, notwithstanding the defeat of the Scottish at Cravant,° brought a new army of five thousand men to the assistance of the dauphin Charles, who having° the victory of Baugé in his recollection gladly received the assistance of a large body of the countrymen of such as had gained it. Their chiefs were loaded with royal favours: the earl of Buchan who had been taken at Cravant° obtained the county of Dreux,° and the earl of Douglas was created duke of Touraine and invested with a certain authority over the French warriors, which perhaps created some national jealousy betwixt them and the strangers, a people who are frequently accused of impetuosity and precipitation, from which the French themselves are not free.

The Scottish auxiliaries were appointed principally to the defence of the Loire and the protection of the province of Berry; it was in this service that Buchan sustained the defeat of Cravant,° and the Scottish army were now doomed to undergo another conflict, the event of which was very like to cause their total annihilation.

The duke of Bedford had formed the siege of Ivry;° the Scots advanced to raise the siege; Bedford on this moved forward towards Verneuil° to meet with Douglas and his countrymen. A sort of war of sarcasm had subsisted betwixt these noblemen of hostile countries. Douglas in ridicule of the slow motions of Bedford had termed him John with the leaden sword, and to repay the sarcasm Bedford sent a herald to inform Douglas that he was come to drink wine with him and hoped to find him provided accordingly. The Scottish earl replied that he had himself come from Scotland to have the pleasure of carousing with Bedford and he would be happy to receive him. Meantime the Scottish and French chieftains went to council and unfortunately differed in opinion. Some historians say that the viscount of Narbonne, the French general, insisted on rushing against the English contrary to the advice of Douglas° and others who preferred waiting for them in an advantageous situation. Others of these historians reverse these opinions of the two generals.[46] It is needless to enquire which out of two nations at least equally rash and fond of battle committed upon this occasion the fault of precipitance. The° one dragging forward the other, they left their advantageous position and rushed on to meet the English, losing ranks, station, and breath° while their enemies of course retained all these advantages. The French and Scottish incurred a defeat which these causes rendered inevitable, and almost all the men of distinction of both countries fell in the field together with the two commanders the Scottish Douglas° and Buchan. The French commander Narbonne, the count du Marie,° and other French noblemen were also found amid the slain. The body of Narbonne was broken on the wheel and hung° upon a gibbet to gratify the Burgundians, who imputed to him a share in the murder of John the Fearless on the bridge of Montereau, at which atrocity he was certainly present.

The immediate succours from Scotland being thus destroyed, the policy of Bedford took the opportunity at the same time of cutting off those supplies which French gold and national antipathy might otherwise have easily obtained from the same country.

James I of Scotland, forced into an English port by stress of weather while a child destined to Paris for his education, had been detained a captive for many years by the injustice of Henry IV and his son. The regent Bedford now set this young prince at liberty, having previously concluded with him an alliance offensive and defensive,° and an English marriage, which of course precluded his yielding farther succours to France.

The French however were not unmindful of the benefits which they had already received from their Scottish allies. Earl Douglas was buried° sumptuously in the city of Tours, the capital of his brief dukedom. The remainder of the Scottish forces, miserably reduced, formed the first materiels of that Scottish royal guard to whom for ages afterwards France entrusted the custody of her sovereign's person.

The effect of the battles of Cravant and Verneuil° were of course very disastrous to France, although it hardly appears that the English made sufficient advantage of them.

In addition to this must be stated the singular disposition of Charles the dauphin, whom we have already mentioned as greatly short of those heroic characters which marked the destined restorer of a ruined monarchy. His excessive poverty was not indeed his fault, but it became one of his greatest misfortunes when it produced in him a reckless desperation, a species of hardness of heart which made him contentedly apply to idle pomp and personal pleasure the small sums he was able to command and which ought to have been strictly reserved for public purposes, however inadequate they might be to their full discharge; hence La Hire, consulted by the prince upon the ordinance of a festival while his affairs were in a very bad situation, answered° him that surely never was there a king who lost his kingdom with so much gaiety as he did. M. Petitot is of opinion that this thoughtlessness has been exaggerated,[47] but his wants scarcely could be, since it was some° time before he could pay the sum of forty livres due° to a chaplain who christened his first son, and about the same time the treasurer of Bourges had in his hands royal treasure to the amount of four crowns only.

Charles appears to have had the common vice of sovereigns which is generally ascribed to weakness of disposition, by which we mean an inclination to favouritism, or rather a disposition to trust everything to those ministers as showed talents to administer the revenues without wearying their masters with importunities or advices. It was neither in favour of the most worthy persons that° the king exercised this predilection, nor does it seem to have been accompanied with much personal liking to those preferred, whom he saw driven from his counsels and put to death though possessed of his full confidence, and that without manifesting the slightest regret,° the only apparent sentiment of the prince appearing to be that if° the support or safety of a favourite would cost him an effort on his behalf it was best and easiest to part with him without making any attempt to prevent his fall.

To give instances of these facts we must recall to our readers'° recollection that duke of Bretagne who had been so loyally educated by the constable Clisson.[48] After the death of John duke of Burgundy this prince, whose accession was of great importance both to France and England, had observed a very dubious line of conduct, sometimes uniting with Philip duke of Burgundy in revenge of his father's death, sometimes expressing himself more disposed to join interests with the unfortunate dauphin. In the meantime Charles VII made an essay to attract to his side the brother of the duke of Bretagne, Arthur count° of Richmond, who had been made prisoner at Agincourt but afterwards inclined° to the English faction in France, had been created an English peer, and was° one of these fierce and martial characters of the age who knew no happiness unless in commanding armies and gaining victories, a rough and ambitious soldier of high talents and dissatisfied with the employment which the English afforded a soldier at the same time ambitious, haughty, and of great politics. The English had showed themselves reserved in gratifying Richmond's ambition, and he therefore entered into terms with the dauphin, and acknowledged his title to the throne who was enabled at the time to gratify him by holding out as an object the baton° of the constable which was then unoccupied. Decency however and consistency dictated to Richmond certain conditions on his own part. He stipulated that Tanneguy du Chastel, the dauphin's° favourite, who struck John duke of Burgundy the fatal blow, should be expelled Charles's councils in future, and also that Louvet,° minister of finance, and several other favourite servants of the dauphin—most part of the dauphin's ministers, against whom he brought a charge of having agreed with the family of Penthièvre, who had laid a plan for making themselves master of the person of John° duke of Bretagne, brother of Richmond the proposed constable—should be dismissed from his court and person in consideration of the count° of Richmond agreeing to serve him as constable.

Charles VII submitted to these conditions, however mortifying, and Richmond, having stated his terms of service, received the staff of constable and departed° to levy an army in his brother's° dominions, where his interest as next heir to the dukedom of Bretagne gave him much personal weight. Meantime the ministers for whose disgrace Richmond, having met with Charles at Chinon, had stipulated° and their master Charles had engaged, resolved that if possible they would keep their places and brave the resentment of the constable. But Richmond was not a man to endure this treatment. He marched towards Charles VII with a considerable body of troops, and the weak king, being ashamed or afraid to meet him under the consciousness of having broken his word by retaining around him the very persons whom he had engaged to dismiss, gave the people of France the strange spectacle of their king flying from place to place closely pursued by his own high constable. Several towns, disgusted by such a spectacle, disposed themselves to abandon the cause of so weak a prince; but the inconsistence of Charles was the means of showing more clearly than ever the union of great qualities with those of a very different description in the character of Tanneguy du Chastel. This faithful subject, ashamed to see his master put to a species of disgrace because he insisted in keeping him around his° person, resolved in a spirit of self-devotion scarce belonging to a person marked by murther and assassination* that he would himself of free accord leave the court rather than see his prince exposed to total ruin by persisting in remaining with him. The king opposed himself to this act of devotion, but the firmness of the subject prevailed, and James and the other ministers who could not plead Tanneguy du Chastel's merits towards that sovereign were placed under the necessity to follow his example, however unwilling.

The constable entered upon the duties of his office with a high hand, and in order to secure a regular supply of money for military expenses he caused the finances of Languedoc to be put under the charge of two intendants, one of whom was to be named by himself. With these precautions, and with an army of about twenty thousand men, the constable laid siege to St James of Beuvron,° a town defended by a strong garrison of French and English. In the meantime the funds of which his precaution seemed to have ensured a regular supply fell short as formerly, and the soldiers began to disband. This was the fault of Giac, husband to the infamous mistress of John duke of Burgundy, who since the murder at Montereau had remained at Charles's court and° continued to raise himself to the full rank of a favourite under protection of Louvet, who recommended him to the dauphin as a useful servant when he himself retired from the court. Invested with some charge over the revenue, this new favourite had no hesitation in diverting from necessary purposes the money which was destined for the war. The constable, finding his forces failing by desertion and otherwise, made an attack upon Beuvron in which he sustained a severe defeat and was obliged to raise the siege, leaving in the power of the English his artillery and baggage. Stung with resentment at this gross breach of faith, Richmond endeavoured to repair his reputation by one or two smaller advantages, and then, having resorted to the king's camp in person, he seized upon Giac of his own authority and put him to death without apprehending or experiencing any rebuke on the part of the king.

Notwithstanding the disastrous° fate of Giac, a nobleman or gentleman entitled Camus de Beaulieu aspired to the dangerous consequence of a royal favourite who undertook the charge of the general finances. This person, like his predecessors, abused his credit by the sacrifice of public funds to the private pleasure of the crown more openly than even Giac had done. The stern constable requited him also with even less ceremony, causing him to be slain by the maréchal de Boussac° under the walls of the castle of Poitiers in which the king was residing, and almost under his very eyes.[49] In this, as in the case of Giac, the constable, say the historians,[50]

---

* Besides the tragedy on the bridge at Montereau Tanneguy du Chastel was also active in the murder of a nobleman called the compte° dauphin of Auvergne, whom he killed in full council and in presence of Charles VII.

explained to the king that he had only acted for the good of the state and found the feeble-minded monarch easily satisfied.

To prevent the necessity of such strange examples in future, and to establish a friend of his own near the king's person, the constable resolved to assist La Trémoille, a young man apparently agreeable to the monarch and who might keep Charles company during the time of his own necessary absence in command of the army, according to Richmond's idea, forwarding not intercepting the military plans. The king himself however showed an unexpected repugnance to the measure proposed, and warned the constable concerning the false step in politics he was about to take, saying these remarkable words: "You insist then, fair cousin, that I shall take this man into my privacy? beware of him: I know him better than you, and I know you will repent of what you are doing."

The constable persisted in his opinion, and Trémoille, left° about the person of the king, soon, like his predecessors, made himself master of his thoughts and convinced the flexible Charles that in Richmond, instead of acquiring a devoted captain, he had got an imperious master who daily° subjected him to the most cruel affronts° and took the life without hesitation of the king's most valued servants. He° shut the gates of several towns against the constable, called to the court the count of Penthièvre, the ancient° and implacable enemy of the reigning house of Montfort° of Bretagne, and had recourse to every measure which could thwart Richmond in his operations for the service of Charles VII.

Chapter 8

While the affairs of the dauphin were in this disorder owing to the quarrels between the manager of his civil revenue and the director of his military efforts, a great quarrel had also come to exist between the duke of Burgundy, and Gloucester the youngest brother of Henry V. The cause was the beautiful Jacqueline of° Brabant, a very great heiress in her own right. This lady was attached to the duke of Gloucester, and though sure by his pretensions° to her large inheritance to disgust the duke of Burgundy, the English prince nevertheless persisted in his imprudent attempt to secure to himself so great an inheritance in Flanders, a legacy° intermingled with the dominions of Burgundy. Gloucester, without regarding the duke of Burgundy's displeasure, endeavoured to seize upon the inheritance of Jacqueline by main force. In doing so Gloucester openly thwarted his brother Bedford, a man of a generous and public-spirited character, who almost by his private talents and resources maintained a war which was left almost entirely upon his hand by the other English nobles, the brothers and companions in arms of King Henry V, but who was now basely engaged in the fatal intrigues which terminated in the bloody civil war of York and Lancaster.

The regent Bedford, thus ill supported, had been obliged to depart to England, where he had acted as peacemaker between his relation the bishop of Winchester and the same Gloucester. With difficulty also he obtained new reinforcements to the extent of about twenty thousand men, from which reinforcement, however, great advantages might have been expected considering the discord and sunk hopes of the French royalists, who as we have seen were furiously tearing each other to pieces. Their affairs were indeed so desperate that Charles VII had resolved to retreat to some strong castle in Dauphiné, and from° that to seek his way to Spain or Scotland, where he hoped to find shelter. Nor did his warmest adherents see the means of postponing this desperate resolution for any length of time.

The English in general felt the superiority over their ancient enemy which was inspired by such victories as Crécy, Poitiers, and Agincourt, any one of° which great conflicts makes more impression on the memory and fills the imagination more fully than any imaginable number of skirmishes lost on the same side. The French also were impressed with the obstinacy which bad fortune had shown in pursuing them, and looked sadly to this new campaign of the duke of Bedford as the last which they should be able to sustain in defence of their independence. Providence however designed, by means which no mortal could have divined, to avert this great calamity, and the progress of events was° so remarkable as to make it worth while to trace them with unusual minuteness.

The plan of the English campaign began with the siege of Orleans, which was valiantly pressed by an excellent general, Montague earl of Salisbury. It was the first in which cannon were employed upon a general scale, and bullets of a hundred pounds weight are said to have been directed against the walls of the town by the English engines.° Within the place was shut up the celebrated Dunois, called by the plainness of the times the Bastard of Orleans, being literally an illegitimate son of that prince of Orleans who was murdered in the streets° of Paris. The English exhausted their skill in mining and in other points of the engineering art, but so valiant was the defence of Dunois and his garrison that the earl of Salisbury was compelled to proceed by surrounding the place with a circumvallation to prevent its receiving supplies and proceeding against the defenders by the slow method of famine. The Bastard of Orleans fought in person most fiercely to prevent the erection of these bulwarks by which the English expected to compel the surrender of the besieged place. But fortune, who had for a long time favoured the English, was now about to change her colours.

A principal tower which was taken by the English had in its highest storey° a grated window through which the captains of the besieging host were enabled to perceive the operations of the besieged and often went to the tower for that purpose. The principal engineer of the city observed this practice and charged a cannon, which he pointed against the aperture. He made his son acquainted with his device, who chanced to be on duty when the earl of Salisbury and two English knights of great account were seen peeping from the grated window. The boy fired the piece as his father had instructed him, and the ball arriving among the iron bars dashed them into the chamber and thus made great havoc, Salisbury being mortally wounded and one of his companions slain on the spot.

The death of this valiant soldier, though much lamented by the English, was compensated in some degree by the entrance of a large supply of provisions into the English lines and the defeat of the French by a person whose name, having been given as a fictitious character upon the stage, is for that reason very familiar to us; I mean Sir John Falstaff. The battle was called the Fight of the Herrings on account of a great many barrels of that fish making a part of the convoy for behoof of the Englishmen in the season of Lent which was now approaching.

The citizens of Orleans were so depressed by this last accident that they resolved to surrender; but desirous even in their submission to inflame the jealousy which they naturally supposed to exist between the English and the Burgundians their allies, they offered to surrender Orleans to Philip duke of Burgundy in preference to the power of England. Deputies were sent to Philip, whose consent would have been ready if the duke of Bedford had not haughtily rejected the proposal of the besieged, saying he would have Orleans surrendered at his own will and not otherwise; neither did he understand being set to beat the bushes while others got possession of the game. Philip is said to have sent orders to recall his Burgundian troops, but their number was small, nor did it much weaken the besieging army.

Lastly, to complete the misfortunes of Orleans, the citizens in despair attempted a general sally, but persevering too long in the design they lost nearly as many men as the besiegers, and as the English were now° rendered vigilant by this last attack all hopes of relief seemed to be effectually cut off, and the siege seemed to be brought to a termination.

Chapter 9

Such were the events which seemed about to conclude the siege of Orleans, but it was to be marked to all posterity by a circumstance much more wonderful than either the death of a great soldier by a chance cannon° bullet or the escape or capture of a convoy of provisions. To understand it in all its particulars we must take up the story at a period considerably earlier than the convoy of the herrings.

Joan of Arc, the peasant girl for whom so extraordinary a part was reserved, was born in the year 1410 or 1411. Her father and mother were villagers living poorly and painfully by the cultivation of the land and the breeding of their cattle. They had three sons and one daughter besides the celebrated heroine who gave distinction to the family. In person Joan of Arc was rather large but well shaped and comely, strong and athletic. In disposition she approached to what is called in her country *une dévote*. She made a point of attending prayers on all occasions, either° in the church of Domremy or in a small rustic chapel dedicated to the Holy Virgin situated not far from the town. She was equally remarkable for observing with accuracy the popular traditions still current among those of her class and handed down to them most likely from pagan antiquity. The village maidens of Domremy were used, since the times of the druids perhaps, to venerate a large tree of great size and venerable age which grew in a forest called Bois Chênes near to their village. It was supposed to be dedicated to the fairies, and the older villagers° pretended to have seen these° ideal beings in that neighbourhood, which was accounted sacred to the fairies.° The Catholics had, as is not uncommon with them, adopted this local superstition into the object of a Christian procession, which the curate of Domremy headed in person upon the eve of Ascension Day. It appears that she was from childhood attentive to the ceremonies of religion alike with the superstitious practices of the country, and as she grew older she became still more remarkable among her companions. Like other persons of an enthusiastic disposition she became accessible to petty scruples and solicitous about trifling° observances.

The sexton of Domremy caused her much anxiety by neglecting to ring the complines with due regularity, and the poor girl not only put this official person in remembrance of his duty, but promised him a small reward out of her own hard-won wages on condition of his being more accurate in future in marking the hour of prayer. In temper Joan d'Arc was mild, gentle, and timid, loving solitude, and remaining if permitted apart from youths of her age and much alone. Although arrived at the age when handsome girls attract the attention of the other sex, she never encouraged the least proposal of gallantry, and was never° seen to distinguish any lad of the village more than another, nor was she ever observed to be present at village dances, festivals, and similar places of resort where the young° people of both sexes may meet with the most innocent purposes.

It remains to notice some personal attributes which have been questioned because they diminish in some degree the marvellous attendant on her character, and to a modern historian therefore appear to render the solution of the riddle more easy. During a part of her life when Joan resided as a kind of helper or assistant with a relation of hers who kept a country inn and dealt in horses, there she accustomed herself to labours which were not strictly feminine,° and learned with ease to ride and to arrange the most untractable horses, to carry and place upon their backs great loads, and to practise all the parts of a robust education proper to a country hostler, a sort of work which at that time sometimes devolved on the women for want of the other sex consumed by the war, and in acquiring which Joan of Arc gained many facilities for her future mission.

In the meantime, thus formed in mind and body Joan of Arc was sought in marriage by a young man whose circumstances rendered him a favourable match, but who being unable otherwise to obtain his wishes pretended that she stood engaged to him by promise, and brought a law suit against her, which was dismissed for want of proof with a sentence in her favour.

In the meantime, and while harassed by this litigation, the girl adopted the fanciful idea that she heard voices whispering in her ear, directing her future course of life and purveying important events to be performed by her means. Under the idea that these suggestions arose° from divine inspiration she promised solemnly that she would dedicate herself to the service of heaven. These mysteries were not in her idea palpable to the imagination alone. St Michael, St Catherine, St Marguerite, and other saints appeared to her visibly and repeatedly,° and assured her that France could not be rescued except by a young shepherdess, and that she herself was the maiden destined for this glorious task. The idea, however it might at first suggest itself, was the more readily entertained because the poor as well as the rich in France were interested in the factions with which the kingdom was torn to pieces, and Joan and all her family had always espoused vigorously the party of Armagnacs or royalists. Being now free of her law suit, an event which she said had been foretold° by the blessed saints as well as by the inspiration of the celestial voices, she declared openly to her relations and friends how it had been revealed to her that she was to go to the camp of the dauphin and bring to Orleans the relief which no one but herself was able to introduce into that unfortunate city. She declared that she was previously desirous of going to Vaucouleurs in the neighbourhood of Domremy, which was garrisoned by a royal force under a M. de Baudricourt. She importuned a brother-in-law of her mother's to escort her on this journey to this place, who at first refused to have accession to so wild a scheme, and when overcome by her entreaties refused positively to have anything more to do with the affair than to conduct her as far as Vaucouleurs. Here she was received by the curate, who conjured her if she were animated by an evil spirit to depart, but if by a good one to approach, when apparently the piety, candour, simplicity, and modesty of Joan made some impression upon her° reverent host, whose attestation made a similar one upon° the seigneur de Baudricourt. The governor, yielding perhaps to the superstition of the times, thought the business at least important enough to be communicated to the king, and wrote for instructions in a matter too much allied to the opinions of the age to be cast altogether aside without notice, yet too improbable (and almost ludicrous) to be rashly meddled with.

Joan was so impatient to commence her supposed mission that she set off for the camp of the dauphin with her uncle and another person, but returned to obtain at least a letter from Baudricourt to attest her identity and to show that she had the countenance of some person of rank. On this second return to Vaucouleurs Joan had an interview with a gentleman of some rank called Monsieur de Metz who addressed her thus: "What do you do here, my child? do you not know that the king is to be chased from his kingdom, and that we are all about to be subjected to the English yoke?" "I am here," said Joan with the dauntless enthusiasm of her character, "that the seignior de Baudricourt may afford me the means of going to the king, but he takes no heed of me and my words; yet I shall see the king ere my Lent° is half over, and I must perfect the rest should I wear down my legs to my very knees. For no person in the world, neither king, nor duke, nor daughter of the king of Scotland,* can redeem the kingdom of France or bring effectual succour to the king except I myself. God knows I would rather remain and spin with my poor mother; but such is not my vocation, and I must go because my master wills it." "Who is that master of thine?" replied Monsieur de Metz. "It is God," answered Joan. The simplicity and tone of inspiration carried along with them the gentleman, who, taking the hand of the maiden, himself° declared that by his faith and under the conduct of God he himself would conduct her to the king. "When," said he, "would you wish to set out?" "Today rather than tomorrow," replied the maiden, but afterwards she delayed her journey till a male dress was provided for her, which she assumed by the command, she said, of the internal voices. John de Metz now, having caught the flame of enthusiasm, pressed the departure of the maiden and was seconded by another gentleman named Bertrand de Poulengy. Permission for Joan to come to court was also received from Charles by Baudricourt, who of course offered no further opposition. The poor inhabitants of Vaucouleurs taxed themselves to purchase the inspired maiden suitable clothes and a

---

* For whom Charles VII was then negotiating as a match for his eldest son and expected with her a supply of fresh succour from Scotland.

horse, for which last however her mother's brother was obliged to grant his security.

Joan of Arc set out for Charles's court in a manner which marked that her mission had obtained a certain degree of credit. The seigneurs of Metz° and Poulengy, each with° an attendant, formed her° escort, to which were added Colet de Vienne and an archer called Richard. (The first was the messenger° sent to Baudricourt from the dauphin.) Such was the commencement of the journey of the singular person° appointed by heaven to do such great things.

The father and mother of the maiden came in a state of absolute despair and certainly made the deepest lamentation, so that the heroine herself said after the commencement of her brilliant career that they had nigh lost their senses. "But," said she, "I have since written to them and obtained their pardon."

On the day fixed for their departure the inhabitants of Vaucouleurs pressed to witness the ceremony which the maiden herself rendered remarkable by her intrepidity. When it was asked at her whether she did not fear traversing so great a space of country infested by the licentious men-at-arms on both sides she answered, "Believe me, I shall find the road free; or if there are men-at-arms,° or if any are seen on the route, the master whom I serve will make me a safe way to the person of the dauphin."

By many of the spectators the youthful heroine was in reality regarded as the inspired person which she certainly believed herself to be. Baudricourt remained still doubtful. He obeyed the court in authorising her departure, and imposed an oath upon those gentlemen Metz and Poulengy charged with her escort to bring her in safety to the dauphin's presence; but he was far from partaking of the enthusiasm which animated a peasant girl of seventeen years old who supposed herself setting forth to deliver a kingdom which nodded to its fall. His last words indeed expressed a wish rather than a hope that this extraordinary mission might possibly turn to good. "Go," he said, "and may such advantage come of it as matters render possible."

The little band of travellers which set out on 13° February[51] 1428 had many difficulties to encounter in traversing the provinces possessed by the English and Burgundians.

It is easy to suppose that King Charles had already obtained full information respecting the heroine who was now by devious routes approaching to his court, and it is probable that he determined to give a stratagem which was suited to the age a fair opportunity of operating in his behalf. It is not unlikely also that Joan should have made herself well acquainted with the personal appearance of Charles, whom she had been so anxious to see, and that she had acquired other information necessary for discharging her character in the scene which lay° before her.

She found the° dauphin Charles in a hall highly illuminated by torches where he was in company of many other lords, he himself simply habited and keeping himself retired among the press of courtiers. Nevertheless the maiden contended that he was pointed out to her by the internal voices, and it certainly appears that, distinguishing him from the multitude, she embraced his knees and said, "God give you a happy life, my lord the king!"

"I am not the king," answered Charles, and endeavoured to impose upon her by pointing to a young nobleman richly dressed on purpose, to which the maiden replied, "Nay, as surely as I am sent by heaven it is you yourself, most noble dauphin, to whom I am sent by the king of heaven in order to relieve this city and to conduct you thereafter to the cathedral of Rheims, there to be crowned and consecrated after the fashion of your ancestors."

The maiden was next examined by several of the councillors, both clerical and laic,° to whom she made such answers as satisfied them on the subject of her divine mission, in which she calmly and uniformly persisted whilst on every other she exhibited the simplicity of a peasant girl of the lowest class. She is said also to have communicated to the king in presence of the duke of Alençon, of the dauphin's confessor, and other persons of trust a secret of great importance which was known only to Charles himself. It was then agreed to dispatch her to Poitiers where the court of parliament was then sitting, which they conceived would be subjecting her to a competent court of enquiry into the truth of her protestations. At Poitiers she underwent another examination, which she maintained with the same prudence and moderation as at Chinon. A Carmelite, a doctor in theology, objected to her that Holy Scripture forbade them to add faith to such words as she used unless they were confirmed by a sign from heaven. "It is true," she said, "and the sign of my mission is that I shall deliver Orleans, and that I shall carry the king to be consecrated at Rheims." "But Joan," said another of the theologians, "you desire the assistance of troops for this purpose, whereas if it was the pleasure of God that the English should return to their native country there could be no occasion for men-at-arms to chase them hence." "True, reverend sir," replied the heroine, "but God works by human means, and although a few men-at-arms are wanted yet the smallest number will be sufficient, so as to remove nothing from the wonder of the miracle." In conclusion the council settled unanimously that the maiden was no enthusiast or impostor, while the women who had been admitted to the examination, and many of the statesmen and churchmen themselves, shed tears of joy in accrediting the mission which heaven was supposed to have sent for their relief.

The maiden, to whom the king now appointed not only a suit of armour but a train of valiant attendants, now furnished herself with a weapon in a manner which gave a new proof of her superhuman character.

Having made enquiry at Poitiers concerning a sword which was said to be at the church of St Catherine de Fierbois° she was asked if she had ever been there herself. She replied in the negative, but described the church so exactly that persons making search there found among a parcel of old iron in some corner a rusted sword-blade bearing five crosses on the upper part near the handle, and caused it to be cleaned and mounted proper for her use.

Old prophesies were now remembered which seemed to announce the defeat of the English by the hands of a maiden, and the credit given to the original story was as in similar cases greatly strengthened by various reports. The dauphin resolved upon accomplishing the relief of Orleans, and collected for that purpose a large stock of provisions to be put under the guidance of the maiden which she conducted so far as Blois, where she waited till she was joined by the troops destined to the relief of the place. Joan had expected to proceed at the head of her convoy right against the circumvallations of the enemy, but to her surprise the Bastard Dunois rather chose to ascend the Loire by water, load the vessels with the provisions at Blois, and thus introduce the Maid of Arc privately and unawares into the city from which she was destined to take her name. It was therefore with some displeasure that she met the commander "of the French." "Are you," she said, "the Bastard of Orleans, and who has directed you to bring us into the city otherwise than by the road most directly exposed to the force of the English?" Dunois defended himself by saying he had acted by the advice of the best soldiers, who considered the proposal of Joan as too rash to be undertaken.

She did not conceal her displeasure, entered the town however with the convoy, and commanded under pain of death that she should be apprised when the English commander Falstaff should approach a certain bulwark of the besiegers which supported the line of circumvallation. At the same time she informed Dunois that his want of faith would have ruined the expedition had it not been for the intercession of St Louis and St Charlemagne, who had petitioned for the city of Orleans more especially as containing the body of his beloved son the duke of that city. The English had already, it would seem, experienced the awe at the approach of a person distinguished by supernatural powers which in the opposite degree had been experienced by the French. They felt as if they were encountering some superior power armed for their destruction, and if they did not respect her as a female inspired by heaven, they dreaded her as a powerful enchantress who had her spells from the nether world.

Meantime she commanded the attack of the forts with which the English had closed the third circumvallation round the place. She herself took arms, which she wielded with the utmost address, and she had borne before her a standard of her own device, being the figure of the Redeemer displayed in a field showed with fleurs-de-lis. But although she carried lance and sword and mail as a warrior in the combat, she always denied that she had herself wounded or killed anyone. She was indeed herself wounded in one of these attacks by an arrow in the neck, and retired for a moment to pull the weapon out of her throat. She yielded to human fear, and° burst into tears. She indulged this feminine° feeling only for a moment, and resumed to the combat in° order to bring back the soldiers whom her wound had discountenanced to the attack of the fortress. "Whither go ye?" she said. "Enter the place, for it is your own."

Accordingly the fort was taken and levelled° to the ground. The Englishmen, apparently discouraged by this superiority of the French, resolved to evacuate their entrenchments within a week after the relief had been thrown in by Joan of Arc, who began to be universally termed the Maid of Orleans.

Her next proposal was to carry King Charles VII to Rheims, there to be crowned after the custom of France, which was the more necessary that as yet he was only termed dauphin by those who most owned his royal claims. In the meantime we learn from a letter of Guy XIV sieur° de Laval[52] some curious particulars respecting the Maid of Orleans, which will no doubt amuse the reader:

> Being in company with the king, his majesty directed that the maid should come before him as we passed at Selles° in Berry where she had been for some time before. This was for my sake, that I might see this singular person. The said maiden gave a° very good reception both to my brother and myself. She was armed all except her head, and had the lance in her hand. After dismounting at Selles° I went to see her in her quarters. She ordered wine to be brought, telling me that she would soon entertain me with such at Paris. It was a divine thing of its kind to see her and to hear her speak. About the vesper hour she set forth to Romorantin° three leagues° further advanced. . . . I saw her mount on horseback, armed entirely except her head, and having a little battle-axe in her hand; her steed was a great black horse and demeaned himself very furiously at the door of her quarters. "Lead him," she said, "to yonder cross at the door of the church of the town," and in truth so soon as he came back he stood as fast as if he had been tied,° allowing her to gain the saddle with the utmost ease. She then turned to the door of the church and said in a voice decidedly female in its tone, "You priests and churchmen, make your processions and prayers to God," and to the others attending on her she said, "Move on; move on." This was addressed to a very genteel-looking page who carried her standard folded, and° a brother of hers who had lately arrived also travelled in her company. . . . The maiden told me when in her quarters that three days before my arrival she had sent to you my grandmother a little ring of gold, and that it was of a very trifling° value, and that she would willingly have sent some better token of her remembrance considering the recommendation which she had received from you.

In this and other passages we find the maiden mixing with persons of rank and holding the high character which she had assumed as the deliverer of the kingdom of France, from whom the slightest remembrance was a gift of importance and the least memorial of her kindness a relict worth preserving. She was applied to also as a favourite of heaven concerning other matters, and such questions she appears to have evaded reply to. Thus we find that a prince of rank enquired at her what medicines° he should use in a particular disease, and received for answer that she professed no skill in that capacity. Another nobleman of the king's party, being the existing count° of Armagnac, wrote to her concerning the schism in the church, declaring himself ready to acknowledge that pontiff to whom Joan should say the popedom was due. The maiden answered with considerable address that she could not answer his question for the present, being engaged in matters of war, but that when she came to Paris or any other fitting place she would hold full communication with him upon the subject of his enquiry.

In other respects the maiden seems always to have acted up to her pretensions° as a missionary from heaven. She sent a summons to the king of England and his subjects charging them to desist from the warfare which wasted France, and she wrote to the same purpose to Philip duke of Burgundy, upon whom her remonstrances might have had more effect.

In general after the relief of Orleans her supernatural character seems to have been perfectly established, both among the French and English of that age. To every enquiry her answer was the same: "It is for five or six years that my brethren in paradise and my heavenly master have made known to me that I am the person doomed, and that I have two parts to perform. First to raise the siege of Orleans, and secondly to conduct the king across several provinces possessed by the English to Rheims, and there be witness to his coronation."

This second enterprise was as wonderful as the first. Sixty leagues of country occupied by the English and filled with strong garrisons and traversed by large rivers which the French had no means of crossing rendered the enterprise in the highest degree dangerous. Nevertheless it was undertaken upon the faith of a young woman of the breeding and quality which we have described. The various obstacles which had been apprehended gave way before the march which this extraordinary person rendered sacred by placing herself at its head. We can hardly trace the steps by which the failing condition of the French was revived under the influence of this strong impression. A battle was fought at Patay° near Beaugency in which the English were defeated and lost eighteen hundred men slain and one hundred and twenty prisoners,° among which last was their general, the celebrated Talbot, to whose lot it fell to protract for a short time the total loss of the English conquests in France. The English conceived° that in opposing the maiden they were placing themselves in unavailing opposition to the will of heaven; and after a feeble resistance they surrendered many places which in the time of the Black Prince or of Henry V they would have defended to extremity. Thus literally° carrying amazement in his van, Charles VII swept through the provinces occupied by England with an army of twelve thousand men, storming and taking whatever ventured to hold out, until he was placed before the city of Rheims which, acted upon perhaps by the surprise of beholding him at° their gates, surrendered without opposition and gave to the Maid of Orleans an opportunity of accomplishing what she always had stated to be the second purpose of her mission.

The solemnity of the coronation of Charles VII took place with every circumstance of pomp which the time admitted.

The king had been in external appearance at least guided and influenced by this supposed inspired person, and had experienced too much advantage from her presence to be willing to relinquish it. When° therefore after the coronation at Rheims the maiden demanded the king's leave to retire in respect of having completed her mission, Charles used every species of remonstrance and command to induce her to remain with the army. If indeed she now wished to resume the simple and rustic life which she led in her native village, and which had been so lately exchanged for a short and brilliant career of existence, the choice was no longer in her own power. Domremy had been wasted and burnt during the period of the maiden's career, perhaps with the less pity that the village had supplied the miraculous heroine who had so wonderfully restored the courage and success of the enemies of the Burgundians who committed the ravage. Having found nothing of her early life left, the maiden was probably prevailed upon with the less difficulty to prosecute that career to which she appeared to be called by a supernatural destination, though it is remarkable that she ceased to make any prophetic averments concerning her fortune or her success, only saying that she would be subjected to the fate which should please God, whose will she had fulfilled in raising the siege of Orleans and attending the king to Rheims.

The duke of Bedford, regent of France in the name of Henry VI, now resolved to take the field at the head of more than ten thousand men with which he defied King Charles to battle. Charles accepted the challenge and met him near Senlis. Both armies drew up on a fair field and were within sight of each other for two days and two nights. Neither prince however saw reason at the time for engaging in a conflict which must have been decisive, and so their meeting passed° away without battle by a retreat on both sides.

It is remarkable that though neither army exceeded twelve thousand men, yet neither King Charles's confidence in his divine guide nor Bedford's trust in° his dreadful force of archery could induce one or other to hazard the consequences of a pitched battle. That two such nations should be only able under such commanders to bring to the field a number of men not exceeding twenty-four thousand in all marks in an especial degree the exhausting consequences of this long and obstinate war.

Charles in the meantime resolved on an attack upon Paris, where he had still a hope of meeting adherents, and perhaps conceived that he would not find the Burgundian partizans very ill disposed towards him.

The attempt was made as proposed, but was totally unsuccessful.

Among others the Maid of Orleans had her share in the repulse, and it is remarkable with what a bitter kind of triumph the English historians record the trifling° disaster of a character whom they had so much national reason to dread!*

In the month of May 1430 about this time the maiden was engaged in a military achievement which ought not to be omitted in a view of her character because it constitutes the only occasion on which she is accused, and then we think falsely, of having been guilty of severity towards a person of the name of Franchet who became her prisoner. This man, commanding three hundred soldiers, assailed the Maiden of Orleans, then lying near Lagny,° but was defeated and forced to render himself a prisoner, and ought according to the rule of war to have received her protection. But Franchet had made himself so hated in the country by many atrocities that he was seized upon by the inhabitants of a town which had suffered by him and put to death in form of law, an example of justice which the maiden had probably no means of preventing even if it had been her wish° to do so, and consequently was not accountable for the criminal's death. Besides, her own course was now near a close, and it seems probable that Joan had little time to interpose in favour of Franchet or seek means of averting the doom which awaited him.

When arriving near Melun, from which the citizens had chased the English garrison, she is said to have expressed for the first time a belief that she was about shortly to fall into the hands of the English. The French having been attacked in Compiègne,° a garrison was thrown into that place under command of an officer named Flavy, said to be a valiant° man of war, but distinguished even at that period for cruelty and rapine. The maiden unhappily engaged in a skirmish in which she was defeated by the Burgundian besieging force, and, it has been alleged, not relieved by Flavy° was at length compelled to yield herself prisoner to a lord of that country, by whose lust of gold she was delivered up to the English at no less a price than ten thousand pounds in money and three hundred crowns in yearly rent. This bargain was made by the English and their party for the sole purpose of obtaining a base revenge upon the high-spirited and loyal though enthusiastic heroine who had so long and often been the occasion of their defeat.

And here we may pause for a very brief enquiry what was the real

---

* "While the French King was," says Holinshed, "at the town of St Dennis and at Mont Martre in the neighbourhood of Paris, he sent John Duke of Alençon and his sorceress Jone la Pusell, with three thousand light horsemen to assault the City and followed himselfe in hopes to get it either by force or treatie. But the English capteins every one keeping his ward and place assigned so manfully defended themselves, their walls and towers with the assistance of the Parisians that they repelled the French and threw down their great godess into the bottom of the Town ditch where she lay behind the back of an ass, sore hurt in the leg till the time that she all filthy with mire and dirt was drawn out by a servant of the Duke of Alençon's."—*Holinshed's*° *Chronicle* [53]

character of this celebrated person, whom upwards of four hundred authors have° made the subject of separate disquisitions, but who have arrived at different conclusions, though arguing upon° the same general premises.

The two extreme opinions entertained almost universally at the period were: first, either that Joan of Arc was, as she pretended, a person inspired from heaven, and gifted with supernatural powers for carrying her forward in a divine mission for the liberation of France; or secondly, that she was a sorceress who had pledged herself to the devil in order to obtain the power of working wonders for the destruction of the English. Neither of these solutions will be willingly received by an age in which it is the general belief that divine providence works its objects by human means, and that the time when the ordinary laws of nature were suspended by supernatural interference is long past.

Dismissing these two extreme opinions of inspiration and sorcery, it remains worthy of enquiry whether Joan was herself an enthusiast in the belief of her own mission, or whether, conscious of the power which she possessed of rendering great services to the cause of her country, she artfully consented to play the part of a willing impostor in order to obtain such an opportunity. On this head as we entertain a strong belief we will not hesitate to express it simply and firmly. We conceive the Maiden of Orleans to have been in no great degree different from the number of enthusiastic persons whose tempers and constitution render them liable to be affected by a hypochondriac imagination. When she began to see her visions and to believe herself destined to deliver France she was at an age when young persons of the female sex are peculiarly liable to attacks of hypochondria, and there are physical circumstances in her case which would induce a physician to ascribe her voices and visions to this source acting upon a modest, solitary, and highly imaginative disposition, and seconded by a spirit too high to yield up its wild fancies. To° the general argument formed upon the dangers with which they must be accompanied slight impressions of imagination verging upon lunacy are often recognised, and are sometimes found to terminate in events of great moral consequence, from the influence of those impressed with such ideas over others in the common ranks of humanity, who, though they seldom entertain fancies of a singular character of their own device and invention, are always proportionably willing to give credit to them when suggested by others, and appear even to feel a certain pleasure while employed in receiving and propagating them. This may be confirmed by reflecting that to become the leader° in any sect requires some degree of talent; to become zealous in following it needs only to be a fool.

Such a temperament as that of Joan of Arc has added many a person to the roll of Catholic saints; nor is it impossible that the visionary ideas of the maiden herself might have terminated in that way, had it not been that they were influenced towards the cause of patriotism by the general circumstances of the country around her. Every village, nay every individual household, was divided after the fashion of the kingdom itself into the jarring factions of Armagnac and Burgundy, and those who adhered to the one were taught to hate the other with every possibility of civil prejudice. The very children also were early brought up to profess the sentiments of their fathers, and to hate the English or love the Burgundians as their prejudices directed. Neither did they° confine their political opinions to mere argument only. In many cases the children of the village divided into bands, and between jest and earnest fought with sticks and stones in supposed defence of their political opinions. When therefore a young woman of great bodily strength and courage found her imagination engaged with war and its terrors, she must be considered as in a great degree familiarized and prepared for the part on which she felt herself called to enter. All the terrors which such a part, such a destiny, would have had for others of her sex and station would for her have been° exciting, or at least familiar.

It must also be remarked that the hallucinations of the Maiden of Orleans were far from those of the vague and shifting character which arise in common minds: they seem to have more resembled the early visions of Mahomet or those fanatical ideas which disturbed the useful career of Oliver Cromwell. Strong minds often create such ideas for themselves by looking too firmly and too long at objects whose bounds are of an uncertain and indefinable nature, till they persuade themselves they become distinct and clear.

It is remarkable that through all the maiden's curious history she is never found to aspire at a wider commission than that which she had persuaded herself she was specially ordained, and that, if her own declarations can be trusted, she was desirous° of resigning her character and retiring into obscurity so soon as the coronation of Charles had taken place; and after that period, though her share of warlike labours was not less than before, yet her success was by no means the same in comparison, and perhaps the spring was in some degree exhausted by use which had contributed so remarkably to her success. In plain words, anything pertaining to the miraculous is subject to fall into disregard if it come too often under the eye of the public.

But if we suppose that Joan of Arc herself was nothing more than an enthusiastic country girl of a masculine character, who had nourished in solitude visions and revelations until they appeared indubitable to her heated imagination, what are we to say of King Charles VII, his court, his parliament, and his doctors of theology?—are we to suppose that so many men acquainted with business and with the world could have entered into an agreement with each other for the purpose of countenancing an imposture so unlikely to succeed, and which detected was sure to overwhelm with indelible ridicule those who were privy to it? This doubt also is only to be answered by attention to the circumstances of the case. The desperate situation of Charles VII is to be considered, which made it as natural for him to incline to a desperate remedy as for a drowning man, in the common phrase, to catch at the support of a straw. His affairs were so bad that, though they might be rendered more ridiculous, they could not in reality have been made worse if by any of those numerous accidents which were° so probable the contrivance that succeeded beyond expectation had instead thereof failed utterly.

At what period Charles determined to make use of the specious miracle of the mission of the maiden, or to what extent he might really entertain the belief in it which he professed, it is impossible for any modern to discover. Enough of time certainly elapsed betwixt Joan's becoming known to Charles and her arrival at court to prepare any of those little incidents which afterwards contributed to her gaining credit. It seems probable that the persons who first declared their belief in the divine mission of the virgin had also insinuated to her what it was necessary that she should know, teaching her how to distinguish the king's person, and perhaps instructed her as to the existence of the sword discovered at St Catherine de Fierbois.° It is usually certain that a person preparing to impose upon others is not very scrupulous in being willing to impose upon himself, nor is it less true that a person who has succeeded in imposing upon himself some extraordinary opinion is anxious to collect and avail himself of all adventitious assistance° by which he can impose the same belief upon others. Thus there probably never was an impostor who was not to certain degree a dupe in his own fancy, nor a dupe so absolutely such as not to be to certain degree an impostor. We may leave Charles and his high-minded prophetess to settle the account between them how far either were impostors or the parties imposed upon. All are to certain degree justified by the object of the deceit which was the safety of the king and kingdom, which was hardly° to be accomplished by any ordinary means, and for which the heroine was entitled to a reward very different from that which it was her lot to receive.

In confirmation of our opinion that Charles VII and his advisers were not such dupes as absolutely to repose their confidence in their heroine's divine° mission we argue from their eluding her purpose of relieving Orleans in the precise manner she herself meditated. Dunois, as we have already said, conducted that operation by making use of the river, and although Dunois was ostensibly placed at their head as their commander, yet their generals made her believe she was following her own intention, while in fact she acted by their delusion—a circumstance clearly showing that they did not regard her as their guide, but as a person who was to give a new impulse to the minds of her soldiers. She then had it only remaining to say that since the divine will had not been implicitly obeyed she could not have been secure of relieving the place had it not been for the intercessions of St Louis and St Charlemagne, to which the deity had yielded rather than that the fair town of Orleans with the body of the duke which was buried there should fall into the power of the English.

The military use made of the maiden's services on the part of Charles and his officers was also such as implied a desire to avail themselves of her influence in the field as what would most likely have an effect of damping the enthusiasm of the English and encouraging that of their own men, rather than entrusting to her the office of leader and general, which, if they had believed implicitly in her inspiration, it would have been natural for them to do.

Accordingly we find Joan generally attended by a band of five or six hundred men, enough to guard her safety and second her audacity, but not a force strong enough for the decision of a battle in which strategy and military manoeuvres° must necessarily be relied on.

While upon this subject, we cannot but remark that the learned and ingenious French antiquary has written a book to prove that the Maid of Arc was not in fact the village maiden which she supposed herself but of very high though irregular extraction.[54] He conceives her to have been the issue of an intrigue between the profligate Isabelle of Bavaria, queen of France, and that same duke of Orleans with whom she was generally charged with a criminal connection, and who was murdered in the streets of Paris in 1407.° Many curious and ingenious reasons were brought to fortify an opinion which seems however as fanciful as that of a child who conceives in its ignorance that a good sword becomes more serviceable if its blade is made of silver, an opinion scarce more ridiculous than that a distinguished history argues the subject of it to be of noble blood. That the two princely adulterers actually had a child from their intrigue ought to be first made certain before arguing upon the allegation that this child, bred up in ignorance and obscurity, proved at length to be no less a person than the famous Maiden of Orleans. The whole theory in fact, though it does honour to the ingenious author, is that of a romancer rather than a serious historian. We smile when we observe our own Shakespeare pressed into M. Caze's° service upon this occasion.

That the great dramatist in forming a slight idea of her character, which it suited him to represent as that of an impostor, makes her throw out some obscure hints of being descended from "ancient but forgotten kings," just as he makes Jack Cade, a peasant insurgent, pretend to be descended from the noble Mortimers, is no° argument that there was ground for such an assumption in the one case any more than the other. It is only a proof that Shakespeare believed° such pretensions the characteristic of imposture. The work however may be read with great interest as one which exhibits how much may be done when assiduity and talent are determined to support a favourite hypothesis, however improbable in itself. The idea that the English poet had access to any traditions concerning the Maid of Orleans unknown to the history of France is so overstrained that it is unnecessary to say more upon the system of M. Caze.

It remains to mention the melancholy fate of this interesting° young woman who, whether princess or peasant, claims a lofty niche° in the page of history. She was accused by the university of Paris, while the bishop of Beauvais,° zealous for the English interest, and deprived of part of his diocese by the French, was employed by the regent, duke of Bedford with other inquisitors of the religious order before whom the Maiden of Arc was charged with heresy, sorcery, and seducing the people from their allegiance. She made a firm and able defence, and her answers to the insidious questions put to her were in every respect sharp-witted and able. But she was in the hands of prejudiced and partial judges, who pronounced sentence against her, although the principal and only° points clearly proved against her were° the wearing masculine apparel and using military weapons contrary to the habit of her sex, though in the defence of her country. For this crime—and we can discern proof of no other, although all manner of aspersions were heaped upon her by her accusers—she was sentenced to perpetual imprisonment, condemned to live on bread and water, to acknowledge her heresies, reconcile herself to the church, and do penance. To this doom, so severe and so disgraceful, the spirit of the unfortunate captive at length submitted, and for some time seems to have obeyed the dictates of this cruel fanaticism. She made her recantation and submitted to her punishment. We are ashamed to say that Charles VII made no efforts to set the unfortunate prisoner at liberty, although so deeply bound by the most weighty obligations. She lingered in her dungeon neglected by the French but still followed by the persevering vengeance of the English. Rouen was the scene of her imprisonment, where she was loaded with irons and treated with the utmost severity. A wretched spy was placed in the prison with her, and when she was likely to escape with a miserable life from the religious court the English cardinal of Winchester used the inhuman expression° on hearing that she was seized with an illness: "The king of England," said he, "would not for half his dominions that she should escape from his hands by a natural death; he has bought her dear enough, and he was resolved to cause her be burned alive." In disembarrassing° the captive from her irons, they threw her a bag with her masculine attire, which she assumed, either because she had no other dress, or from a secret partiality to the habit in which she had wrought so many wonders. This action, though in some degree compelled by her persecutors, was interpreted as a relapse on her part into the guilt of heresy and branded as such by the spiritual court. She was delivered up to the secular arm as a heretic° relapsed into her errors, with the usual insidious prayer that the judges would not shed her blood, by which in fact it was implied that they° should put her to death by the cruel mode of burning alive. She bewailed herself in a melancholy manner when she learned that she was destined to this conclusion, but on the scaffold which was erected in the market place of Rouen she resumed the courage by which she had hitherto been distinguished, and met her death as befitted one whose life had exhibited such feats of intrepidity. On the place of her execution a statue is now erected to her honour, Orleans still shows the house which she occupied when she came as deliverer of the city, and of the names which have been recorded in French history few are either so well remembered or so worthy of memory as the village heroine of Domremy so distinguished by her courage and her misfortunes. It is possible, and certainly it would be no exculpation to Charles VII, that the maiden's catastrophe took place at a time when the prestige of her mission could hardly be much longer maintained, and it is probable that the pile of Rouen, while it brought her career to so lamentable a termination, was also of some service to those who might be still inclined to believe in her miraculous mission.

Chapter 10

We have somewhat anticipated the course of events in order to keep in view the origin, progress, and unfortunate final end of the Maiden of Arc, whose fate forms such a remarkable incident in French history. We must therefore draw back a little in order to have a view of the character of Charles VII, upon which at this period so very much depended. We have already said that, although bred in the school of adversity and destined to bear the name of restorer of the French monarchy, he had not learned those qualities of military enterprise, attention to business, and similar qualifications which one would think indispensable° to his destination. His appearing but rarely at the head of his troops might be through the advice° of his leaders, who were sensible that too many of the French princes of the blood had already become captive during these English wars, and were conscious that death or captivity on the part of Charles would be a final termination to his party and cause. This however will not account for his love of pleasure, his idle dissipation, and his spending those funds upon pleasures which ought to have supported the warlike exploits of his constable. For these he must still remain answerable, and it was well that one object of his attachment was of a character so worthy of his admiration as to have deservedly attracted that of future ages.

The object of this passion was Agnes Sorel,° famous for her beauty, her accomplishments, and her public spirit in making the king's regard to her person the means of advancing his own glory and the reestablishment of his kingdom, his° best-known and most recognised connection. She used to contend with him, and exert the utmost of her influence over him to induce him to exertions worthy of his birth and dignity, and which his situation demanded. Upon one occasion, a person pretending to astrology was introduced to Charles VII and his mistress. Being asked the destiny of the fair Agnes Sorel,° he replied with the dexterity of his profession that it was her fate to be long beloved by a great king. "I must then," said Agnes, addressing herself to her lover, "quit your court, and attach myself to that of the English monarch, who is upon the point of adding to his dominions the crown of France which you are losing for want of the constancy of mind necessary to exert yourself in reclaiming it." This sentiment, so sarcastic and so noble, coming from the lips of a beloved female, had a decided effect upon the spirit of Charles, and spurred him to greater and more noble exertion than he had yet appeared to manifest.

Still, except in the confidence which he reposed in the Maid of Arc, the extent and nature of which we have attempted to ascertain, Charles gives no example in his person of that chivalrous valour which was characteristic of the age. He still adhered to his plan of maintaining the count of Richmond as his constable or general-in-chief, while he entrusted the management of his revenues to La Trémoille who, relying upon the king's carelessness, if not by his express encouragement, made a use of them totally inconsistent° with affording the constable the supplies requisite for carrying on the war. This minister rendered himself infamous by marrying the Lady of Giac, who had so deep a concern in the murder of her former lover John duke of Burgundy, and which person he° had brought to be slaughtered at Montereau.° He also formed a league with several other lords at the king's court, and with the counts of Clermont and of Marche,° princes of the blood royal, agreeing to exclude Richmond from the king's presence and to act against him as a common enemy. They also invited to the court of Charles the count of Penthièvre, whose family had contended for the sovereignty of Bretagne with the constable's predecessors, and who was the most mortal enemy of Francis I,° reigning duke of Bretagne, Arthur the constable (count° of Richmond, his brother), and the whole house of De Montfort.° Thus there seemed even among the small court and camp of Charles VII° friends who waited but an opportunity to burst out into all the exasperation of a civil war.

But Charles had one consolation in the disunion of his adherents: his wife, whom he had married during the lifetime of his elder brothers in the year 1413,[55] was a woman of an excellent character and many virtues, which seldom attend a crown. This lady, Mary by name, was daughter of Louis II, titular king of Sicily and Jerusalem. Being descended of the house of Anjou, she brought the friendship of that powerful branch of the blood royal to her husband; and her own good qualities were of a kind yet more valuable. She was gentle and indulgent, and seems to have taken no offence at her husband's gallantries, while her ingenuity and active spirit full of resources gave the king and his councillors comfort in the utmost desperation of their affairs. During° the disastrous period in 1427 and 1428 it was the exhortations of Queen Mary which prevented the king from taking the ultimate resolution of retreating into Dauphiné and abandoning the provinces upon the Loire. In the extremity of his pecuniary distress,° he was always at liberty to command such slender resources as were within the power of his affectionate consort. The emblems of her royal dignity, her personal decorations and the plate of her chapel, were repeatedly sacrificed to raise the necessary funds either for carrying on the war or for supporting the expense of the court of her husband.

In other respects also the disposition of Charles himself was popular. He received with thanks and gratitude all such adventurers as were willing to join his slender band of partizans, and was so very gracious that amid a proud nobility he obtained adherents whom he was unable to have gained over, either by the example of his own deeds of chivalry or by the wealth which he no longer possessed.

The course of conquest still continued to set in upon the French side, and although the Maid of Orleans was dead, and in a manner so shocking, her spirit appeared still to lead her countrymen to victory. Dunois, La Hire, and other champions now led them in successful skirmishes. Towns revolted against the English, nobles deserted the odious cause of the aliens, and even the presence of Henry VI himself, whom his uncle Bedford caused to be brought to Paris and crowned there as king of France, had only the effect of exposing him to considerable personal danger. Paris was surprised by a French nobleman in the interest of Charles, and had his party not quarrelled concerning the division of the spoil before the resistance was ended, the person of the young king would certainly have fallen into the hands of the enemy.

In the meantime the internal feuds of the partizans of Charles continued to rage with the same inveteracy as when his fortunes were at the lowest ebb. Montargis was taken by the English, and a bold attempt to recover it failed, as it was said by the open treason of La Trémoille, minister of the finances, of whose turbulent disposition the king had given warning long before, when at the command of Richmond himself he first° preferred him to his service, and when he predicted to the constable the probable event which was now realised.

Richmond was not a person long to endure the open manner in which his authority was thwarted, nor was he nice in selecting his means of vengeance. He° united himself therefore with several principal persons about the court, and particularly with the count° of Maine, brother of Queen Mary, whom he won over by holding out to him as an object the succession of La Trémoille in the management° of the king's revenue. Thus fortified, the constable showed little hesitation and experienced less danger by seizing upon La Trémoille in the castle of Chinon when the king was in the next room, and in the scuffle the minister of finance, wounded and made prisoner, was carried off by his enemies to the castle of Montrésor, where he long remained captive. This attack upon the king's favourite minister was at first regarded by Charles as a gross affront, as formerly had been the case with those upon the lord of Giac and Camus de Beaulieu, both trusted by the king in the same important offices, and both murdered, as seemed like to be their successor's fate, by the sole authority of the constable Richmond.

"Not to be however either a coward or a fool,"[56] Charles VII was a sovereign who most easily reconciled himself to affronts. He saw the rashness of breaking with the constable, who with all his impetuosity and violence was of high character in his military capacity, and invaluable° as a public servant, besides his interest as brother to the duke° of Bretagne, from whose dominion he raised several bodies of men. Charles therefore taking all this into consideration, and the queen interposing her intercession, he passed over the offence of Richmond by a third time changing the ministry° by violence, and at an assembly of the states held at Tours plainly announced that he did not hold the act of those who had seized La Trémoille as an offence, but was willing to regard it as good service.

This source of discord between his partizans being thus patched up rather than removed left the king at leisure to undertake a treaty of the greatest consequence, and which he carried through in a manner more statesmanlike than any political measure in which he had yet been engaged, proving thereby that his want of application to business did not at least arise from incapacity.

We have already hinted that Philip duke of Burgundy had been in a manner forced into the war with France and alliance with England to seek revenge for his father's death, murdered on the bridge of Montereau,° an injury which according to the opinions of the time could not have been left unrevenged.

In pursuing this object he allied himself closely to England, although sacrificing his interest as a member of the blood royal of France, which could be but in a small degree made up by the alliance between the duke of Bedford and duke of Burgundy, by the marriage of the former to the sister of the latter.

Unquestionably the duke of Burgundy saw the distresses of his country prolonged by a long and bloody war with great pain, even although the object of his continuing to add to its evils was the natural feeling of revenge for his father's death. These feelings must have been deeply aggravated° by a separate cause of quarrel arising out of the English duke of Gloucester's claims upon Jacqueline of Hainault and her rich possessions. The domestic ties which yet existed between Philip and the house of Plantagenet were dissolved by the death of the duchess of Bedford, whom her husband replaced by a second wife who had no connection with the Flemish prince. The quarrel between the two potentates was rather inflamed by a measure adopted to bring them to an amicable interview at St Omer.° Both princes came to the place, but as the duke of Burgundy insisted on the duke of Bedford making the first visit and was disappointed in this etiquette, they withdrew worse enemies than before, and each preparing to follow his own measures without paying any attention to the wishes of the other. In this Burgundy had considerably the advantage, since the French were willing to grant to the duke Philip the most favourable terms, on condition of his withdrawing himself from the English interest; while on the other hand the English nation could gain nothing by a separation of their interests from that of the duke of Burgundy.

The interest of the dauphin obviously turned upon a speedy peace. Both France and England had suffered extremely from the war. Their population was thinned, their wealth exhausted, and neither nation had been able for the last two or three years to carry it on without the most severe exertions. A peace, were it but for a few years, was absolutely necessary to recruit the funds of France especially, within whose territory the contest raged, and which suffered therefore in a peculiar degree all the evils of war. In this view of the case Charles and the duke of Burgundy easily united, agreeing to send plenipotentiaries to Arras, and prevailed upon the English court to do the same. The latter nation's accession was necessary to secure the duke of Burgundy from the reproach of having made peace without consent of his English allies.

Some insurrections in Flanders about this time added to Duke Philip's difficulties, and to his desire to° extricate himself from the war. The treaty at Arras opened with a proposal from the French plenipotentiaries that for the sake of peace they were willing to surrender Normandy and Aquitaine, ancient possessions of the kings of England, under the same articles of fealty and homage under which they had been formerly held. Unquestionably it would have been wise to have accepted terms more favourable than the situation of the country permitted them to look for gaining arms. The English however, although weakened in power, were not humbled in pride, and rejected with scorn conditions which fell so far short of those under the influence of which Henry V drew his victories. The envoys of England therefore withdrew from Arras, disdaining as it were the terms which were offered, while the king of France, as he was now generally styled, and the duke of Burgundy, under direction of one legate from the pope and another from the council of the church acting as mediators, agreed upon the terms of a pacification.

No article stipulated by the duke of Burgundy, however much to the disadvantage of France, was tenaciously defended, and a treaty therefore was soon made by which that powerful vassal of the French crown was rendered still more independent of the kingdom of which he was a vassal; and this second treaty of Arras was nevertheless attended with as much advantage to the French king as the first had been to its loss and danger. About the same time also two persons of note in this history also died, and A.D. there can be little doubt that the death of one of them at least was acceler-
1435° ated by the treaty we have mentioned.

This was the celebrated Queen Isabelle of Bavaria, widow of the unfortunate Charles VI of France, and the unnatural mother of the present king. The work of the first treaty of Arras which united Burgundy against the power of France was accomplished in 1419[57] under the mediation of this profligate princess, and the dissolution of this league was excessively mortifying to her haughty and vindictive spirit. She had enjoyed a transient importance by the marriage of Henry V, the most accomplished prince in Europe, to her favourite daughter the Princess Catherine. This° however had been dissolved by his untimely death, and it is said that the English no longer treated her with the same respect, and dropped hints before her face upbraiding° her that Charles VII was in fact no lawful son of his supposed father. These and other insults offered to her by allies for whom she had made such sacrifices are supposed to have contributed to the revenge of the country upon the person who was alike a bad queen, a bad wife, and a bad mother. She died, partly it is said of mortification and disappointment, in the space of a week after the conclusion of the second treaty of Arras, which withdrew from the English the alliance of Burgundy and gave some hope to her only son Charles, whom she hated so unnaturally. As the latter part of her life was spent in unhonoured privacy, so her funeral rights were hurried over in the most negligent manner. No prelate assisted at her funeral obsequies, and four of her own domestics conveyed her body in a boat to that royal cemetery at St Denis° where she was hastily interred with as little ceremony as her rank could possibly dispense with.

The second person of note who died at this time was the duke of Bedford, who was regent of France on the part of the young king of England, and who had so long maintained the interest of his nephew in that kingdom. He was a prince almost equal to his brother Henry V in military talents, and more than his equal in political prudence. For some time he supported a losing cause with great courage and address, but unhappily he did not see the necessity of relaxing the terms which he was willing to grant to the French in proportion to the exhausted state of England during the war and to the civil discords which began to rise in that country. The very great loss which England suffered by the death of the regent Bedford was not remedied by the appointment of the duke of York, who for a prince of talent was of a temper too fiery and haughty in these adverse times to recover the English interest in France. Other important events followed in succession, and upon the whole favourable to the affairs of Charles VII.

Paris for example had continued faithful to the English interest so long as the duke of Burgundy, who possessed a high hereditary interest in the city, was united in league with them, but after the treaty of Arras had dissolved this connection the city of Paris entered into negotiations with the constable Richmond, and having obtained a general indemnity for past crimes and a confirmation of their privileges, delivered up one of their gates to the French and besieged the English garrison, which departed *A.D.* from the city and agreed to evacuate Paris being° conveyed safely to *1436°* Rouen by land or water, which capitulation was strictly executed.

After this success the advance of Charles's cause was generally acknowledged by his being universally termed the king, whereas dauphin was the highest title of sovereignty which had yet been commonly bestowed upon him. Yet the course of his success was not uniform, and although the duke of Burgundy laid siege to the English possession of Calais he was compelled to remove from before the place by his old enemy the duke of Gloucester, who came over from England with forces for that purpose. The courage of Talbot, one of the ablest English officers, took advantage of a snowstorm, and having dressed his soldiers in white approached the town of Pontoise° which he surprised. Charles VII was stung at these losses and became desirous of showing his real character by an attack upon Montereau,° a strong place and which commanding the river Seine gave great anxiety to the city of Paris. The king ordered the constable therefore to collect a body of troops which he took under his own command, passed the ditch in person, the water reaching to his middle, mounted° a scaling ladder, and was among the first who stormed Montereau.° The fame of this exploit seemed to contradict the character of a disposition for love of ease and avoiding personal danger, of which he had been hitherto accused. The Parisians welcomed their king into his metropolis on 12 November° 1437, and the rather on account of his having removed the severe check or bridle° held over their heads by the garrison of Montereau. The king had been upwards of nineteen years absent from the metropolis, during most part of which time it had acknowledged a foreign yoke, neither did his return produce the immediate effect of restoring his prosperity: the plagues of famine and of pestilence signalized the entrance of Charles into Paris, and the bounds between savage and social nature seemed to be broken down; for we learn that parties of wolves repeatedly entered the remote districts of the city and carried off women and children: a° circumstance, being perhaps the most striking, which marks the universal exhaustion of a war which had in a great measure extinguished industry and lessened the means of protecting human society in almost all cases.

Although Charles VII was judiciously anxious to gain and preserve the character of a brave soldier and hazarded his person frankly at Montereau and upon other occasions, yet in reality he was no less desirous to deserve the character of a great statesman, and in that capacity to operate changes in the court of France which laid the foundation of its independence, and which tended gradually to increase the power of the crown to an enormous degree.

The first innovation regarded the Catholic Church, or the power of the pope at that time, which was of a character to interfere with the liberties and privileges° of every Christian community in separate countries. Now about this time the council of Basle had a formal dispute with Pope Eugenius IV° as an universal council of the church. They claimed the right of controlling by their canons the authority of the pope himself.

Having agreed upon these heads of complaint, they digested them into a set of ordinances calculated to abolish or limit the power claimed by the pope both to nominate persons to ecclesiastical dignities, to grant expectatives, pensions, and exemptions,° and other acts of influence and favour in the French church, which were in future reserved to the king himself.

A council of the church was then held at Basle,[58] which was disposed° to lower the authority claimed, and in fact much of it usurped, by the pope. These° canons were sent from the council of Basle to the French king by five ambassadors, who had orders to defend them if challenged, and to obtain Charles's consent to declare them current through his kingdom. The king entered with great form, and having heard and examined the propositions of the council in an assembly of the French clergy held at Bourges, at which the princes of the blood and the principal nobility of France were present, the° regulations were formed into a law approving of and confirming them in every point, which was afterwards well known by the name of the *Pragmatic Sanction,* and being adhered to by the French monarchs was generally considered as the foundation of the liberties of the Gallican church. It is not likely that Charles in his comparatively weak state would have been able to have thwarted thus effectually what must have been a favourite object of the Roman pontiff, but about this period several schisms had taken place in the church, in consequence of which a great deal of the reverence once entertained for the pontiff by temporal princes was diminished by perceiving that the right of either depended much upon the selection of the temporal princes themselves. A feeling of this unquestionably induced the popes to submit, which in other prosperous circumstances it is probable they would have been very loath to have done. We may also consider from the conduct of the English parliament in the matter of the church lands at the beginning of Henry V's time that Christian princes generally had their attention strongly fixed upon the exorbitant° wealth of the Catholic Church, and were determined to abridge its resources in future, if not to seize upon part of its present possessions.

Charles VII, after having thus extended in an important degree the privileges° of the French national church, took next in hand an improvement or innovation at least equally difficult, which was that of taking the power of the sword from the feudal nobles and vesting the command of the army of France in the person of the crown exclusively. But before detailing this great change it is proper to acquaint you with Charles VII's domestic affairs, which were in such an unpleasant state as might be supposed to counterbalance the warlike success which he had now begun to attain ever since the relief of Orleans.

The young dauphin, afterwards well known as Louis XI of France, already began to display those unamiable qualifications which distinguished him as one of the worst men, though certainly one of the ablest politicians, of his time. The first matrimonial alliance of this prince was with the Princess Margaret of Scotland, when it was no small object to preserve the friendship° of those ancient allies of the crown of France. She never obtained her husband's affections, although she was a princess of great spirit and genius,° and finally broke her heart concerning some false reports spread against her° by the scandal of a foul calumniator, and which her high spirit would not permit her to survive. In extreme youth by his disposition to treachery and insubordination he joined with several princes of the blood and the disgraced minister La Trémoille, who, expecting to be received into his former office of minister of the finances, readily united to seize on the constable, Arthur count° of Richmond, of whose character and talents they stood in considerable awe.

This distinguished general and statesman escaped from his enemies, and made his way to the person and protection of the king, who exclaimed with joy upon seeing him and said with much glee, "Now that my constable is restored to me I fear nothing." Shortly after, however, the king began to talk of retiring into some castle or place of strength, from the association of his son with the princes of the blood. On this the sagacious Richmond dropped the ominous words, that before adopting such a resolution his majesty ought to remember the fate of Richard II of England.

Stirred up by more manly thoughts, the king marched against the insurgents, and openly accused the duke of Bourbon of seducing his son and his subjects from their allegiance. Many of the towns supplied Charles with troops and money, and Bourbon, the dauphin, and some others of the nobles resolved to submit to the king. Trémoille, Chaumont, and De Prie took the same resolution, but the last were prohibited from approaching the presence of Charles. Bourbon and the dauphin himself were received with a degree of sternness which had not hitherto seemed part of the monarch's character. The duke of Bourbon Charles received with a stern warning, saying, "This is not the first time you have offended me; take a serious advice and let it be the last." Louis the dauphin was ordered from his father's presence and afterwards when he represented that if Trémoille and his companions were not admitted to grace he° himself would leave the town of Chinon and retire from his father's court, "Go," said Charles, "with all my heart; the gate is open, and if you do not think it wide enough you are at liberty to break down twenty yards of the city wall." Louis made his dissimulation answer his purpose by affecting a profound submission to the king his father. This scene of discord among the princes of the French court is called in history the *Praguerie* or *Briquerie,* and is remarkable as giving rise° to the first explosion of the inordinate temper of Louis XI. It was ended however by a reconciliation with his father, in consequence of which the dauphin was entrusted with the government of the place betwixt the rivers Seine and Saône,° which trust he acquitted° himself of to the king's satisfaction. Dieppe was taken from the English, being attacked by storm.

King Charles furnished his son with a fresh accession of distinction. John count of Armagnac, son° of that famous constable who gave name to the royalists and was massacred at Paris in the year 1418,° had forged some pretended rights upon the County of Comminges,° and proceeded to seize upon and defend such places of strength as lay near, and deviating greatly from the loyalty of his master entered into a treasonable correspondence. The dauphin surprized the count and made him prisoner. He was pardoned by the king, but not without confiscating some part of his estates.

About the same time[59] the king, to gain credit with the citizens of the metropolis, resolved to besiege Pontoise, a place of great consequence from its vicinity to Paris and keenly defended by the English. The duke of York and the lord Talbot relieved the place five several times, and many of the nobles having served out the time to which they were bound by their feudal tenures, the king was under the necessity of retiring to Poissy.° He was sensible that should he persevere in his purpose of retreat he would not make such a figure in the eyes of his subjects as would be the case with a prince who meditated a total change in the national system of defence and was yet afraid to venture on his own experiment.

Learning therefore that his repeated failure before Pontoise had injured his character with the Parisians and exposed him to their jests, he suddenly returned before Pontoise when totally unexpected, stormed the breach, and carried the place at the head of his army, exposing himself so bravely as at once to establish his reputation and turn the satires of the Parisians into panegyrics.° It would appear that the great vassals of the crown entertained a general sense that the schemes of Charles went to diminish their individual importance and consequence. The dukes of Burgundy and Bretagne, the ancient malcontents of the Praguerie, the dukes of Bourbon and Alençon, together with the duke of Orleans, who was now set at liberty after a long captivity by the generosity of the duke of Burgundy, who paid a large proportion of his ransom, joined° together in remonstrances concerning their rights, to which Charles VII returned grave and temperate answers expressive of goodwill to the princes who were indisposed towards him—a moderation which strongly recommended him to the sound judging part of the public, who welcomed his° plan for the public defence from the evils of free quarters and military exactions, by which hitherto the country and particularly the trading towns had been almost totally ruined.

To understand this you must remember that the duty of a feudal vassal was that of assisting his superior in the wars and defending the *fief,* that is the castle and lands held by him, against the enemy, for which purpose he either took into his service a body of hired soldiers, or, as was more frequently the case, called out his own military retainers, who held lands of him as he himself held them of some great lord, or of the crown itself.

It will readily occur to you that a war the subordinate parts of which were thus maintained by the exertions of individual vassals was not in a situation to be easily carried on by the prince who was indeed the nominal and ostensible, but not the real or absolute, chief of the national defence. In fine weather doubtless, and where the war was popular or signalized by advantages of a peculiar nature, the military spirit of the age determined the greater part of those who aspired to the name or character of gentleman to perform his stated attendance upon his lord's banner. But in the course of a protracted warfare this species of feudal militia was exhausted, not only by the consequences of great battles, by disease, by famine, and the other maladies which infect every camp, but more especially those of the early times when the art of preserving health was but poorly understood. But Charles VII, whose lot it was to be so long engaged in war, was sensible of the advantages which he must obtain by substituting instead of actual bodies of troops rather the pay at which these troops were sustained and the necessary expenses to enable them to keep together, by which means he would unite under his own authority a kind of standing army, well disciplined and ready at his call, while they were not liable to the flighty changes of great men and were always found to come readily forwards; while the country itself, instead of being loaded with the severest taxes—those of military men, namely, collecting the means of their own subsistence—on° the contrary gained a considerable advantage by the money necessarily spent by these troops at the expense of the community in paying for articles of subsistence; and lastly the soldiery themselves were much better provided for than they could possibly have been if left, as heretofore, to the irregular resource of their own licensed pillage.

Such was the change introduced by Charles VII, who thus substituted the foundation of a standing force under the king and officers appointed by him instead of a seditious and uncertain feudal militia. The state of his long wars smoothed a way for his innovations, and when his nobles stated that their means of furnishing men for the defence of their *fiefs* were exhausted, he took good care not only to relieve them of the burden° at present, but likewise to prohibit their having recourse to it hereafter.

In this manner the foundation was laid for a levy of troops which were called companies of ordonnance. Each village or township supplied a soldier, who, although called an archer, was often equipped° with firearms, spears, or some weapon different from the bow and arrow. These regular troops, for such they might be called in comparison to the feudal army, were perpetually ready for the field, and were constantly paid and furnished at the expense of the king. In order to encourage these necessary bodies of men, they were excepted from all sorts of taxes paid by other subjects, from which they obtained the name of *les francs° archers,* or free archers, a° total alteration of the French system of defence, which was adopted the more willingly as the king pledged himself to bestow the proper funds levied for that purpose, and as he brought in gradually a coinage sufficiently adequate to the nominal value, and could in no respect be charged with having harassed° his subjects by unnecessary impositions.

Meantime the war between France and England continued, not without attempts at peace, particularly in the year 1444,° when a truce was concluded to last two years from Easter in that year to 1 April in the following.[60] In the meantime the English took an opportunity of marrying their young king Henry VI to Margaret, daughter to René,° titular monarch of Sicily and duke of Lorraine and Bar. The French considered the English as having gained a great advantage by the temporary pacification, although the English authors, in despite of Queen Margaret of Anjou's talents, unite in painting her as one of the most unfortunate sovereigns who ever sat° on the English throne, and affirm that her haughty and ambitious temper and spirit of intrigue were the principal means of inflaming the dreadful quarrel of the factions of York and Lancaster, which finally occasioned the° long civil war which ended in the deposition and murder of her husband Henry VI.[61] Accordingly the counsellors who framed that marriage were many of them prosecuted for treason and condemned to die for their share in that unfortunate negotiation. The virtues and vices of Margaret of Anjou belong however to English history, and need not therefore be noticed here. The French king in particular lent the assistance of a body of troops, for° whom he desired to find employment, and he himself besieged Metz in the quarrel of René° of Anjou, duke of Lorraine, with one army, while he sent another body of his troops to assist the house of Austria in their calamitous wars with Switzerland, which were at this time beginning. It was an early proof of the dauphin's penetrating and prudent disposition that he made peace with the Switzers after having made himself master of Montbéliard° and defeated a body of the Swiss themselves. It is very remarkable that the first of the numerous peaces between the French and the Swiss cantons should have been formed by one of the wisest of kings and most artful of men. The king and the dauphin, having now returned into France with their forces, endeavoured to carry into effect by numerous reviews and strict discipline, which enabled them to maintain a body of troops which scoured the roads, kept order in the country, and effectually rendered the French troops a protection instead of a scourge to the country, which those had been who were formerly raised on the old feudal system. The king provided for this expense by large sums of money, which the people of Metz were contented to pay him as an allowance for his expenses during the war.

While the war between France and England was thus at a momentary pause, and while the French king was carefully preparing his troops° for victory the moment the war should again commence, those of England on the contrary were neither disciplined with sufficient care, nor recruited with sufficient regularity to admit of their making an adequate defence. The garrisons, exposed to numerous losses during the war, were in many instances too weak sufficiently to guard against a surprise, and the necessity of guarding against it subjected them to unnecessary hardships. They were also naturally jealous of the French with whom they still acted, and considering them as persons who on every occasion were ready to take advantage against them, they used them with a degree of suspicion and severity which only rendered them the more willing and ready to take the first opportunity of deserting to their countrymen. Soldiers that are not exactly paid or kept under strict discipline are always formidable to the country where they reside by their rapine, violence, and misbehaviour;° they have in such case the power to do evil without the fear of being punished. Thus the English garrisons got the blame of plundering and committing other outrages on the high roads, where disguised in fantastic° dresses they acted the part of devils both in external appearance and in reality.

Lastly, the war with France, which had once been so popular in England, was now from long misfortune and a continuance of constant expense become very much the contrary. The nobility of England were already agitating those conspiracies and plots which broke out presently afterwards in the bloody war of York and Lancaster, and the common people, alike to their own misery and that of the country, were engaged in tumultuary civil broils, augmenting the distresses of the country, but neither producing nor like to produce any advantage to themselves. Owing to this it happened° that the English power in France grew every day weaker, while that of France on the other hand was every day improving, and becoming more fit to prevail in the final struggle between the nations.

The French king had likewise acquired new allies and renewed his connection with his old national friends. The alliance of Scotland was revived, a league with Castile was formed, and the° duke of Bretagne, long dubious, seemed at length fixed to the French side. The army on the one side was well supplied, numerous, and disciplined, while on the other side the troops were weak, poor in numbers, and ill supplied with everything of a military nature.

A.D. *1448* At this important period, and just two months before the truce would naturally have expired, the effect of the factions in England began to display themselves in France. The duke of Somerset, one of the Lancastrian faction, was sent over from England to replace the duke of York as regent of that kingdom. He appears neither to have brought with him supplies of men and money,° nor resources of art and valour by which the part of these might have been supplied. Above all this nobleman does not appear to have foreseen° that the truce had already served France for all the purposes in which it could be of use to her, while England had neither men nor money in readiness to resume the war, and her scattered troops were hardly able to maintain a numerous line of garrisons which the French might attack in succession without their enemies having the means of relieving them or providing them against danger.

An adventurer in the English service, by birth a native of Aragon, a Knight of the Garter however, and commanding for the English in the marches of Normandy, was attracted unhappily by the wealth of a Breton town called Fougères, which he took in gross violation of the truce and pillaged at the same time. The duke of Bretagne summoned promptly the regent Somerset to account and atone° for the outrage done the duke's subjects; to whom the Englishman returned° the unsatisfactory answer that Surienne,° who had done the deed, was not his master's subject. This answer was transmitted by the duke of Bretagne to his liege lord the king of France, to whose cause he was now, as we have already said, begun to incline and wanted but some injury to decide his adherence to his cause; and, glad of such an opportunity to show his readiness to protect his vassals, he prepared four several armies to invade Normandy, and the fate of Rouen its capital may be now mentioned as showing how little it required of encouragement to put Charles in possession of that important place.

As his first exploit the sovereign of France appeared before the walls of

Rouen, and received a private assurance that the citizens would at night open their gates. They had accordingly mounted the walls for that purpose when they were surprised in the fact by the English general Talbot, who threw the citizens from the ramparts and interrupted for the present their purpose of giving over the town to Charles. On the next morning however the whole of the citizens united to give up the town, and they blockaded the duke of Somerset and Talbot and the few English in the old palace or castle, until they were obliged to give a pledge to yield up all the places which they possessed on the east side of the Seine, preserving only Harfleur, Henry V's first conquest. The king of France was about to have completed° his conquest of Normandy when a body of three thousand English were landed under Sir Thomas Kyriel. They came too late to be serviceable, and were° defeated near Formigny,° and the consequence of this action, fought 15 April 1450,° was the completion of the reconquest of Normandy, including Caen and Cherbourg, places of considerable strength.

We may here finish the story of 1451 when Count Dunois the Bastard of Orleans began and completed° the conquest of Guienne, although a hereditary succession of the English and much attached to those whom they considered as the descendants of their ancient princes. This feeling doubtless was greatly weakened, if it was not absolutely destroyed, by the estrangement of the Gascon° barons from their English sovereigns; nor indeed is it probable that their attachment ever survived after the attempt which was made to impose upon them a capitation tax in the last years of the Black Prince. Bordeaux made an obstinate resistance, and did not surrender till 17 October[62] 1453. The place was reduced by famine, notwithstanding which the citizens obtained an amnesty for themselves. Thus Charles VII obtained possession of the whole kingdom of France, though the greater share of it belonged at one time to England, and the principal motive for the long wars between England and France° was now removed.

It must also be added that Calais, the first conquest of Edward III, remained long in possession of the English after they had lost the rest of France. Its strong situation among sands and swamps, and the circumstance of its being garrisoned° with native English, rendered° it unlikely that it should be the° subject of treachery like so many other English garrisons.

The only circumstance by which the total loss of France was for a time retarded was the opposition of the valiant Talbot, created earl of Shrewsbury, with whose life as a specimen of ancient English chivalry these wars seemed destined to close.

In the autumn° of 1452 five thousand English troops were thrown into Bordeaux, surprised the French garrison, and overran° the various places held by Charles's adherents in the neighbourhood, till at length by the impetuosity of the Gascons Talbot was urged to make an attack upon the fortified camp of the French, then lying before a town called Castillon.° His son was present in the battle; the father, according to his wont, gained every possible advantage till, his horse being struck down by a culverin, he ordered his son to extricate himself from the battle and reserve his valour for another day. The young knight was of opinion that he would best vouch himself to be his father's son by dying at his feet.

The defeat of Castillon° and the loss of these two heroes° formed the close to the conquest of Guienne,° and Bordeaux itself returned under the French allegiance, under no worse conditions than that twenty adherents of the English should be punished with exile. This battle of Castillon° furnished almost the last of the blood which had been drawn in France through such a period° without serving essentially either of the kingdoms.

In the meantime, while the° breeze of success was thus seconding Charles VII's efforts in recovering his native kingdom, he was still experiencing the lot of humanity, and suffering through the caprices of his son Louis a species of family misfortunes which balanced the national advantages which affixed to his name the title of *victorious*.

Chapter 11

We left the father and the son apparently on good terms about the time of the death of the dauphiness, when it certainly appears that Louis had treated his wife with unkindness. At° about this time[63] the dauphin had acted against the rebellious Armagnac and against the Swiss confederates, and in both cases in° such a manner as highly to merit his father's approbation. It° is not clear from what immediate sources the growing disaffection between the king and the dauphin originally took its rise, though its existence can be clearly traced. It is indeed no easy act to trace with actual certainty the origin of family quarrels, the beginning of which is often slight and obscure, such as° neither of the parties concerned are very willing to acknowledge. They therefore substitute° offences of a more ostensible character instead of those of which the parties are ashamed, but which really contain the rankling and irritating grounds of original quarrel. It is said among other reports that the celebrated Agnes Sorel,° who was his father's mistress, was not treated by the dauphin with that respect which would have been prudent at least, as well as decent; and although we see room to doubt that the dauphin was guilty of the unmanly and brutal indelicacy of actually striking a person so handsome as to be known generally as the *Lovely Agnes* and the *Lady of Beauty,* yet Louis, who possessed a sarcastic and piercing wit, could be at no loss for methods sufficiently acute as blows themselves by means of which to mortify a person in her situation, and it is not improbable that the quarrel between the father and son might originate in some insult of the kind.

Nor must we here omit to mention that the death of Agnes in 1450 was ascribed to disease contracted in that year in a rapid journey made to join the king in the neighbourhood of Rouen to discover to him a treasonable design which had been formed against his person. She died in a few days, leaving behind her the rare character of a woman of so much beauty who could yet esteem her lover's glory as of more importance than a sacrifice to her own charms.

Exact° proofs and examinations tend° to show that the dauphin was accused of tampering with the archers of the Scottish Guard, to whom his father's personal safety was entrusted,° for the purpose of revolutionizing the court of Charles VII and displacing him from the throne, or perhaps even taking his life, though considering the relation of the parties a plot so unnatural ought not to be rashly taken for granted. Such very suspicions Louis is certainly declared to have made use of by the count of Dammartin. The° declaration was made in the king's presence. Louis himself was also present, and told° Dammartin that he lied. "You are the son of my sovereign," said the count; "to any other person I would prove what I say body to body." The dauphin left the apartment in fury, swearing by his head he "would be avenged of those whose calumnies excluded him from° his father's house."

A.D. 1446 ⁶⁴ In a few weeks accordingly Louis left the court under pretence of spending some months in Dauphiné, in which province the eldest son of France had the privileges of any other peer of France. But though this was° chosen as the pretence he resided near ten years instead of a° few months in his own appanage.

Upon his arrival in Dauphiné, Louis had the art to obtain from the state a gratuitous° gift of forty thousand florins. Some historians have told the story more favourably for the dauphin,° yet scarce destitute of culpable malevolence to his father's° servants.⁶⁵ His dislike, they° say, whatever was the immediate pretext, was always excited against those who enjoyed the favour, love, and confidence of his father, and especially such as he suspected of giving him advice unfavourable in respect to the trust he should commit to his son. Thus a principal object of the dauphin's dislike was Peter de Brézé,° seneschal of Poitou, a man of rank and merit, against whom the dauphin and his adherents brought a long accusation comprehending a numerous list of crimes. The king gave way to the charges against a minister whom he respected; he removed Brézé from his seat in council, from his employments, and from his presence. He replaced however all these advantages to an innocent man, since he appointed the accused to be tried before upright judges, who upon a full enquiry into the charges acquitted him in the most honourable manner. He was of course restored to his offices and to the king's favour, while Louis, mortified by his justifying himself from these treasonable charges, desired leave, so we formerly noticed, to withdraw for a short time into his appanage of Dauphiné where, by the constitution of France, he acted as already stated with the authority of a separate sovereign, and affected an estate as independent° of the king of France as the dukes of Burgundy or of Bretagne within their own principalities. He replaced all the exhausted machinery of a feudal government, for which he was greatly lauded by those whom he employed in lucrative offices, and much censured by others who had little to do with him besides° paying the expenses, and regretted the quiet and frugal management of his father.

The dauphin's personal taste seems to have been chiefly displayed in an affectation of independent power. This independence Louis exerted in a manner peculiarly offensive, so that he affected personal preference as° well as an emancipation from parental right in proposing himself as a match to Charlotte, princess of Savoy, not merely without the king's consent, but° against his express command. At this decisive contempt of his authority Charles was so much hurt, both as a sovereign and as a father, that he declared war against Savoy, and assembled an army at Bourges for the purpose of carrying it on. The sudden landing of the English supplies under

Talbot, and the revolt of many of the Gascons and the inhabitants of Bordeaux, prevented the king from following up this resolution. He was pacified also by the cardinal d'Estouteville,° who prevailed on him to regard the Savoy match as an advantageous one, especially at a moment when the English were obtaining a footing in Bordeaux which might have been of a very different permanence, had it not been crushed by the victory of Castillon° and the death of the two gallant Talbots. Nay, what is even more remarkable is that the king consented to a double alliance between his own royal family and that of Savoy, not only acquiescing between the dauphin and the princess Charlotte, but also to a° union between his own daughter the princess Galaude and° the duke of Savoy's son.

This act of free will in a matter highly encroaching upon the king's paternal power did not exhaust the freaks or disobedient humours of the dauphin, who certainly paid such obedience as became a son to such commands as came from the king himself directly; but whenever he could trace them to the ministers of Charles, Louis seemed to rejoice to find an opportunity of paying disrespect to them as of no account whatever. He also treated in his own name and by his own authority with the princes, and this species° of self-willed obstinacy, as well as the unpleasant temper which it displayed, was highly offensive to Charles, nor can we imagine° anything which could perfectly account for it except a strain of insanity which can sometimes be traced in the actions of very able men like Louis XI, when from some inward feeling they are apt to prefer the gratification of their humour to their direct and solid interest. Thus upon the invasion of Guienne by the English the dauphin offered his services to reconquer the province, but this offer of filial assistance was clogged with the condition that any part of the province which he reduced should form in future a part of his own° appanage of Dauphiné.° King Charles answered contemptuously that as Guienne had been conquered from the English without the dauphin's assistance, so there was no doubt that it would now be pacified once more without troubling him for his help in this matter. The king's resentment against his son increased every day, and at length Charles resolved positively that he would treat the dauphin as an insurgent vassal of the crown, standing under no more ceremony with him than with a distant ally independent of the nation. The dauphin's appointments were therefore suspended, as encouraging that prince in his disrespectful mode of treating his father, and in order to put an end to his affectation of independence Anthony de Chabannes,° lord of Dammartin, had orders to advance into Dauphiné and seize on the dauphin's person for disobedience against his royal father. Dammartin was at the same time assured by the king that the dauphin would receive no assistance, either in troops or money.

The dauphin at first had some idea of standing on his defence, but the stopping his appointments° had removed all means which he might have otherwise retained of a purpose so desperate as resistance. He left his province,[66] and the count of Dammartin, succeeding him in government of Dauphiné, proceeded to destroy all marks of the innovations which the prince had introduced, and instead of which the government of the king was restored.

It was part of the dauphin's policy to maintain a close intercourse by means of spies with his father's court. So soon as he found himself in great danger of being laid under arrest while the king's commands were thus executed Louis saw° the necessity of pursuing his flight. He set off with only two attendants[67] and took refuge in Brabant, a part of the duke of Burgundy's territories, the prince he probably conceived to be the most able of his father's vassals to protect him, and the most willing to do so.

Philip the° duke of Burgundy however well deserved upon this occasion the epithet of the *Good* which was generally bestowed upon him. Instead of exasperating the breach between the father and the son he took every mode of composing it, and so unwilling was he to assume the appearance of protecting Louis against his father that he refused to see him even in his own dominions until King Charles's pleasure should be known, and immediately dispatched to Chinon, the king's habitation, to notify the extraordinary arrival that had taken place, and with a request to know what was the king's pleasure in the circumstances. Charles VII, sufficiently hurt no doubt at being exposed at his vassal's court by means of his own son, yet looked at the emergency in a manly and dignified° manner. He directed the duke of Burgundy to receive his son with the same honour and courtesy which he would use towards himself if any occasion should call him out of his own dominions into those of the duke, and assured him that whatever respect was paid to his son's person he should always consider as rendered to himself while the dauphin abstained from taking any share in such point of dispute as might arise between them while his son was in Burgundy.

Upon other occasions, having thus received the king's permission, the duke of Burgundy hastened to fix upon Louis a large sum of annual allowance, and allotted him the palace of Genappe° for his residence. When Charles heard of his generosity he could not help sending a sarcastic remark mocking what was in his own opinion his° son the dauphin's temper: "Tell the duke of Burgundy," said he, "that he is following a fox who will one day eat his poultry." Charles VII behaved with so much moderation and paternal indulgence towards his son that even Louis himself seems in some degree to have been softened by it.

Thus when Charlotte of Savoy, the young dauphiness,° was delivered of a son[68] the king wrote to Louis a letter of congratulation with his own hand and caused public rejoicing to be made for the event; again when the dauphin wrote to his father saying that some of the ministers did not pay a proper regard to his requests, the king replied that he had no reason to apply to anyone of his council, since he himself was always willing to receive his reasonable requests, and exceedingly desirous to grant them. By this generous acquiescence in his wishes Louis's hard temper was so far softened that he wrote to his father a very submissive letter of thanks and gratitude. It is difficult to say upon what exact footing the king of France and his son now stood towards each other, but we shall be justified° perhaps in supposing that Louis, being now upwards of thirty years old, was desirous to administer a part of the royal power for which his years and talents rendered him by no means unfit. He nevertheless invited the duke of Burgundy and his son to be godfathers upon the occasion of christening this young prince, a compliment not probably meant civilly or so taken by his father, and introduced by an extravagant compliment that he himself, his wife, and his child were all the property of the duke and duchess of Burgundy and the count of Charolais, a compliment which his father could not feel very kind, in as much as it excluded him from all interest in this grandson. The dauphin's son died in infancy, nor had Louis any surviving son till the birth of Charles, afterwards his successor on the throne by the name of Charles VIII, and the last French king of the house of Philip of Valois. The king, perhaps from his love of pleasure, perhaps from motives of ambition merely, might be unwilling as the common phrase goes to pull off his clothes before he went to bed, or despoil himself of any part of his power before he should be summoned by death to account for the exercise of the whole; nor is it to be kept out of view that such was the character of the dauphin that the king his father might not by any means feel that the term of his own life was more secure if another person, even his own son and heir, should have any temptation to lay schemes for shortening it. The intrigues of Louis among the archers of the Scottish Guard could not be easily forgotten, and the independence affected by the dauphin did not argue great respect or excess of filial affection on the part of this prince. These fears, doubts, and jealousies were not, we shall see, thoughts to which the king's mind was inaccessible, and the manner of Charles's death, which was° finally produced, it is uniformly said, by the desire of guarding against poison, was such as to render it very possible that the fear of Louis's machinations against his life° might haunt his dying moments.

It is striking that at this time the duke of Burgundy had, like his sovereign the king of France, a son whose temper was turbulent, haughty, and untractable, who was strictly and with difficulty kept in order by his father, and proved most willing to consort with Louis the dauphin, strengthening each other by mutual disobedience. The dauphin however appears rather to have sustained a more literary character than Charles count of Charolais, which was the title of the young heir of Burgundy. He had round him many men of wit and pleasure, who composed stories for his amusement, of a very coarse character indeed, but of some merit as far as the taste of the times permitted. Meantime the king had the mortification to see his son remain a sort of hostage at the court of his potent vassal, while some circumstances which were in debate between them were gradually assuming a more irreconcileable and hostile aspect. Nor can it be doubted that it must often have saddened his reflections when he thought on the probability of being engaged in war with Burgundy before his son Louis had left the duke's court.

At this time another affair of consequence broke out owing to the schemes of the duke of Alençon. This young prince, ill construing the situation either of England or of his own country, entered° into correspondence with Henry VI for the purpose of bringing the° English into Normandy, in consequence of injustice suffered, as he alleged, by himself at the instance of Arthur of Bretagne, constable of France, who had succeeded to the dukedom of Bretagne by the death of his brother.

When this scheme of betraying Normandy was drawn out at length and enclosed in a hollow staff, a messenger was dispatched to convey the cane and letter to the king of England, but suspecting the nature of his commission he° brought it to Charles VII. When the treacherous paper was discovered Charles exclaimed with deep feeling, "My God, whom shall I now trust when my nearest relations betray me?"[69] He° then commanded the arrest of Alençon, which was performed by the king's old servant the count de Longueville, formerly the Bastard of Orleans. After a fair trial,° at which all the privileges and prerogatives of the peers of France were fully observed and the duke's own confession left no escape from conviction, he was formally condemned to death. The sentence was not however executed, owing to the interference of Arthur count° of Richmond, who requested that it should be changed into perpetual imprisonment. While some° reports said that the duke of Burgundy and the dauphin were not strangers to this plot of Alençon, such rumours seem to have contributed to the gloomy and low fever which formed Charles's last disease, which was now fast approaching.

The king, already dejected and broken in spirit, had been told by a captain of his guard[70] whom he trusted much that there was a scheme on foot to dispatch him by poison. Instead° of using ordinary precautions to discover and detect this alleged conspiracy, the unfortunate king took the melancholy resolution of refusing to swallow any food in order to avoid the possibility° of executing such a plot. In this he persisted for seven or eight days, until his stomach had collapsed and from want of sustenance refused to perform the functions necessary to life. He then submitted to the last ceremonies of the church, and died at Mehun-sur-Yèvre° 22 July 1461.

Though a monarch generally beloved and unusually fortunate, neither his good qualities nor his services to his country could save him from the frequent fate of princes to have their obsequies treated with negligence while those who were near their persons, instead of minding the dead, make haste on the contrary to hail their successor. The whole of the noblesse of the French court contended with each other in hastening to attend the heir of the crown at the court of Flanders. One favourite of the late king alone, Tanneguy du Chastel, who was his first favourite and un-happy in serving him in the death of John duke of Burgundy on the bridge of Montereau, showed his fidelity at this° moment to him whom he had borne° in his sleep through the bloody terrors of the night in which Paris was surprized by the Burgundians.[71] This faithful though un-scrupulous adherent had once, as you may recollect, subjected himself vol-untarily to a sentence of exile rather than that his presence should be a bar to a league so necessary as that between the king and the duke of Bur-gundy. Upon this final occasion he again manifested his irreproachable faith by discharging at his own expense in a manner not unworthy of a king the obsequies of Charles VII, whom in youth he had borne in his arms from among the bloodshed and slaughter of the Burgundians who had surprised the city. Having performed this last important duty Tan-neguy du Chastel, not perhaps desirous° of trusting himself with a king so nearly connected with the house of Burgundy as the present, retired to his native country of Bretagne, and long survived in traditional memory as a model of ancient loyalty and fidelity.

Upon Charles VII's tomb was inscribed an epitaph terming him the *vic-torious* and the *well served*. He might also have been called the fortunate if he had had a better mother than Isabelle of Bavaria and a better son than Louis XI, as his° domestic vexations occasioned° by the bizarre and unnat-ural conduct of these two near relations gave him perhaps as much distress as his unexpected national successes yielded him satisfaction.

Chapter 12

When the news of Charles VII's death reached Flanders, which it speedily did by means of the servile courtiers who left the dead body of the monarch to make interest with the heir by hastening to his presence, the young king was considerably alarmed by the false position in which he had placed himself with his father's ministers, and alarmed at the same time at the only measures which he had left within his own power to remedy it.

Out of a spirit of contradiction, rather than any motive else which historians can fix upon with certainty, Louis XI while dauphin entertained a particular aversion to all who were trusted or beloved by his father, and rather supported the effects of poverty at the court of Burgundy, where he had neither a penny of money to spend nor a whole garment to wear, and besides these deprivations rather than submit to his father or his father's ministers he had thrown himself almost upon the charity of the duke of Burgundy, from whom he received a pension, and who assigned him for his residence the palace of Genappe, where he resided at variance with his father and his father's ministers, and scarcely in friendship with the duke of Burgundy or his son the count of Charolais. Indeed he took every public opportunity of acknowledging his gratitude, and even magnifying the obligations which he laboured under towards his generous entertainer. "I owe it to you," said he, "and to your munificence that of my wife and that of my child." Yet while making such professions he secretly nourished the discontents of the citizens of Liège against their superior the duke of Burgundy, to whom he stood obliged for his own support and that of his family.

In these circumstances, distrusted by all who had intercourse with him, and distrusting them in a like degree, Louis XI was naturally apprehensive that those ministers of his father towards whom he had shown himself so relentlessly disposed might take the opportunity of excluding from the crown a prince who had in some degree placed it in their power and wishes to do so by making known his extreme dislike to them, and rendering them personally afraid° of his vengeance upon his mounting the throne. On the other hand he had it in his choice to throw himself even more absolutely into the power of the duke of Burgundy and count of Charolais° by requiring their assistance to ascend his father's vacant throne and return into France with an army of their subjects. He was conscious of the private suspicions which his tampering with the insurgents of Liège and other towns of Flanders had given occasion for; and he was also not unmindful of many causes of misunderstanding which must have taken place betwixt his hosts and himself, during his residing with them in a state of absolute dependence;° but he felt himself obliged to run the risk of their calling all these circumstances to recollection, and of their being seen under the worst light, and he applied accordingly to the duke of Burgundy as a great vassal of France, as well as to his son as a friend, to attend him with as large an army as he could muster in order to see his new sovereign consecrated at the cathedral of Rheims, under the imaginary fear that, considering his own unpopularity and absence of anything like real power, the nobles and ministers might substitute in his place his youthful brother Charles duke of Berry, who was already commonly called, with an eye, it was thought, to such a pretension,° *le petit Seigneur.*

Obedient to the call of his new sovereign, the duke of Burgundy assembled an army of no fewer than one hundred thousand men under the walls of Avesnes upon the frontier of France. This great aid was no sooner supplied than Louis became alarmed at the amount of the auxiliary arm of Burgundy and the use which might possibly be made of it. He was assured by letters from the privy council that his subjects were all prepared to receive his accession with the usual signs of love and duty, and he began therefore to desire to get rid of so large an auxiliary force, lest it should encourage his powerful vassal to apply his great army to some purpose which might inconvenience his superior. His fears on this side proved as imaginary as his suspicions of the fidelity of his French subjects. The duke of Burgundy, the candour and justice of whose disposition had procured him the surname of the *Good,* had not the least intention of availing himself of Louis's presence in his dominions, or of the strength of the army which he put on foot at his request. Immediately on receiving a hint that his army was too numerous for the purpose intended, he dismissed the whole, except four thousand choice troops to serve as a guard of honour at the coronation of Louis.

At the consecration of the young king he endeavoured by a studious attention to pay honour and respect to the duke of Burgundy, in order perhaps to wipe out the impression which the want of confidence implied in the order to disband his army might have been supposed to have occasioned.°

It was remarkable however that on this high occasion, when princes are usually disposed to grant favours to those who are entitled to ask them, the young king refused a boon which was asked him by the duke of Burgundy to whom he was so much obliged, although it was a favour which in no respects could have gratified° the duke himself, while it might if granted have contributed greatly to the quiet of the infant reign of Louis himself.

The ceremony of the coronation at Rheims had gone on with the usual form, except that the king requested the duke to bestow upon him the order of knighthood, although it had hitherto been the custom in France to suppose that in the case of a dauphin he received this honour at the font of baptism. At length the royal banquet was spread, and the twelve peers of France, or the persons representing them for the day, had feasted with the king when (says Monstrelet)[72] the tables were removed and the° noble duke of Burgundy out of his own generosity stepped forth and kneeled down before the king, and conjured him for the sake of the Holy Passion and of the blessed death of our Saviour that he would be pleased to forgive all those who had in any respect incurred his suspicion as being suspected of having occasioned the misunderstanding. Louis had not the generosity to see that this, while it was a civility to the duke of Burgundy, and an example of beneficence towards his own subjects becoming the beginning of his reign, was also an act of sound political wisdom. He nevertheless replied coldly that he would gladly pardon all those persons *seven excepted;* and thus, as he named no one, he retained it in his power to exclude from amnesty whomever he had a mind. It need hardly be added that so unseemly a reservation maintained the feeling of jealousy and distrust of the king's intentions in the breasts of many powerful persons, who could not easily deem themselves in safety while they were marked in the memory of this cold-hearted and vindictive young man.

Philip duke of Burgundy was not offended by this ungracious refusal of a boon which he had probably asked for the sake of Louis, rather than with a view of any personal pleasure which its fulfilment° could give to himself. In a point of personal observance he displayed the same moderation. By the treaty of Arras, which healed such deep wounds between France and Burgundy, it was declared that during Philip's life he should not be liable for any homage to be paid either to Charles VII of France or any of his successors. The meaning of this remission was doubtless for the purpose of preventing this claim of homage from being made vexatiously, and when perhaps it could° not be paid with strict safety to the vassal; but Duke Philip, finding that no such real danger existed, to prevent all occasions of misunderstanding would not avail himself of this exemption at the consecration of a young king of France to whom he desired to pay all the respect which his station could demand, and at whose hands he had not to fear, considering the terms on which they had lived, anything approaching to personal injury. He therefore voluntarily performed in the fullest manner the homage which was due for the duchy of Burgundy and his other dominions.

Shortly after the coronation at Rheims Louis, at the head of a numerous body of French and Burgundian noblemen, entered Paris, where splendid feasts amused the imagination of the young and the vulgar, while the king privately arranged his purposed mode of taking vengeance upon the servants of his father who had displeased him.

Louis in prosecution of these plans made a complete change, not only among the high officers of the crown, but through all the channels of finance and coinage, removing the experienced officers of his father and substituting such as were totally° void of experience. The zeal too even of those whom he preferred to stations of trust was considerably cooled by the observation that even a faithful service to the reigning sovereign did not avail those who could plead such merit at the beginning of a new reign, but that on the contrary approved talent and merit were dispossessed of their offices of power and trust without the least hesitation.

But it was chiefly against the count of Dammartin, who had his father's orders to arrest him in 1456, and against the procurator general, the president, and counsellor[73] of the parliament of Grenoble that the resentment of Louis was most bitterly directed.

Of these Dammartin, whose declarations had impeached the dauphin of tampering with the soldiers of his father's Scottish archer guard, had given the greatest personal offence, and his fate was most remarkable. All his estates were confiscated by the king's private authority, the count himself fled for fear of personal punishment, and his wife, despoiled of everything, would have perished for want, had she not been supported by one of her tenants during the absence of her husband. The procurator general and other persons employed in destroying the regulations which Louis had introduced into Dauphiné were tried for the singular crime of having assisted the late king to obtain possession of Dauphiné against the dauphin himself, the true and only lord of that province. The accused were found guilty of treason, their public offices taken from them, their effects confiscated, and their persons driven into exile, and thus Louis made good his vow to take vengeance on those by whom he was banished, or induced to banish himself, from his father's house.

As a counterpart to this severity against his own personal enemies, or those whom he considered as such, Louis granted pardons to such as in his father's time had been condemned for public crimes. Such were the duke of Alençon, guilty of plotting to bring in the English, and the count of Armagnac, which last was not only guilty of public crimes but accused of those of murder and incest. Thus to have incurred Charles VII's displeasure, however justly, seemed to be sufficient reason for obtaining the forgiveness and favour of his successor Louis.

In so far it was only the nobles who were of consequence sufficient to attract the notice of the king, but in the matter of revenue, which alike affected the nobleman and the private citizen, or rather was peculiarly incumbent upon the latter class of subjects, the conduct of the king was equally unpopular.

His father when he set apart a taillage, or capitation tax, for the maintenance of the standing forces, had promised that it should not be enlarged for any other purpose, and his savings had produced a sum of two hundred and fifty thousand livres, which was deposited in the treasury. The revenues of the royal domain had been amply accommodated to the annual expenses of the crown, to which economy had rendered them adequate.

Without any apparent necessity for such a step, and without respect to the promise of his father pledged to the contrary, Louis XI, whether out of sheer love of money, or covetous of that despotism for which the way is

most surely paved by possession of wealth, established the extraordinary
taxes which were highly unpopular through all his dominions. The people
of Rheims in particular, conceiving° that they had obtained from the king
a promise that no new taxes should be imposed, which was given at the
time that he saw it greatly for his own interest to have his consecration
celebrated without delay, burst out into a species of insurrection, massacred the officers of the revenue, and pillaged the records of taxation.

Louis XI, as expert in meeting danger as he was rash in provoking it,
caused an officer named the marshal° de Rouault to introduce into the
town a party of men-at-arms disguised as merchants, artisans, and labourers. The royalists, having thus obtained the superiority, caused the head of
the insurgents to be capitally executed by quartering, besides beheading
several other citizens,[74] cutting off their hands, scourging them with rods,
and imposing upon them fines to a large amount. Similar revolts broke out
at Angers, Alençon, and Aurillac, which were suppressed and punished
with the like severity by the young monarch.

Meantime the experience of the duke of Burgundy became aware of
the danger which his late guest was incurring by the violence of his proceedings in direct contradiction to his father's rules of government, and
took an opportunity more than once of advising Louis to have patience,
and not provoke public discontent by forcing forward at the same moment so many subjects of discontent. Finding his caution was not regarded, the duke dropped to the ear of one of his counsellors the ominous
expression concerning the king of France, "That young man will not long
reign until he involve himself in marvellous great trouble." Shortly after, he
took his leave of the French court, and from that time the intercourse between the house of Burgundy and the king of France, although it is impossible to say that the appearance of cordiality was not preserved, was
nevertheless so hypocritically conducted as easily to betray its own falsehood.° One principal subject of quarrel between the princes was the private intercourse which the duke of Bretagne naturally maintained with
the duke of Burgundy, a wealthier and more powerful vassal of France
than himself, and for whose support he therefore hoped in matters where
their mutual interest was concerned. This Louis was disposed to regard as a
league offensive and defensive between two of the most powerful crown
vassals of France against their superior. So great was his resentment of
these proceedings that he attempted to raise taxes in Burgundy, and stirred
so many other questions between Philip and himself that Philip sent to his
court the lord Chimay as a special messenger with directions to bring him
special answers upon all his subjects of complaint. Chimay, finding that he
was refused an audience, attended the king as he came out from his bedchamber and complained without ceremony of the little attention which
was paid to him, although the representative of so powerful a prince.
Louis, shocked at the familiarity of the remonstrance, asked scornfully if
Philip was then made of a different metal from other princes. "It must be

so," answered Chimay° boldly, "since he maintained, subsisted, and supported your majesty against the inclination of King Charles your father,
upon whom God have mercy, at a time when no other prince either
wished to assist you or dared to have done so." The king immediately
turned back into his chamber and sent Chimay° back to his court, whom
the duke of Burgundy replaced by another envoy. Louis at the same time
learned through a hint of Anthony de Croy,° the favourite of Philip, that if
the duke was pushed to the extremity he would be driven into a treaty
with Edward IV, king of England, who had already made him some advantageous propositions. The king of France, surprised at the hint of a
danger which had not, it° seems, occurred to him, immediately hastened to
yield to the duke of Burgundy both the point concerning the taxation of
salt which he proposed to exact in Burgundy, and also a dispute betwixt
him and the duke concerning the succession to the Duchy of Luxembourg.° Both these points, after being obstinately and ungraciously de-
bated, were only yielded when the conduct of the king must necessarily
be attributed to fear; but the intercourse between the duke of Bretagne
and Philip of Burgundy continued the more close that both these princes
were convinced that, though force or fear might be a reason for Louis's
concessions for the present, it would still be his final resolution to deprive
these formidable vassals of the more important part of their privileges.

Another intrigue of Louis's augmented the general discontent which
prevailed against him. He° undertook to assist John, king of Aragon, against
his subjects, who had taken arms to revenge the death of a son by a former wife termed the prince of Viana, who had been poisoned by his step-
mother. For this service he exacted that the counties of Roussillon° and
Cerdagne should be delivered up to him, redeemable upon payment of
three hundred thousand pounds. The king of Aragon and Henry IV, king
of Castile, had some disputes together which they at length referred to the
mediation of the king of France. They met upon the banks of the Bidas-
soa, and the difference of their appearance and personal equipment was so
great that both nations entertained for a considerable time a great contempt for each other. The person of the Spanish king was richly attired,
and his dress was a habit blazing with gold and jewels; the very boat of his
favourite minister was covered with an awning of cloth of gold. On the
other hand Louis, although fond of gay apparel° in his more youthful days,
had by this time adopted a kind of short coat of coarse cloth, neither in
point of manufacture nor form such as was then used among persons of
rank. The covering of the king's head was a sort of cowl or hood, worn
threadbare and secured by the leaden image of a saint which was its only
ornament. The French ridiculed° the affected pedantry of the Spaniards,
who no less laughed to scorn the poverty and miserable appearance of the
French court. The historian however says that Louis XI resembled an able
merchant who transacts his business with great advantage, although not
caring for any refinement of dress, and wrapped up in a coarse frieze°

great-coat.[75] It is certain that Louis XI made himself master of the hearts of the ministers of both monarchs of Castile and Aragon, and through them obtained a road to the state secrets of their masters for which he paid very liberally. On his return from Spain, or rather from his own frontiers, an experiment was made on his temper respecting his unfortunate enemy the count Dammartin. This gentleman appeared suddenly in the king's presence, introduced by a nobleman called Charles de Bost. He threw himself at the king's feet. "What is it you want," said Louis, "from me? is it justice?—or do you ask compassion?" "Justice, my lord," answered Dammartin, too proud to repress the answer which rose to his lips. "In that case," replied the king, whose credit for justice depended on his maintaining that which he exercised towards persons in Dammartin's situation, "you are banished for° ever from my dominions."

As the count of Dammartin had the reputation of civil and military talents, he would have risen to preferment in the duke of Burgundy's service, but unable to live out of France he afterwards re-entered his native country and submitted himself to prison. He was tried before the parliament, by which he was a second time declared guilty of treason and banished to the isle of Rhodes, to which however he was not actually transported.

At the treaty of Arras certain towns upon the river Somme° had been expressly ceded to Burgundy in support of the expenses which were to be laid out by that state in the war with England. They were declared to be redeemable by France upon the payment of four hundred thousand crowns of gold, which was presumed to be the amount of the expenses incurred by Burgundy. In° fact no such expenditure had been made, and Burgundy received the full advantages of this barrier treaty° without having expended any considerable sum in the war, which was taken into view when the agreement was entered into.

The redemption of these towns had been long a considerable object both with Louis and with his father; the latter had made a considerable reserve of treasure, and Louis had suffered himself to be tempted into indirect means to augment his revenue for the same purpose. The influence of the king with John de Croy° and others of that family, gained as usual by extravagant largesses, was not sufficient to obtain this object, and he was compelled to propose an interview with the duke himself, which took place at the town of Hesdin,° at which he was no otherwise successful than in obtaining a change in the government of these places rather favourable to the interests of France. In fact during this interview Louis hoped to carry his point by means of a stratagem which, considering the person against whom it was directed, was singularly base and ungrateful. He entrusted a person generally known by the name of the Bastard of Rubempré,° a species of pirate or buccaneer, whom he directed to embark aboard a French frigate, sail to The Hague on the coast of Holland, where the count of Charolais was then on a tour visiting the coast, and attended by a crew of forty or fifty desperate men to° take an unexpected opportunity to secure that prince's person. In the meantime the king himself with the troops that attended him, who were lawless and desperate men like himself, intended to make sure of both father and son, who should thus fall all at once into King Louis's net. The plot was discovered by means of the imprudence of Rubempré° himself, who was made prisoner and detained.

When Louis saw that his design was penetrated he sent an embassy to the duke of Burgundy consisting of Morvilliers,° president of the parliament of Paris, the archbishop° of Narbonne,[76] and others,° who by their master's direction took a very high tone, complaining of the duke of Burgundy and count of Charolais for° circulating reports to his prejudice, or at least permitting them to be circulated among his subjects; declaring that Olivier de La Marche° and a minister of the same province[77] had made violent reflections upon the king's conduct, and desiring° that they should be delivered up to him. The Burgundian duke would not pay the least attention to the charge of the king, and the count de Charolais, replying with great animation, declared he would have spoke his mind yet more plainly had it not been out of reverence to his father.

In fact the said count had already arranged the means by which he intended to take a severe vengeance on the king for the various insults and displeasures to which he had subjected him ever since his hospitable reception in Burgundy. Neither was he so prudent as to keep his purpose to himself.

When he took leave of the archbishop of Narbonne, the last of the French embassy with whom he spoke, he desired to be recommended very humbly to the good grace of the king, "and tell him," said he, "that he has sent me on this occasion a sharp lecture by the mouth of his chancellor, but before a year be out, it is ten to one that he shall repent having offered me such an affront." These words being carried to the king, who well knew the fiery and vindictive temper of the prince by whom they were spoken, satisfied him that he had some signal vengeance to expect at the hands of the count of Charolais, although neither by means of spies nor the treachery of ministers he had been able to descry its exact nature.

Chapter 13

In fact the time was now arrived which was presaged to Louis XI by his gentle and benevolent friend Philip duke of Burgundy, and had been in a great measure prepared by the vengeful intrigues of Philip's son the count of Charolais, who had felt the king's ill usage and returned it with a resentment better corresponding with its nature. It was indeed long seen that this king's selfish and ungenerous policy, by which he sought to gratify the meanest passions of envy and of malevolence, had gradually succeeded in spreading through his kingdom a flame of general disaffection. The present duke of Bretagne was the successor of that Arthur count° of Richmond, who long held the constable's baton° and faithfully served the king of France in his wars. That distinguished general in the extremity of his life succeeded to his brother in the dukedom of Bretagne, which was a great fief of the crown, but died after a very short reign of a few months, bequeathing his territories to his nearest male heir the present duke.

This prince was the particular object of jealousy and hatred to Louis XI, who was of opinion that he had not power to make his pretensions° avail to the extent of those high privileges which there was no disputing with the duke of Burgundy; he therefore intimated his royal pleasure by the mouth of his chancellor Pierre de Morvilliers,° that he should not presume to strike golden money, nor to make by his own authority any extraordinary levy of his vassals, nor to receive them as if altogether depending on himself, and other restrictions tending to degrade the duke from the character of a high crown vassal of France, retrench his privileges, and diminish his importance.

In the event of the duke's refusal the chancellor had directions to proclaim war, and the king held himself ready to invade Bretagne with an army which he had assembled for the purpose at the city of Tours. Francis II, duke of Bretagne, was not a man of great talent, on which account he was despised by Louis, who confided very much in a fine-spun web of policy which sometimes had the effect of involving the manufacturer in unexpected difficulties. He did not make allowance for the exercise of that dissimulation on the part of others which he practised without scruple himself. The duke of Bretagne had also good counsellors capable of supplying at this crisis the expedients which his own genius might not be ready to devise.

By their advice Francis of Bretagne apparently humbled himself to the storm, submitted in appearance to the mandates of the king, but pleaded that he was under the necessity of consulting his estates of Bretagne before consenting to such impositions, and obtained a truce of three months for this purpose. Louis accordingly dismissed his army and granted the truce proposed.

In the meantime the duke of Bretagne, or those by whose advice he acted in this emergency, drew still more close the bonds of alliance which had long existed between the duke of Burgundy, or at least the count of Charolais, and their master, soliciting the attention of that powerful prince to the tyrannical injunctions of Louis, and pointing them out as being the same which, if it were ever in his power, he would desire to impose upon Burgundy himself.

Numerous other emissaries, disguised as begging friars, pilgrims, or the like, were charged with letters from Francis II, duke of Bretagne, to the various men of rank who had either received, or who apprehended, injustice at the hand of King Louis. We have already stated that these were very numerous, and that they were powerful was manifest when it was considered that the strength of Burgundy was at their head.

The king had increased the unpopularity of his measures by renouncing the Pragmatic Sanction, which was generally reputed one of his father's wisest and most public-spirited measures. Louis nevertheless recalled it in order to obtain the countenance of the pope respecting some claims which he had upon the succession of Milan. The French clergy especially were deeply offended at a measure which greatly affected the liberties of their national church, and among the various motives of a general war by the vassals of France against the crown this of the recall of the Pragmatic Sanction was certainly one of the most legitimate apologies.

The affair of Rubempré, the agent of Louis XI, being made prisoner in Holland, gave a new force to this conspiracy, and as the emissaries of different princes who were inclined to join the general league against the king always held their meetings in the churches, which were places of open resort, they escaped all ordinary modes of detection or causes of suspicion, and a conspiracy in which many hundred persons were engaged remained altogether invisible to the eyes of Louis XI, one of the most jealous, suspicious, and sharp-sighted of monarchs. He lost also his means of intelligence in Burgundy by the fall of the family of Croy,° who had been long his intelligencers in that quarter. But Duke Philip, whose favourites they had been, was now unable to maintain his predilection in their favour against the more natural influence of his son, who succeeded to the exercise of his father's sovereignty as extreme old age and feebleness rendered Philip gradually more incapable of exercising the ducal authority.

The king of France meanwhile insisted upon his complaints against the duke of Bretagne, and laid them before a great assembly of the grandees of the kingdom held at Tours in December 1464. Most of the assembly assented to the proposals of the king that they should stand by him with their lives and treasure against a vassal whose disloyal conduct had commenced under the reign of Charles VII. The duke of Orleans alone, not deceived by the artful style in which Louis conducted the accusations, conceived himself at liberty to prefer a sort of defence, or at least an apology. The king upbraided° him in the harshest terms with taking the part of a revolted vassal against his sovereign, and the duke took the reprimand so much to heart that he fell ill and died in consequence.

The duke of Bourbon also took his departure for the court of Burgundy, for, having considerable influence over Duke Philip, he hoped at this time to obtain his consent to his son's measures, which involved a general alliance against the king and an immediate war. These however were measures too decisive and violent for Duke Philip, and were indeed contrary to the whole tenor of his quiet and peaceable life. He could be brought no further than to give his consent to levy forces and put the country himself in a state of defence, and he remained obstinate upon this point, although he was induced to submit to the banishment of his favourite ministers of the family of Croy,° who dreaded so much the violence of the young count of Charolais, or were so conscious of their own criminal correspondence with Louis, that they dared not even take the last leave of their old master. A large body of men-at-arms amounting to about fourteen hundred with eight or nine thousand archers took arms at the summons of the count of Charolais; they were well mounted and well equipped,° but indifferently disciplined, because Burgundy had been at peace since the treaty of Arras about thirty years before. Many princes, vassals of France of higher or lower degree, joined this formidable confederacy, and the nearest prince of the blood royal escaped from the king's camp for the purpose of putting himself at their head, and the war assumed the name of one carried on for the public good, because it was supposed that if the noblesse of France did not make common cause with the dukes of Burgundy and Bretagne they would be one by one crushed and deprived of their former privileges.

Some foreign negotiations may be mentioned as tending to inflame the quarrel between the king and the princes during the war as it was called for the public° good. Edward IV, heir of the house of York, had now seated himself firmly on the throne of England, and Louis XI already rejoiced in an alliance which had been proposed betwixt this young monarch and his own sister[78] Bona, for which a negotiation had been some time in dependence. This treaty however was set aside, owing to the inordinate affection which the king of England had formed for a beautiful gentlewoman, Elizabeth Woodville,° the widow however of a simple knight. The duke of Burgundy did his utmost to show honour and approbation of this match, and was generally understood to have drawn still closer those bands of alliance with England which were always the subject of suspicion to the French, and even to Duke Philip's own subjects of Burgundy. The sudden breaking out of the war of the public good astonished Louis, who had no idea that a conspiracy so general could have existed in his kingdom without coming to his knowledge. It must have been a great surprise to him when not only the princes nearest to him in blood, but the Bastard of Orleans, his father's ancient and faithful servant, appeared engaged against him. The new persons whom he had made depositories of his power possessed neither rank, talents, nor influence for serving him in such a crisis, so that he more than once repented bitterly of the usage of his father's experienced and faithful servants, which had estranged them from his standard, among whom we may notice Anthony de Chabannes,° count of Dammartin, who had escaped from the Bastille° where the king imprisoned him, and had joined the ranks of the insurgent nobility. Both armies were now in the field and adopted their various plans for the campaign. The count of Charolais upon his part resolved to advance to Paris, in hopes of renewing some of those parties which his ancestors had long possessed within that city, and possessing him of the capital as his grandfather Duke John had contrived to do in 1418.° The king on the contrary, unwilling that his enemies should obtain such an advantage over him as the possession of the metropolis, must needs have been pressed forwards at the head of the companies of ordonnnance as they were called, the francs archers that were° levied upon the plan adopted by Charles VII,° and anticipated the Burgundians and took possession of the city of Paris upon 28 July[79] 1465.

The count of St Pol, a descendant of the imperial house of Luxembourg,° at this time a favourite and follower of the count of Charolais, in whose history the death of St Pol makes a dishonourable chapter, who was quartered not far from the castle of Montlhéry, sent to inform the count of Charolais that the enemy from Paris had sallied to attack him, and he prayed the count to come to his relief. Some time was lost in mounting and again dismounting the Burgundian men-at-arms, who broke with little difficulty the French force opposed to them, rode down and totally broke the Burgundians,° that is their own section, and with the count of Charolais at their head pursued rashly and carelessly. Being at length informed by an old gentleman of Luxembourg,° who came at full gallop with the news that the French, after flying some space from the field of battle, had rallied, the count of Charolais saw the necessity of retreating in his turn, in doing which he incurred several dangers; one was from the archers of the French guard who were in possession of the castle of Montlhéry; these however, though they shot, did not advance to attack the count. But the count of Charolais fell in with a party of fifteen or sixteen French men-at-arms, who killed the esquire of his little escort and several others, beat the count himself down by a wound in the throat, of which he retained the scar during his whole life, and called to him to surrender, if he would not be slain on the spot, which would have been his only alternative if an individual gentleman-at-arms of his own attendants had not charged into the melée with a large and powerful horse and thus extricated the duke, who after this rescue was succoured by the arrival of the count of St Pol and others, amounting at length to about eight hundred men.

On the other hand the battle on Louis's part was equally partial and in-decisive. His soldiers fled with as much confusion as those of Charolais, and finally many were killed and wounded, and many on both sides fled above a hundred miles from the field of battle without being pursued by any one of the opposite party. The enquiries which were made on this oc-casion bore traces of the same confused result: some persons were dispos-sessed of their offices and employments for having fled from the battle, and the very same offices were in some cases conferred upon persons who had fled ten miles further than those who had before held them. There was seldom a battle in which were engaged troops so much esteemed for their gallantry, and so many nobles renowned for their high birth and re-doubted valour, yet judgement and military valour was seldom less dis-played on either side. Even the means of refreshment seemed to alter their nature after the battle of Montlhéry and become applicable to creatures of a different species, for the excellent historian Philip de Commynes tells us, as one who was present at the battle, that his horse, which was quite ex-hausted, was equally refreshed by plunging its head into a pitcher of wine and taking a good full draught of a liquor which he probably tasted for the first time.° [80]

But the most unfortunate effect was experienced upon the count de Charolais himself. This was his first campaign, and he had no reason to be ashamed of the part which he had individually played. He had at least showed sufficient bravery, if he had made no display of military knowledge beyond his age and experience. On the other hand he was certainly wrong in esteeming that his own conduct at the field of Montlhéry was that of a great leader as well as of a brave soldier, and the consequence of his adopt-ing such an opinion of himself was that he ever after became unadvisable and obstinate, which terminated in the downfall of the house of Burgundy which had been raised so high by the wisdom of three experienced and skilful° princes, his ancestors.

The king after the battle retired to Corbeil, which was a convenient station for recruiting his army from Normandy. On the other hand the count of Charolais resolved to extend his quarters and form a junction with the army of Brittany and their other allies on the south of the Seine. A bridge supported upon empty casks and boats was thrown across for this purpose, and the force which the allies had now assembled amounted to a hundred thousand men,[81] a number sufficient to have carried any of these objects which they pretended to have in view for the public benefit. No such plan was however brought forward in their councils. On the contrary, the various members of this confederacy, from its head downwards, had al-most all personal objects to transact with the king of France, and if° these could be secured in their own favour they were very willing to neglect the general purposes of the "war for the public good."

A prince so acute as Louis was naturally could not but perceive the ad-vantage which was likely to accrue to himself, a single monarch, while negotiating with an alliance of nobles who could not form any general system of terms, and must consequently be always helpless and indecided in anything like negotiation which might take place between them and him.

Accordingly he set every engine at work, and spared neither money nor preferment where either was necessary to seduce a person of importance from the present confederacy, or deter such from engaging in any which was similar. The° duke of Burgundy and duke of Bretagne insisted upon such terms as were directly for their own interests, all which Louis granted with sufficient readiness, under the secret reservation to execute these terms with as little fidelity as he could possibly avoid. In° the meantime he threw into his mode of negotiating as much frankness and confidence as if such had been the real turn of his genius and disposition.

Thus upon one occasion, being embarked upon the Seine with four or five persons only, and perceiving on the other side the° count of Charolais and several of the confederate nobles of his party, Louis called out, "My brother, my brother,[82] do you give me assurance?" "Yes," said the count, "as a brother I do." Upon this assurance the king caused his boat to be rowed to the enemy's side of the river, and without hesitation leaped ashore followed by two or three persons, saying, "My brother, I now well know that you are a gentleman of your word as becomes one of the blood royal of France." "In what manner do you know that?" said the count of Charolais. "Because," said the king, "when that fool Morvilliers used such language towards you, you sent me word by the archbishop° of Narbonne, who is a gentleman of blood, that you would cause me before the end of the year repent words which the said Morvilliers had used towards you."

This he said with a smiling countenance, and as one who was rather glad that the count of Charolais should know what were his sentiments on that head, and that, being tired of the war, he was willing to come to a reconciliation. They proceeded in this confidential manner to discuss several stipulations in favour of the principal insurgents. Thus it was proposed that the duke° of Berry should have the whole duchy of Normandy without any stipulation on the king's part except that of homage, and that Monsieur de Charolais should have his life's possession of the towns upon the Somme.° Both these demands the king seems to have evaded for the present, while he consented that the count of St Pol should be created high constable of France, and in this manner they departed in apparent good humour with each other.

Chapter 14

The frankness exhibited by King Louis in this memorable interview seems to have gained his point by convincing the count of Charolais that there would be no difficulty on the part of King Louis in submitting to any conditions which might be required, and therefore it was unnecessary to insist upon such as might deprive him even of the likeness of a crown. Louis on his part became satisfied that he had in a great measure by his appearance of sincerity and candour removed the envenomed sting of the affront which he had given the count of Charolais, and of consequence had taken from the personal resentment of that haughty prince whatever it had of bitterness. In doing so Louis, from his knowledge of mankind,° was aware that he had taken out of the road the greatest obstacles to the peace, and that, whatever other conditions he might be obliged to submit to, he might find some opportunity of shaking himself free from them, either° by fair means or foul, providing the passions and especially the pride of this Charles count of Charolais were not implicated in the discussion.

Mean agents and men of indifferent character were employed in forming the treaty between the parties which went on irregularly, the° skirmishes which took place every day having no effect in interrupting the pacification, which indeed concerned so many various persons whom private disaffection had driven to become parties in this war which was carried on under pretence of the public good, and whose interest was to be consulted before a pacification could be obtained.

There are no great military feats to be told in addition to the battle of Montlhéry; nevertheless two little incidents may be mentioned as illustrative of the simplicity of the times, and how low military° discipline was reduced among the Burgundian troops.

The armies, as you are aware, being lying opposite to each other on opposite banks of the Seine, sallies and attacks were frequent, and King Louis's suspicions of some treachery on the part of his garrison were gradually increased, especially when one night, making in person the round of his defences, he found that the postern gate of the Bastille° which led to the fields was open and unguarded; the artillery therefore on both sides thundered upon each other when an attack was apprehended on the part of either, though without much effect. One night about the hour of midnight the attention of the besiegers was called by the voice of a page, which loudly cried across the river that some good friends of the lords who were in the besiegers' camp gave them notice that those within the town were that night to make their great enterprize, which the besiegers understood to be a general attack on the camp of the Burgundians and their allies, in the course of which they were to assault it with their whole force on three sides. Taking this therefore for certain, the whole host was in alarm, and great confusion ensued. The camp was put under arms, somewhat after the fashion of the ancient Gauls, for it appears that the baggage waggons were used as a species of circumvallation against the attack of the Parisians. The princes and honourable persons present in a camp which held so many of them sheathed themselves in their armour, and bodies of cavalry were sent out to see what was doing in the interval between the besiegers' camp and the city walls. These reconnoitering parties went so far in the twilight of a very thick morning that they saw an object which appeared to them to be several large phalanxes of lances held upright, from which they° concluded that the king himself was in the act of sallying at the head of all his companies of ordonnance° or of gens d'armes° and of all the citizens of Paris who inclined to bear arms in his defence, and the conflict° was more immediately and more certainly expected; the confusion was augmented in proportion, and the count of Charolais himself called out, "The time is come now which we have long desired; the king with his friends are sallying from the city; let everyone do his duty, and we shall measure out the Parisians with the long yard which is the measure current in their own town."

So far it had come ere the parties sent to reconnoitre° had taken courage to advance near enough to the supposed lances, when they° discovered them to be in reality clumps of overgrown thistles, which in their confusion and trepidation the Burgundian cavaliers had taken for divisions of lances, nor did any consequences follow after so much confusion worth relating.

The other incident is also trifling° of itself, but worthy of preserving as marking one step in the history of gunpowder. It seems that a man in the host of the allies had learned or invented the art of making fireworks somewhat similar to those which are now in common use of children and are called squibs. This *fire-worker* had gained the appropriate name of Jean Bouttefeu° or John of the Serpents. This fellow chanced to be amusing himself with some of his fireworks near a house where the leaders of the army were assembled, and one of the squibs dropped between the count of Charolais and the duke of Berry, that is the real and the nominal chief of the war, and there exploded. The quantity of smoke, the noise, and appearance of flame which accompanied its explosion carried in that suspicious period the conviction that one of these princes had designed foul play to his ally; the camp consisting of so many men of different nations was soon in arms, the bodyguards of the duke and count armed themselves cap a pie, and the tumult was nearly as great as on the day when the thistles were taken for lances; nor can it be known what violence might have arisen if John of the Serpents had not come into the presence of the princes and candidly avowed his own manufacture, craving pardon on his knees for the confusion which he had inadvertently been the cause of exciting, so that cause of alarm also passed away without any real mischief.

We are now to return to the negotiations of the leaders in which King Louis himself participated, to favour his own purposes. He was particularly anxious to extirpate from recollection an error which his practice in the first administration of sovereignty had impressed on the mind of every one as part of his character. He opened negotiations with Count Dammartin and several other persons whom he had accounted his enemies during his father's lifetime, and upon whom he had taken severe revenge at the commencement of his own reign; and in this conviction of his error in this particular he was, notwithstanding his suspicious temper, perfectly sincere. We have seen how severe he had been in the persecution of Count Dammartin before the war of the public good commenced. Since that time the only advances on the count's part towards the king had been his making his escape from the Bastille° in which he was imprisoned, an exile and an impoverished man, and in carrying to the camp of the count of Charolais the military conduct and civil talents for which he had high reputation. Louis now saw that by taking away all hope of his favour from this eminent person he would convert into an unforgiving and constant enemy a man who would otherwise be for his own sake a faithful servant, and, convinced that this was the case, the king hastened to make such advances as should again reconcile Dammartin to his service. Accordingly he restored him all the effects which he had forfeited, and was so bountiful in making up to him his past severity that Dammartin is said to have died in his service in possession of appointments worth no less than seventy-five thousand livres a year.

Having thus secretly diminished the strength of the league, both by reconciling himself with his old enemies, and by using unbounded generosity or profusion in order to acquire new friends, Louis began really and effectually to lay the foundation of a general peace. He fixed the place of treaty at the castle of Conflans near Paris, and went thither in order to hold meetings in person with the count of Charolais. He took with him in attendance on his person few excepting about a hundred archers of his own Scottish Guard. The count of Charolais was also thinly attended. Upon their meeting together Louis, with apparent candour, took the first opportunity to tell the count of the removal of one great obstacle to peace.

This was the provision which the allies made for Charles the duke of Berry and who, as we have already said, they insisted should have the fief of Normandy instead of that which he now possessed, and so number among the great vassals of France. This article of the treaty Louis had hitherto eluded by every means in his power; but at length it had become inevitable.

This was owing to the agitation of the friends of the allies in Normandy itself. The duke of Bourbon had transferred° himself to that province, and made so much interest there in behalf of the duke of Berry that the county itself had in general seen its own advantage in replacing its

existence in the shape of a separate grand fief of the kingdom having a parliament, a prince, a duke, and a separate existence of its own; and so very
keen they became of this object that the capital city of Rouen was delivered up to the duke of Bourbon as representing his relative the duke of
Berry, and most of the official and powerful persons in Normandy ap-
proved° of the proposed change of government and took their oaths to the
duke of Bourbon as representing the prince° of that province. Louis therefore saw plainly that his opposing the allies in this favourite object would
serve no purpose but to inspire them with an idea of his obstinacy and in-
tractability° which would render them more difficult to deal with in future.
As° the province was effectually won, the king therefore made a merit of
guaranteeing the cession of Normandy to his youngest brother under condition of paying the usual homage to the king of France, and thus one
great difficulty of the treaty was removed. Another less insisted on was
however as generally felt and as unexpectedly removed. The count of
Charolais, who was not always remarkable for the accuracy with which he
adjusted his means to the ends which he pursued, seems to have undertaken this important siege or blockade of Paris without adequate preparation. His ranks had been considerably thinned both by flight, desertion, and
slaughter in the battle of Montlhéry, and he suffered since that time from
scarcity of provisions and of money. It was therefore with the greatest pleasure that at this critical state of the treaty he received into his encampment°
a reinforcement levied by the command of his father Duke Philip's cham-
berlain° Monseigneur de Saveuse.° This force consisted of two thousand[83]
men-at-arms, fifteen hundred archers, and treasure to the amount of six
score thousand coined crowns of gold, besides military weapons and provisions. This large reinforcement, so opportunely° furnished by the sagacity of
Duke Philip his father, removed any apprehensions that Count de Charolais, or Charles the Bold as he began to be termed as much from his rashness as from his courage, should be obliged to abandon his undertaking on
Paris from weakness: in fact these supplies, and the humour of acquiescence in which he found the king of France, impressed Charles with a belief that their agreement was almost perfected, and he continued discours-
ing with the king on such matters as remained unsettled with so much
anxiety that he did not observe which way they were taking, and before his
attention was called to the danger to which he exposed himself he had accompanied Louis into the interior of a bastion or bulwark which had been
erected to guard the entrance of a trench or covered way, which led himself
and the four or five persons who followed him to observe that he was as
much within the king's absolute power as his unfortunate grandfather had
been in that of Charles VII at the bridge of Montereau, when he was slain
in the dauphin's presence. The chiefs and favourites of old Duke Philip
were exceedingly alarmed at the danger into which Count Charles had
thus wilfully° chosen to involve himself. The marshal° of Burgundy particularly, whose family name was Neufchatel, said to his companions aloud, "If

this young prince has cast away his person like a madman, it is not our business for that reason to incur the loss of his father's house or our own. Let everyone retire to the post where his duty calls him, and we are enough, providing we keep ourselves prudently together, to regain the boundaries of Hainault or Burgundy in safety." With these expressions he took horse in company with the count of St Pol and rode in front of the encampment to see what news were coming from Paris, or what intelligence he could collect of the count of Charolais.

They were not long in perceiving forty or fifty horses, which in fact proved to be Charles the Bold. He had taken leave of the king so soon as he felt himself too absolutely in his power, and maintaining at the same time the best countenance he could, since to express any suspicion would have been to hasten the danger he suspected. Louis, without showing the least inclination to avail himself treacherously of the count's absence of mind, dismissed several of his own train to guard him until he regained his own army.

When coming up to his own soldiers Charles showed himself something afraid of the marshal° of Burgundy, who had been upon one occasion bold enough to say to him, "Remember, sir, that during your father's lifetime my service is only yours by the right of loan." Notwithstanding his haughty temper Charles deigned to deprecate the censure of this plain-spoken officer.

"Do not scold me," he said, "for I acknowledge my great folly; but the truth is I did not perceive the danger until I was entering the outwork." The marshal° then told him what he had said, and the regulations which he had adopted on the supposition that he might have been detained within the city. The prince said nothing, but hung his head, and rode into his camp with an air of mortification at his own incautious conduct, while the soldiers welcomed him with shouts of congratulation, and such exaggerated praises of King Louis for his observing good faith on an occasion so tempting to break it, that we are led to conclude that the value of a character for honour was not at that time generally understood or believed in. We may indeed see that Louis XI himself felt the advantage which he would possess in regaining a character for faith and honour, which was by no means the consequence of his public life as far as hitherto known. The opportunity afforded him to break his faith in the instance of the count de Charolais was by no means tempting in itself, nor had his father gained so much by the murder of the duke of Burgundy at Montereau as he had lost by the general execrations of all who lived at the time of that abominable action of treacherous murder. It does not appear that Louis XI was one of those determined villains to whom the commission of crime gives actual pleasure merely from its own nature. We only conceive that he was so far an immoral man as not to be deterred from any expedient by its mere deficiency in moral fitness, but that he was aware that he must incur difficulty and prejudice in proportion to the obliquity of the means which he made use of, and resolved therefore to carry his point by fair means while such remained in his power. We have heard of a celebrated gambler of our own day, or that which passed immediately before our time, who said that he would willingly purchase a general character for fair dealing although he should pay twenty thousand pounds for it. One° of his companions replied to him, "You forget, my friend, that in your possession the best character must necessarily be lost in the course of a week after having acquired it." "True," answered the gambler, "but before I lost my reputation I should even in that week have made a hundred thousand pounds by my bargain." It is more than probable that Louis's motives for neglecting to take the advantage of the count de Charolais was a motive similar to that above expressed, or perhaps it resembled one of those sallies which the domestic cat uses to permit its victim, until the time comes when he feels perfectly secure of tearing it to pieces.

The very next day, 28 October° 1465, Louis showed a disposition to improve the visiting acquaintance which had been commenced by Count Charles. Without° sending any previous message or requiring any security, he appeared at the head of about a hundred horse only,[84] and was present at a review of the Burgundian army upon which he bestowed considerable approbation. The count and he then agreed that the old castle of Vincennes should be a place of neutral meeting for concluding the treaty of Conflans. The great personages concerned all repaired thither, and everyone according to his importance was gratified with offices or estates at the expense of the king of France, providing always they were of importance sufficient to render their consent to the peace an object of importance; for if anyone had no more to say for themselves than to state the general principle of the public good, which was the pretence of the war, we have already stated enough to show that such a person was paid very little regard to.

A curious jotting exists of the conditions required from the king at the conclusion of this peace. Louis on the other hand has made a satirical° and jesting recapitulation of the attributes of the princes and great nobles whose allied power had attempted to impose such terms upon him. The note states that the above conditions have been preferred° in consequence of

> The youth of my brother of Berry,
> The prudence of my fair cousin of Calabria,
> The profound sense of my fair brother of Bourbon,
> The malicious wit of the count Armagnac,
> The great pride of my fair cousin[85] of Bretagne,
> and the invincible power of my fair cousin of Charolais.

The treaty however which made this progress in jest was concluded in earnest, and the particular pardons, deeds, and grants, whether of offices, treasure, or estates; and the league for the public good, having obtained its end for the present in the satisfaction of so many persons respecting their private interest, was declared to be dissolved and at an end. In order to put as complete a° close as possible to the arrangement, Charles took upon him the character of duke of Normandy, and did homage to the king in that capacity, while Louis XI bestowed that great fief upon him in the fullest form of such grants, retaining the purpose of not carrying the gift into existence if he should find the least possibility of eluding it.

The dukes of Bretagne and Berry having matters of consequence to transact in Normandy in which they claimed a joint interest set off together for that province. The count of Charolais commenced his retreat to his own country of Burgundy intending to take possession of the towns of the Somme which Louis had been obliged to restore to him, notwithstanding his having ransomed them by the payment of four hundred crowns of gold. The king, as if loath to part with his company, accompanied him as far as Villiers-le-Bel, about four leagues from Paris. Louis was at first attended but by a small train, but being joined by two hundred men-at-arms to escort him homewards again the count of Charolais entered into great suspicion of his purpose and caused to bring up many troops in order to guard against surprise. "Thus," says the historian Commynes, "so numerous are the grounds of suspicion daily arising between persons of such rank it is scarce possible for them really to love each other or to hold a personal correspondence together unless by employing good and wise envoys on either side."[86]

3
NOVEMBER
1465
On this day the two princes separated after a last sacrifice to decorum in some phrases which were probably dissembled on both sides. The count de Charolais again took possession of the towns which had been pledged to him by Louis in the barrier treaty of France to° that effect, and having accomplished his purpose proceeded to Flanders to assist his aged father in a war in which Duke Philip had been engaged with his rebellious vassals of Liège, who had been excited to rebel against him among other things by their own restless disposition and the private encouragement of King Louis XI.

Louis on the other hand moved towards the skirts of Normandy with the purpose of depriving his brother Charles of the sovereignty of that province, the aborting of which from the crown of France had been one principal object assigned for the war of the public good.

Chapter 15

Neither of the great vassals of Louis, the duke of Bretagne nor his brother Charles, formerly of Berry, now duke of Normandy, had any share of his piercing, acute, and self-interested disposition. With them the treaty which ended the war of the public good was considered as a solid and effectual arrangement to be bona fide executed according to its tenor in favour of all who could claim an interest in it.

On the other hand, as we have already stated, Louis XI considered the war for the public good as a mere pretext assumed in order to wring from the French crown some of its most valuable prerogatives, to subject it to the control of its own vassals; and the general treaty of Conflans by which it was concluded he viewed as nothing else save a compulsory arrangement to which he was obliged to yield his assent at the time, but to which he intended to adhere no longer than circumstances should give him an opportunity of receding from the concessions which he had been forced to make. In this mode of calculating he kept two principal objects in view. The first was, as we have already hinted, the recovery of the province of Normandy from his brother Charles, whose right he was determined should not have existence according to the arrangement settled by the treaty.

The second point was that of entangling the count of Charolais, whose father Philip of Burgundy soon after died and left him actual possession of his dominions, which he already had for some time governed in fact, in such and so difficult affairs at home as might prevent him from interfering in behalf of his late ally Charles, once of Berry and now, by the late treaty, of Normandy.

Both these points, of which in fact one depended on the other, Louis began to provide for with an ingenuity not the least embarrassed by shame at breaking his own word or regret at destroying the work of his own hands. His purpose of involving the dukes of Normandy and Bretagne in a quarrel together was facilitated by the causes of division which existed between these two sovereigns, who were not long in disputing vehemently concerning the division of the booty which they had rather seemed to acquire than gained in reality by the close of the war and the concessions of Louis XI in the treaty of Conflans.

The neighbourhood of their different territories, and the uncertain state of Normandy, had occasioned the duke of Bretagne getting possession of several strong places which Louis foresaw° must become so many bones of contention between him and Duke Charles; he therefore resolved to approach the scene of action at the head of such an army as should enable him to take the field for his own interest.

Accordingly no sooner had such discussions given rise to discord betwixt the duke of Bretagne and Normandy than it followed that many of the strong places in dispute between them fell into the hands of the king, who had troops in readiness to occupy them in his own name. The duke of Normandy soon found himself in such personal danger that he was glad to retreat for safety, and at length both the princes of Bretagne and Normandy came to be so much afraid of the predominant power of the king that they accommodated their own differences, which they ought never to have permitted to exist, and in consequence of this accommodation Charles of Normandy, very poor and in an extremely desolate condition, was compelled to fly to the court of Bretagne, where he was forced from absolute poverty to dispose of his plate in order to defray his subsistence.

Louis meanwhile accomplished his purpose of quietly retaining possession of the great appanage of Normandy, which he had so lately bound himself solemnly in the eyes of his friends and enemies to deliver up to his brother. And now Charles, so lately the nominal head of a league strong enough to control his brother, received no title save that of Monsieur as the meanest existing son of France.

These proceedings in diametrical breach of the late treaty of Conflans did not pass unobserved by the count of Charolais, who in vain endeavoured to prevent by negotiation the downfall of that structure which had been so lately reared up by the treaty of Conflans or Vincennes, but he was not able at this moment to use the peremptory mode of association, that more effectual remonstrance which was in his nature to appeal to more readily. This was owing to the winter season which rendered the weather unfit for marching to Normandy or Bretagne, and still more to the disaffection of° the duke's Flemish vassals of Dinant and Liège, which were nearly in a state of absolute insurrection. Standing in no awe therefore of the duke's arms, the king did not permit his remonstrances greatly to interfere with his own views upon Normandy. If you take the trouble to look back to the first series of Tales[87] in the time of Edward III of England, where an account is given of the insurrection of the Flemings under Philip d'Artville, you will find some general account given of the towns and communities in the Low Countries which held of the house of Burgundy, and which certainly, being possessed of a principal part of the manufactures of the period, were consequently remarkable for their population and wealth, while on the other hand from their democratical constitution they were the most fickle, most rash and bloodthirsty people in the world, engaging in wars with their princes on slight provocation, and supported by the perfidious excitements which were constantly supplied by their insidious neighbour the king of France; who, although he seldom gave them actual support, was constant (and none more so than Louis XI) in maintaining amongst them these continual intrigues, which kept up a bad understanding between the Flemish citizens and their native° princes.

Thus it happened that no sooner was Count Charles of Charolais returned° from the campaign of the public good than he found himself called upon to chastize the citizens of Dinant, who at that time were a very numerous people chiefly employed in the manufacture of utensils° made of copper. They rendered themselves particularly obnoxious to the duke of Burgundy, with whose haughty and resentful character they were sufficiently acquainted. He° appeared before Dinant, which then being abandoned by the people of Liège who were their allies, the place was taken, and the duke, acting according to his natural violence of character, sacked and laid it waste with all the extremities of hostility. Meantime the people of Liège, unmoved by the dreadful example of their near neighbours, revived their insurrection after a short truce, and Charles duke of Burgundy, having succeeded to that title by the death of his father, took   *15 JUNE* the field against them with a large army of feudal cavalry, while the citi-   *1467* zens were chiefly armed and regimented as pikemen and hoped to bring the horsemen of Burgundy to a battle in ground which was much cut up by rivers and canals, which° rendered it unfit for the operations of that force. In the meantime the duke formed the siege of a town called St Trond,° which the natives of Liège were desirous of relieving.

While the war stood thus in Flanders and fully occupied the duke of Burgundy's attention, Louis XI resolved to persevere in his plan, and to crush the duke of Bretagne as he had already reduced Charles of Normandy to exile and to poverty. For this purpose he designed to have such an explanation as should prevent the duke of Burgundy from interfering with what he proposed. For this purpose he employed the count of° St Pol, a nobleman who had gained the prize of constable with the leading of a large band of men-at-arms and other considerable advantages of estate and territory in the lottery of the treaty of the public good. Since he had been so successful he had assumed, in appearance at least, a complete dependence upon the king, although there was no doubt from what happened afterwards that he had already formed the rash and delicate project of maintaining his own separate independence and keeping the° balance between France and Burgundy, shifting from the one power to the other as he should find most effectual for his° own interest. He now appeared in behalf of France, having with him the cardinal Balue° and other envoys of Louis, upon whose suggestion he acted.

Their audience only lasted one day, in which the constable told the duke of Burgundy that the people of Liège were allies of France and included in the treaty between Burgundy and that kingdom, and that if he attacked them Louis must necessarily give them succour; nevertheless they added an alternative, that if the duke of Burgundy would renounce all interference with the war in Bretagne the king of France on his part would avoid taking any part in the war between the duke and the citizens of

Liège. The duke replied by saying that the breach of the truce had commenced on the part of the citizens of Liège and not upon his, and that therefore he could not be justly charged with having broken it. He also gave the count of St Pol, who had become by his interference the great man he at present was, a plain hint of the delicate game which he was choosing to play. "Fair cousin," said he, "we are at present good friends, and I would therefore advise you to take care that the king does not deal with you as he has done with many others. Should you choose˚ to remain on this side of the frontier or the French boundary, believe me you will take a very wise resolution." A final parting took place between them, which expressed in a remarkable manner the different characters of the two princes, Louis XI relying upon his astucious and nicely balanced policy, and the duke of Burgundy on the other hand throwing his sword into the scale with the natural bluntness and fierceness of his temper and appealing in support of his cause to the speedy determination of battle.

As they were about to mount on each side, Charles of Burgundy called on the French king's envoys to warn his majesty seriously not to make any aggression upon the province of Bretagne. To˚ this the count of St Pol replied, "Monseigneur, you do not treat fairly, for you insist upon having everything your own way, and wish to make war at your own pleasure upon our friends, while you would have us remain quiet without injuring yours; these are not equal terms, nor will the king admit of them." The duke answered with his wonted promptness and decision, "The people of Liège are assembled in force, and I expect to have a decisive battle within three days. If I lose it I have no doubt you will decide upon all these matters in the way most agreeable to you, but you will˚ also do well to remember that if I gain the expected action against the men of Liège you must not again speak of disturbing the province of Britanny." With these words he mounted his horse and set forth at the head of his army to cover the siege of St Trond.˚

The battle which was speedily expected by this adventurous sovereign took place, and was in fact much more desperately disputed than he himself perhaps apprehended. The people of Liège in the conferences respecting peace had agreed upon certain conditions and given˚ to the duke the custody of a hundred hostages as pledges that these should be faithfully observed, and now that they had broke off the treaty and broke through the truce it was matter of doubt in the council of the duke of Burgundy whether these hostages should not be put to death in resentment of their countrymen's breach of faith. The seignior de Contay, contrary to his usual strain of opinion which was humane and moderate, gave here his vote for the severer judgement and for the death of the hostages, while the lord˚ of Humbercourt[88] was so much shocked that he whispered to the historian Commynes, "Do you mark that old man so strong and healthy?—I would wager a great deal that he is not alive at this time next year, which I say on account of the terrible opinion which he has just now expressed."

The more mild and favourable sentiment having prevailed respecting the lives of the hostages, the duke of Burgundy was informed that the people of Liège were advancing to raise the siege of St Trond° as near as a place called Bruestem° within half a league of his camp. "He immediately drew out his forces and prepared for action," says Commynes, "with more skill and prudence than I had observed him to use upon similar occasions."[89] The pikemen of Liège lined with their infantry the various canals° and brooks which lay between them and the duke's army. The Burgundian men-at-arms and the archers assailed them with great violence, with such force that at length the men-at-arms by the superiority of their weapons and their good order, and the archery by the advantage of their shot, had the same advantage over the artillery of Liège. Thus at length the Liège insurgents were forced and broken upon all points. This was not accomplished without a desperate resistance, and the slaughter, which was much augmented by the report of the victors, amounted to about six thousand men, the rest of the fugitives being concealed by the darkness of the night. Had it not been for the latter circumstance more than fifteen thousand men would have fallen by the pursuit of the duke of Burgundy's cavalry.

The seignior de Contay died soon after this battle,[90] as had been prophesied by M. Humbercourt when he gave the cruel opinion for putting the hostages of Liège to death. He had however done great service to the duke in this battle of Bruestem,° which depended much upon the exertions which he had used to preserve to the duke's men-at-arms the full advantage of their discipline, which was their principal cause of gaining the victory. The battle was fought on foot upon both sides, the nature of the ground not permitting the men-at-arms to act upon horseback. That night Duke Charles, the instant he had laid aside his armour, wrote a letter to the constable and his late colleagues, envoys from King Louis, warning them of the battle he had gained, and intimating his pleasure that, the men of Liège having been defeated, the king should abstain from making war upon Britanny. This message seems to have given considerable anxiety to King Louis, whom it finally drove to the most hazardous expedient which in the course of his life he ever had ventured upon.

Meanwhile, although the victory of Bruestem° had by instant means decided the surrender of Liège, yet the citizens who had been engaged in that action returned in great numbers and gave new spirits to the popular insurgents when the° event of the action had struck them with dismay. It is true that the duke, having first received the surrender of St Trond,° had advanced towards Liège with his army when three hundred of the most respectable citizens of the place approached his presence in their shirts with their feet bare, bringing the keys of the city in evidence of their surrender to all extremities of war at the duke's pleasure, excepting only those of fire and pillage.

But although the submission° had been made by the better orders with every sincere wish on their part to avoid the threatened extremity of fire and sword, yet the inferior classes, having less to lose and being still in in-surrection, declared against all surrender, and refused to give up their gates either to Humbercourt or to the duke himself, and it became a great question whether they would permit the treaty to be executed, or whether they would not rather make a sally, which the great numbers and desperation of the mutineers might render a dangerous one to the duke and that part of his army which had arrived first before the city. But the management of Humbercourt was so judicious that the people of Liège were at length contented to admit the duke into their gates, a ceremony conducted with such marks of indignation as showed the sense which the prince entertained of their rebellion. Declining to enter by any of the gates of the city, Charles caused a breach to be made in the walls of twenty cubits wide, the ditch of the city to be filled up to the same extent. Through this opening he entered on horseback, armed cap-a-pie, sur-rounded by his officers, and escorted by two thousand men-at-arms also in complete armour. The procession being closed by ten thousand archers, and a large army being still collected before the place, the duke then pro-ceeded to execute his pleasure, putting to death five or six of the persons of those who had formerly been his hostages, and imposing° upon the city new taxes in consideration (as was the pretext) of the expenses to which he had been put by their breach of conditions. At the same time he car-ried off such store of artillery and armour as was in the city, and caused the towers and walls thereof to be pulled down and razed. Having° thus punished the mutinous and tumultuous city, and rendered it incapable of resisting his arms in case the humour of insurrection should again seize upon them, he began° now to think seriously of putting a stop to the king of France's operations in Brittany and elsewhere, which had for their ob-ject the destruction of the treaty° which so lately had concluded the war for the public good.

Louis indeed had to plead that, although he had ostensibly subscribed and authorised every particular of that treaty,° yet it was under a secret protestation taken in presence of some confidential crown officers, before whom he insisted upon the evil consequences of many of those stipula-tions which were pretended to be for the public good, but which he con-tended would operate in a manner quite the contrary. Louis endeavoured to plead his own cause more fully in an assembly of the states of France at Tours, to whom he represented the great loss and distraction which must necessarily arise from the execution of the treaty of Conflans in its literal extent, and he made a case so specious as to obtain the assurances of the estates that they would stand by him with lives and fortunes in resisting the impositions he complained of, and thus in some measure sanctioned° the infraction of the treaty. Thus fortified by° the support of his subjects, he obtained their consent that the appanage assigned to his brother Charles should not exceed twelve thousand francs° in landed rent and sixty thou-sand payable by the crown in form of pension, instead of the separation of all Normandy from the crown as had been arranged at Conflans.

Thus fortified in his purpose, Louis proceeded to make war in Bretagne with a view of compelling the dukes of that province and of Normandy to submit to such terms as he should please to dictate. Accordingly he prevailed upon these two princes, neither of them men of great firmness or talent, to agree to renounce a proposed settlement of Normandy, that the pension of sixty thousand francs should be accepted in lieu thereof, and that on consideration of his brother the king's granting the same Charles should renounce alliance with all foreign princes whatever, and especially with the duke of Burgundy. Such a treaty was accordingly dictated by the king to the duke of Bretagne and his brother Charles, and a herald belonging to the duke of Bretagne was sent to the duke of Burgundy intimating that they could no longer profit by his interference with King Louis. In consequence of the terms of this treaty the duke of Burgundy's wrath was extreme upon finding how completely° his feeble-minded allies had suffered themselves to be overreached by the astucity of the king, and as he supposed the monarch capable of any species of fraud, his first idea was that the treaty announced by the herald was entirely a forgery on his part, and the messenger had some difficulty to escape being hanged in the first burst of the duke's passion.

The news of Charles's rage embarrassed Louis considerably, for he saw he must necessarily make some great act of confidence in order to obtain a reconciliation with Charles, or else he must encounter all the inconveniences arising from the distrust and jealousy of a man of this prince's impetuous and ungovernable temper. Louis had some reason to think that he had learned to understand completely° the nature of the duke's disposition by the intercourse which he had with him under the walls of Paris, and had perhaps rather calculated too much upon the effect he had been able to produce upon him by his personal intercourse; and by a bold neglect of all the usual precautions attended to in the meeting of persons of their rank, he therefore resolved of his own account to offer a visit to his cousin of Burgundy, without expressing more than a desire for assurance of the° safety of his person, and to have a simple safe conduct under the duke's hand. The few counsellors whose advice the king used on this occasion gave different counsel according to their habits of education and profession.

The count of Dammartin, whom we have often mentioned as a valiant soldier, and who after having been much persecuted by Louis for offences given against himself while dauphin was now trusted and employed by him, gave it as his opinion that the king ought to bid the duke of Burgundy defiance and move against him at the head of the forces of France before Charles could fully assemble his own. This was the opinion of a soldier and was certainly the most manly course which the king had to pursue, but it was not that which was most agreeable to his inclination, for Louis was possessed of an idea of his own powers of superiority in personal argument over most people with whom he had occasion to negotiate, and his celebrated minister the cardinal Balue° together with the bishop of Amiens[91] encouraged him by their advice, approving of his proposed meeting with Charles, and assuring him that his own intellectual powers of superiority were so great that if Charles could but only meet him personally it must follow as a matter of course that the duke must yield up every point of debate between them. The mode of negotiation was therefore adopted instead of that of war, and a safe conduct to Péronne,° a strong town of Flanders where Duke Charles then was and where the meeting was to take place, was granted to King Louis as he required.

On this remarkable occasion, as Louis's object was not to irritate or provoke the powerful duke of Burgundy but to soften any prejudices he might be actuated by, and if possible to gain him over, he adopted no measure which could excite Charles's suspicion in the least degree. In particular he brought with him no troops nor guards, not even those usually attendant on his own body, and indeed brought nobody with him of any kind except three or four favourite statesmen. The duke of Burgundy came to meet him about a league from Péronne,° saluted him on the knee, and showed every mark of satisfaction at his arrival.

Louis was lodged honourably within the town of Péronne,° the castle of which was a rude ancient tower of great strength, but not then thought fitting for the reception of a crowned head, nor were its° recollections at such a moment such as could have been agreeable to the feelings of the king of France, since it is said to have been the place where Charles the Simple, one of those monarchs called in history *rois fainéants,*° was put to death by his insurgent vassal Herbert count° of Vermandois.

Upon entering the town of Péronne Louis became aware of the banners of several powerful persons who although born his subjects had embraced the allegiance of the duke of Burgundy, and having been irritated by preceding acts of severity at the hands of the king might° be supposed capable of advising the duke to use the king with rigour now he had placed himself in his power.

The effect of these observations was such that Louis, becoming alarmed for his safety, instead of retreating from Péronne,° to which no opposition would have been offered, made it his personal request to the duke that, leaving the more convenient apartments° assigned to him in the place, he should be permitted to retire to the castle of Count Herbert as a place of greater security.

This was readily granted by Duke Charles, who saw, perhaps not without satisfaction, that Louis put himself more into his power by this change of residence from one fastness to another still more secure. It is probable nevertheless that Charles, among whose faults treachery is not reckoned, would have abstained from taking any dishonourable advantage of the king's situation if he had not himself given an example of bad faith at the time when the success of his politics depended on a display of the utmost candour on his own part.

It must be remembered that the interference of the king of France with the insurgents of Liège was one of the points upon which Charles had shown himself anxiously sensitive, and Louis was so much aware of this that he resolved to renew and carry on his own machinations in Liège and influence the inhabitants, of whom° the lower classes were more numerous and desperate, still exasperated against the duke on account of the severe chastisement they had received at his hands after the battle of Bruestem.° Louis therefore, very incautiously as well as treacherously, took the very time of his own journey to Péronne° to send two of his most skilful° agents for the purpose of again stirring up the people of Liège against their sovereign, whom they had lately so highly offended and by whom they had been severely punished.

Apparently they had little difficulty in setting tumult afoot among the multitude and enrolling° them under their former leaders, while the numbers and ferocity of the citizens and their habit of using the pike or spear compensated for the want of other weapons. The insurgents sallied from Liège for the purpose of attacking the city of Tongres in the vicinity, to which the bishop of Liège had retreated along with the seigneur de Humbercourt with a few Burgundian forces. The Liège citizens had little difficulty in storming the place, for their numbers were overpowering. They were guilty of sacrilegious cruelty in putting to death and tearing to pieces a number of the canons and religious persons who were in attendance upon the bishop, and they seized rudely upon the bishop himself, although a relation and near ally of the duke of Burgundy their lord, whose part he had warmly espoused during all the disputes betwixt the duke and his subjects of Liège. The bishop himself and Humbercourt were made prisoners, and the life of the latter was spared at the request of a knight called John de Wilde,° who had taken upon him the command of the insurgent citizens and prevailed upon them in this instance to adopt the rules of reasonable and humane warfare.

As these tumultuary soldiers returned from Tongres° to Liège they indulged their innate cruelty by tearing to pieces some of the bishop's confidential servants and throwing the gobbets of their flesh at each other's heads in derision. They brought with them their bishop also as a captive, and imprisoned him within the city of Liège. Some of the Burgundians they set at liberty, considering it necessary for their own safety to maintain an affectation of stating that these proceedings were not directed against the duke, with whom they intended the peace lately made, but were directed against the bishop alone, against whom they had separate causes of quarrel.

These news soon flew from Liège and Tongres to the proudest residence of Charles of Burgundy at Péronne, to which they were carried by the scattered soldiers and officers who had been in attendance on the° bishop and Humbercourt. These fugitives did not omit to mention the share which the emissaries of King Louis had taken in exciting these bloody proceedings on the part of the people of Liège, and like fire set to

gunpowder the news gave occasion to a violent explosion of the duke of
Burgundy's naturally hot disposition. He conceived himself as treated by
the king after the manner of a mutinous child whom his keeper affects to
indulge and humour while in fact he is imposing upon and deceiving
him. The idea that the king should have dared to have thrown himself so
completely in his power, while at the same time he feared not to take the
readiest course to affront and provoke him by acting with such breach of
faith by instigating to new rebellion a people who had been so lately and
so severely chastised, and attacking and endangering the life of a ruling
prince bishop, the duke's own ally and kinsman, implied not only contempt of the duke's power, but an idea that he could under any provocation be soothed by the art or intimidated by the power of the king of
France, who thus openly and barefacedly trifled° with the danger in which
he himself stood. The first burst of the duke's displeasure at this treatment
inferred° a fixed purpose of taking an awful vengeance by seizing advantage of the false step Louis had made by putting himself into the power of
the duke on the one hand, while on the other he provoked his violent
temper by provoking it in a very sensible point. The evil news also came
in an exaggerated shape, for it was reported that the bishop was not
merely imprisoned but slain; a report which was founded on the slaughter
of priests who attended on him.

The first orders of the duke were to mount a strict guard upon the
king's person, and particularly upon the gates of the castle of Péronne in
which he had unwisely requested to be lodged. The day before this exasperating intelligence the duke had assured the king on his expressing some
slight degree of suspicion that, did he see an arrow come in the direction
of his majesty, he would esteem it his duty to receive it in his own bosom.
Now on the contrary the king beheld a strong guard posted on the walls
of the town, the gates of the castle in like manner shut, and nobody admitted except by means of the wicket and under the halberts of the
warders. Above all he was now impressed with the ominous reflection that
he was lodged by his own folly in that massive and ominous tower which
had already witnessed the death of one king of France, and was likely° to
see that of Louis the sagacious, slain by his own vassal as Charles the Simple had been treated by the count° of Vermandois. Louis's instinct however, or his habitual cunning, had brought with him resources which few
other persons would have thought of in such circumstances. He had, as we
have said, ventured to Péronne unattended by guards or military force, but
he bore in his hand that which, well applied, possessed the same power of
making an impression. Foreseeing that he would have occasion to make
friends among the duke's familiars, he had brought with him a sum of
treasure equal to the load of six horses; this he distributed with great liberality among the attendants of Charles, each of whom for regard to his own
character was° desirous that their master should not abuse the advantage
which had been afforded him by the rashness of Louis's confidence, and

felt that they were parties like to profit more by soothing than inflaming the resentment of their master Charles.

The first day after the arrival of the news from Tongres the duke openly expressed the most severe intentions of vengeance. He indeed alleged a specious cause for the strict guard which was kept upon the castle and town of Péronne, namely the loss of a casket of valuable jewels which had been stolen from him. But his own violence of deportment plainly showed to what a vigilance so unusual was really to be attributed, and that the guards were designed to prevent the king from attempting an escape from Péronne castle. The first day after the tidings the duke intermitted all communication with the king by visits, and it seemed that Louis was to expect very severe measure at his hand. On the next day however the news of the bishop of Liège being alive and other mitigating circumstances reached Péronne, upon which occasion the duke held a council of his own principal followers, amongst whom the liberality of Louis had already made a party in his favour. Most of those, and perhaps some who had no° selfish motive for forming such an opinion, declared that the safe conduct granted to King Louis under the duke's own hand could not be honourably or creditably broken, but that the opportunity might be taken to compel the king to subscribe without discussion such a treaty of peace as the duke had already determined should close the interview at Péronne.

Others gave it as their opinion that the king should be seized upon without any ceremony and placed under the duke's arrest as having forfeited his privilege and immunity by his own duplicity. It was added by some that Charles the king's brother should be presently sent for, and a treaty entered into of a nature more advantageous to the princes and vassals of France than that of Conflans which Louis had shown so much desire to elude. And so popular was this opinion in the council of Burgundy that Commynes tells us that he himself saw a messenger ready booted and prepared to depart for Charles of Normandy, who was then residing in Bretagne. It is by no means unlikely that if this course had once been taken Louis XI would have been compelled to resign his throne in favour of his brother; and it is probable that since the king's talents and duplicity were the subject of general apprehension he would in that case have been sentenced to perpetual imprisonment, if not to a darker fate.°

The sagacious king was not however awanting to himself in so imminent a crisis. He offered in order to procure his own personal freedom to submit to what articles of treaty should be proposed by the duke of Burgundy, and he named as hostages the duke of Bourbon and the cardinal the duke of Bourbon's brother, the constable count St Pol, and other persons of consequence presently at Péronne, who expressed no doubt of the king's observing good faith towards them.

The council was adjourned from one day to another, and on the third night Duke Charles continued in a state of agitation which was finely described by the historian Commynes,[92] who was himself in attendance upon the duke in his bedchamber: "During° that night which was the third of the debate the duke did not undress himself, only threw himself twice or thrice upon his bed, and then paced his chamber as was his custom when troubled in mind. I walked with him on these occasions for some time. In the morning he was in greater resentment than ever, making use of threats as if about to execute some great and violent resolution. However he was at length so much calmed as to say that he would content himself if the king of France would be pleased to confirm the peace as it had been already treated of between them by a solemn oath, and would go in person with him to Liège to see vengeance taken on the insurgents and the deliverance of the captive bishop who was the king's relation as well as the duke's."* A private friend to Louis (undoubtedly Commynes himself) transmitted to the king the very useful information that if he consented to these two points there was no danger, but that by disputing either of them he would put himself into great peril.

Immediately after receiving this private information Louis was surprised by a visit from the duke, who came in person to propose to him the two conditions on which he had privately resolved to set him at liberty. When the duke addressed him it was with an agitated voice, so much was he moved and so ready to break forth into rage. His demeanour was gentle, but his gesture and language were rude and peremptory, which probably the rather induced the king to observe the friendly hint which he had received. To the first question, which was whether the king would pledge his oath to the treaty of peace that had been already drawn out, he answered in the affirmative, and declared himself willing the same on a crucifix of peculiar sanctity, and in the virtue of which he was a known believer. Nothing was indeed altered so far as the duke of Burgundy was concerned, but with respect to Charles the brother of Louis it was stipulated that, since the king had deprived him of the duchy of Normandy, he should receive instead the territories of Champagne° and of Brie. This would be more effectual to the prince Charles as placing his territories near those of Burgundy, so that no attempt could be made either to limit or dispossess without his having immediate power to apply for the protection of his ally, to which king Louis did not venture to make any objections.

The duke of Burgundy's second proposal was that, in order to disown any accession to the villainy to which the citizens of Liège had charged the king of exciting them, Louis should himself march against that city in company with the duke Charles of Burgundy and to assist him to revenge the injury done to the bishop of Liège, who was a relation of both princes. King Louis, prepared for this request also, said that he would° most willingly consent to join the duke of Burgundy on this occasion, either with a small or large force, whichever should be most agreeable to him. The stipulation was no doubt a triumphant one on the part of the duke of

---

* The prelate alluded to was Louis de Bourbon, brother of the duke of that noble house.

Burgundy, since it tended to show his insurgent subjects that though the king of France might instigate them to courses displeasing to their prince, he was compelled to disavow them when the question came to concern their impunity or punishment; nor can it be denied that Louis of France, thus moving in arms to punish the very insurrection which he had himself excited, made a mean and unworthy appearance. He did not however hesitate to sacrifice to the emergency of the time, for without such a sacrifice he could hardly have obtained his demission from Péronne, and he long after, upon Commynes's° exchanging the service of Burgundy for that of France, remunerated him amply for the sound advice which he had furnished him in such a crisis, or rather the private information he had conveyed to him of what the duke intended° to insist upon as conditions of his freedom not to be dispensed with.

Chapter 16

No sooner were the princes agreed upon the treaty than they sent for the holy relic° before mentioned, being a cross called the Cross of Victory and believed to be a part of that on which our Saviour actually suffered. On this both princes made their oath faithfully to observe the articles of the treaty. The question was now with what attendance Louis should make this forced campaign against Liège, and it seems to have been limited to three hundred men-at-arms as a number sufficient to show that the king was in earnest, yet so inferior to the host of Burgundy as not to give any occasion for suspecting to what purpose it might be applied.

Meantime, the news of the treaty of Péronne having gone abroad, the count of Dammartin, grand master of France, showed his fidelity to the service of Louis by remonstrating with the duke of Burgundy[93] on the violence which he had used towards the king, and declaring that if he was not at perfect liberty the whole kingdom of France would come to fight for his freedom, and with the purpose of making such° military execution in the territory of the duke of Burgundy as the duke himself proposed to deal° to the city of Liège. "For Monsieur the king's brother," said Dammartin, "is not dead, nor is France so thinly supplied with men of gallantry as seems to be supposed." This bold language, although it did not alter Louis's resolution to submit to the faithful execution of the treaty of Péronne, was certainly very efficacious in inducing the duke of Burgundy to take no further advantage of Louis's situation than he had already gained.

Meanwhile the duke, approaching the city of Liège with the king, held a council what mode of attack should be resolved upon. A bold proposal was here made, not as was supposed without the hope of pleasing the duke's rash temper, the purport of which was that they should send backwards a part of the army, as their force was too great to be applied to taking a town in whose walls there existed such large breaches as the duke had made in those of Liège last year, especially as the ditch had been filled up and the towers destroyed at the same time with the walls. But Charles, with a moderation and sagacity which was probably suggested by his apprehension of danger from the practices of King Louis, resolved upon a safe and prudent mode of conduct which should leave nothing to chance. It was resolved in his council° that the marshal° of Burgundy and the seigneur de Humbercourt should command the vanguard of the army with a large number of men-at-arms. These had instructions to lodge themselves within the city, either by consent of the citizens or by force, while the duke and the king approached at the head of the other part of their forces, both the Burgundians and the men-at-arms of France, in order to support the vanguard. Meantime° a great number of that foremost° body had precipitated their march, and, desirous of being the first who should obtain the plunder of the city, had taken possession of a suburb° of the place, though the citizens could not be prevailed upon to introduce them into the main body through the gate which connected the town with the suburb. In the meantime John de Wilde° and other captains of the insurgents observed that the Burgundians who had taken possession of this suburb kept very bad order; they therefore took heart, and resolved so far to profit by the breaches in their walls as to lead forth great numbers of spearmen (whom the place contained) and by fetching a slight compass attack unexpectedly the enemy who had possession of the suburb.°

This was in a great measure successful, the surprise being complete and more than eight hundred of the besiegers being slain, one hundred of whom were men-at-arms. On the other hand the besieged were obliged to retire after daybreak with much fatigue and the loss of John de Wilde° and one or two of the principal popular chiefs, who were slain or desperately wounded and great part of whom afterward died.

The duke received notice of this sally and pushed forward a body of men-at-arms, carrying with them supplies of various kinds for refreshment of the vanguard, and to restore the order which had been lost, and which reinforcement sufficed until the main body came up to keep the besieged from attempting further sallies.

In the meantime the situation of the princes was so extraordinary as naturally inspired them with mutual distrust of each other and gave the operations of the siege a very singular and suspicious aspect. Charles, who considered King Louis as being in some degree a captive, was afraid lest° he should throw himself into Liège and combine with the citizens in defence of the place, or, what was equally dangerous, that he might march off with his own guards and men-at-arms.

Louis on the contrary, although conscious of nourishing no intentions hostile to the treaty of Péronne, was yet sensible that the duke had no cause particularly to trust him and was a man likely to act to extremity upon any suspicion which he might adopt, however causelessly. It became the object of the princes therefore closely to watch each other's motions, and the king, who had no intention of trusting his person to the fickle faith of the popular party in Liège, was extremely desirous by every means in his power to satisfy the duke of Burgundy of the fairness of his intentions.

For this purpose two villas, or country houses, situated beyond the walls of the town and nearly opposite to the breaches which had been made in them the year before by Duke Charles, were allotted the one for the quarters of the duke and the other for those of the king of France. Charles had thus the means for maintaining from the vicinity of their residence close observation on the motions of his slippery captive or hostage, in whichever

light Louis is regarded in his present singular position. A large barn was situated nearly between these two villas and a good deal in advance of them
both. In this barn Duke Charles posted four or five hundred men-at-arms,
the flower of his household troops. The walls of the place were made full
of loopholes, that it might be defended in case of necessity against any
treacherous attempt on the part of the French who lay in the adjoining
villa, or any sally by the besieged through the breaches of the city wall like
that which they had already attempted. Louis on the other hand, attended
by his guards and men-at-arms, conceived that his situation on the other
side of the barn in the large country house was tolerably safe.

In the first night of their taking up these quarters there arose considerable confusion and alarm in the army, although no just cause could be discovered. The darkness and badness of the night, together with the fatal effects of the former sally, had impressed a terror on the minds of the
besiegers which broke out into an open and alarming confusion. The duke
of Burgundy, the king, and the constable of France hastened to the spot
from which the alarm was said to come, and it was remarkable, considering how military the duke of Burgundy's general character was, that Louis
displayed a readiness of resource and a presence of mind which indicated
the depth of understanding and readiness of thought which he possessed
in a degree superior to his impetuous and fiery rival, who fell into confusion, not for deficiency of courage, says a historian whom we have already
often quoted,[94] but for want of presence of mind; and indeed it is in such
circumstances that a great and powerful mind really assumes its ascen-
dancy.

The king of France therefore took the word of command, naturally as
it were directing the besiegers to fire on such and such points, since if the
besieged came at all there lay their way. The Burgundians saw with some
mortification that their duke's military talents and resources fell considerably below those of the king who displayed so much judgement and decision. The alarm, being in a great measure imaginary, at length subsided, but
the anecdote is worth preserving to illustrate the characters of those two
remarkable rivals.

The besiegers lay thus blockading the town for about a week, during
which neither the duke nor any of the men-at-arms laid aside their armour, expecting always a sally from the besieged to which the first attempt gave so much encouragement. At length the duke of Burgundy determined to assault the town and fixed to his attack 30 October 1468. He
directed all men-at-arms to disarm themselves in the morning of that day
in order to take some repose, but at the same time commanded them to
be in readiness to resume their armour before eight o'clock, and to hold
themselves ready at that hour to commence the assault so soon as they
should hear a signal which was the discharge of three pieces of artillery.

On the contrary the city which was about to be thus assaulted was already reduced to the last extremity. John de Wilde° their principal commander was dead, and there were no longer any knights or gentlemen among the insurgents, for the few that had° adhered to their cause were killed or wounded in the first sally. They had° neither gates, nor walls, nor towers, nor ditches, save what were completely indefensible. King Louis, from whom they had been taught to expect assistance, had appeared in the army of the besiegers and acted as their enemy, nor was there a quarter from which they could expect any relief or assistance. They had no forces whatever except the numerous populace of the town and a separate body of countrymen, inhabitants of the district of Franchimont, a little district belonging to Liège, who had at all times borne° a high character for courage. With such inadequate forces however they came to the desperate resolution of venturing upon a decisive sally, the execution of which was fixed for the night preceding 30 October, being the very night before the day which the duke had fixed for the general assault.

The intention of the people of Liège, bold and desperate in itself, was also ordered with considerable military skill, from whatever quarter that was derived. It was agreed that the men of Franchimont, on whose courage great reliance was placed by the townsmen of Liège, should sally forth by the breaches in the wall, having for their guides the two proprietors of the villas where the king and the duke were quartered, who undertook from their knowledge of the ground to conduct two columns to the attack of the quarters occupied by the king and the duke. They hoped to attain the quarters of these princes without being discovered, by moving under cover of a rock which formed a species of hollow way and observing strict silence. These men of Franchimont therefore would, they concluded, have every chance of surprising the persons of the king and duke, and at the same time the mass of the citizens armed with lances were designed to sally from the gates into the suburb and assault the part of the besieging army there stationed. The enterprise of these desperate men, to whom the attribute of much courage and some conduct cannot be denied, seemed to be undertaken in consequence of their having received some information of the duke's intention to proceed to the assault on the same day, though at a later° hour. The coincidence of time was however merely accidental, but as it happened had very nearly been successful.

On the night therefore before the 30th, or early in the morning of that day, the weather being dark and the besiegers having most of them laid aside their armour according to the command which had been issued by Charles, six or seven hundred of these men of Franchimont issued from the town in silence through the breaches of the city wall, surprised such scouts as had been placed as sentinels in the space between the breaches in the walls of the city and the quarters of the princes, and put° them to death; and had they pushed on to the villas where the quarters° of the latter were established they might have succeeded in killing or making them prisoners, and by that means throwing the besiegers into irretrievable disorder. Unfortunately however for their enterprise the men of Franchimont engaged in an attack upon the barn already mentioned which stood in front of the quarters of the king and duke. This was garrisoned by three hundred chosen men-at-arms, not so much indeed as apprehending any attack from the town as to protect the duke of Burgundy from any treachery on the part of the king of France. Although these men were disarmed, they had time to cast on their cuirasses and defend the house by thrusting their long lances through the loopholes which had been made for that purpose. The duke of Burgundy meanwhile caught the alarm. His bodyguard consisted only of ten archers,⁹⁵ who when the alarm was general were amusing themselves with playing at dice, and two or three gentlemen who waited upon his person. His attendants armed him hastily, throwing on his cuirass and placing a headpiece of steel upon his head, and endeavoured to issue forth. But before they could get into the street the archers were busy defending the windows of the house against a strong party of the men of Franchimont, who had been guided by the owner of the house from the attack upon the barn to that of the house itself, which was now fiercely assailed. Loud cries of different kinds were now raised on all hands, some calling "France," some "Burgundy," some "Long life to the king" and "Kill";° but the chance of success in so desperate an attempt as that of surprising two princes in the middle of their host must have depended entirely on the secrecy° and surprize with which it was commenced, and this had been destroyed by the alarm given by the assault upon the barn. If the men of Franchimont had followed implicitly their two guides it is probable they would have taken these princes in their beds without much chance of resistance. The owner of the villa where the king was quartered led thither directly a part of the men of Franchimont entrusted to his charge, but on coming hither they found an hundred of the Scottish archer guard awake and in good order and were° received with a ready and continued shower of arrows whose discharge killed° the guide and most of his followers, and a great number of Burgundians besides. In the meantime the camp got under arms, and those citizens who were to have sallied from the gate became afraid of being overpowered. Thus therefore the sally of Liège ended with the loss of almost all the poor peasants of Franchimont who had acted as the advanced party and behaved with so much resolution and bravery during the night.

When the tumult was somewhile over a communication was made between Louis and Charles in which the king, afraid of some mistake in consequence of their mutual suspicions, would have been well pleased to have taken his departure. But the duke's distrust was so great that he would not consent to the king departing farther from the host than Namur, which Louis declined to do; and it was finally agreed between them that the storm of Liège should take place in the same manner and at the same time as had been originally intended.

The signal guns were accordingly fired at the hour appointed, the trumpets of Burgundy began to sound to the assault, and the standards advanced at the head of the troops. No resistance whatever was made to the advance of the besiegers, and of course the slaughter was very inconsiderable, but the pillage was universal and extended as well to churches as to private houses. Many of the poor inhabitants who fled from the city were plundered and slain by the people of the country, their neighbours,[96] who° had hitherto pretended to be their friends. The weather which set in extremely hard killed many others who died with cold, of hunger, fatigue, or want° of sleep.

The duke of Burgundy remained in Liège, which he treated with great rigour; yet he had injuries to complain of which might have provoked a more patient man than himself, for this was the fifth year in which he had been compelled by repeated mutinies to bring an army before the town, nor had he ever been able to obtain any fulfilment° of such pacification as he had upon former occasions accomplished with the fickle populace of this mutinous city. The peace which was accomplished one year being° no more an assurance of its being continued the next year than the lowering° of a tempest tonight is an argument that the day will be fair tomorrow, it° was not therefore to be wondered at that Charles of Burgundy, a severe prince in a cruel age, distinguished himself by a signal vengeance upon a city by whose mutiny and breach of faith he had been so often provoked.

Meantime King Louis, having accomplished all that was stipulated on his personal part by the treaty of Péronne, was now desirous° of returning to his own country. He was conscious however of the policy of moving with extreme caution in intimating this wish, which if misinterpreted might again awaken the suspicions of the jealous duke. He caused it to be intimated to Charles therefore that he had ratified the peace of Péronne upon the duke's desire, and had most willingly been present at the well-deserved chastisement of the citizens of Liège, and further that if the duke had anything farther to command him he would remain with pleasure along with his army, but if the duke was satisfied with his services it concerned the interest of both sovereigns that Louis should return to his own country in order to obtain the accession of parliament to the treaty of Péronne and have the same regularly recorded. To this claim of the king's freedom the duke of Burgundy could make no reasonable objection and accordingly took leave of his royal hostage, having limited his revenge upon him for his duplicity to a course which was rather of a dishonourable than of a prejudicial character.

After the departure of the king and his body of troops, the duke proceeded finally to execute his vengeance upon the city of Liège, which was to burn the town, all except the churches which were to be carefully preserved. Accordingly this severe sentence was executed. This conflagration was executed on those several days fixed for the purpose, and nevertheless so great was the attachment of the inhabitants to the site, and so much were they determined by the vicinity of the churches, that the town was repeopled again in a surprisingly short space of time.

The small territory of Franchimont was dreadfully laid waste, its houses burned,° and its inhabitants slain on account of their having furnished the bravest part of those who defended Liège.

2
NOVEMBER
1468

The king having, at° the expense of much flattery and many fair words to the duke, of which he was by no means sparing, at length obtained permission to depart from the duke of Burgundy's host to his excessive joy lost no time in employing his liberty to regain some of the advantages which he had been obliged to resign by the treaty of Péronne, the principal of which was to endeavour if possible to obtain an alteration of that article which assigned Champagne and Brie° to Charles the king's brother, instead of Normandy as had been settled by the treaty which closed the war of the public good. For this purpose he endeavoured to work upon the flexible disposition of Charles himself, who is described as a prince who never formed any resolution of his own but was entirely managed by those who acquired his confidence. On the present occasion the duke of Burgundy sent ambassadors to Prince Charles for the very purpose of pointing out to him the advantage of possessing the county of Champagne and Brie,° because it lay so near Burgundy that if the king should wish to dispossess his brother of this territory, as he had done with that of Normandy, he might be immediately supported by the forces of the duke. He is even said to have added as an inducement to Charles to keep firm on the present occasion that he had thoughts of bestowing upon him in marriage his own eldest daughter, and that Champagne and Brie° would naturally fall to° unite with his great possession of Burgundy, Artois, as well as Flanders &c., which he would of course intend with his daughter. To what extent the duke pledged himself it is not easy to state. It was certainly a strong motive to encourage this young French prince to firmness on his own side, and it was more requisite to bring him to such a decision on the duke of Burgundy's side because before King° Louis parted with the duke the former had artfully extracted from the latter a promise which he could not decently refuse to fulfil,° although he hoped that the firmness of the prince would render it nugatory, especially with so advantageous a match° in his eye as that with the heiress of Burgundy. The king when about to separate from the duke° had taken him aside and put a question of the consequences of which Duke Charles was not at the moment fully aware.

"What shall we do," said Louis, "in case this brother Charles of mine shall reject the appanage of Champagne and Brie° which I have agreed at your request to settle upon him?" "In that case," replied the duke unthinkingly, "I shall leave you to settle between you upon a substitute which may be agreeable to you both." He had however no doubt that it would be perfectly possible to keep Prince Charles of France firm upon a point so much to his own advantage, and he sent the embassy already mentioned for the purpose of preventing any alteration in his mind.

Louis however, who had calculated on the feebleness of his brother's temper, spared neither treasure nor promises in influencing those who were his brother's favourites for the day and pointing out to them the large advantage which they themselves would gain by his brother becoming count of Guienne and governor of Rochelle instead of accepting the appanage of Brie and Champagne, secured to him by the treaty of Péronne. Without considering therefore the risk of the duke of Burgundy's friendship, or the splendour of a match with his heiress, or even sufficiently regarding that duke's wishes on an occasion so important to his own interest, the weak prince suffered himself to be decided in his choice of an appanage by his favourites who had been suborned° by his brother Louis; and the prince Charles had the weakness to announce that his brother had agreed to give, and he himself to receive, the province of Guienne instead of that of Champagne as had been provided for him by the intervention of the duke of Burgundy at the treaty of Péronne. The duke was greatly mortified at finding his purpose thus eluded by the subtlety° of the one royal brother and the simplicity of the other, to which his own rash assent had given force to bind himself; for the whole was brought within the predicament stated by the king in his parting question to the duke, "What was to be the rule of decision in case his brother should refuse the province of Champagne?" Nor was it possible for the duke to extricate himself from the terms of his own answer, "that in such case he himself would remain satisfied with any arrangement which should please the two brothers." Thus evanished one principal advantage which Duke Charles conceived he had secured by the treaty of Péronne.

Another point which Louis failed not to secure was the gratification of his revenge against certain of his own counsellors and ministers who had acted with treachery towards him as well during the treaty of Péronne, as upon other occasions during their ministry. These were the celebrated Cardinal Balue, bishop° of Evreux, and the bishop of Verdun. Louis had trusted Balue° in a degree very unusual for so suspicious a person, although his mode of talking of him implied no great real trust. "Just now," he said in his peculiar phraseology, "the prelate is a good enough devil of a bishop, but I cannot tell what he may turn out in a future day."

During the affair of Péronne at which both these churchmen were present they took the opportunity to desert their master in his difficulties, and to attach themselves to the duke of Burgundy. They also interfered with the intrigues about Prince Charles's appanage, and addressed themselves to him, advising him strongly to adhere to the provision made in his favour at the treaty of Péronne, which was of course naturally considered by the king as an act of disloyalty to his interest. For this he resolved to subject the two culpable prelates to a most signal punishment, and caused them to be shut up in state prisons where their persons were enclosed° within a species of grate or cage made of bars of iron, in which a prisoner could neither sit upright, nor stand, nor recline conveniently at full length. The prelates were the less pitied in this situation because the bishop of Verdun° was believed to be the original inventor of these° detestable contrivances, in which he and the bishop of Evreux were detained for several years.[97]

The common people, according to their custom of insulting the fallen, devised° doggerel songs upon their confiscation and imprisonment.*

We may here mention that although Louis by his policy recovered some effects of the treaty of Péronne, and also took vengeance on some faithless ministers who took that occasion to betray him, yet he continued to remember his precipitation on that occasion as a painful and offensive jest, and when the people of Paris taught their magpies and jays to say *Péronne Péronne* the king not only caused the birds to be put to death, but a list to be preserved of the owners' names who took this mode of preserving in memory the most disagreeable incident of his life.

To return to our history. Under the auspices we have shown, Charles of France, after being disappointed successively of Normandy and Champagne, became at length duke of Guienne. The brothers afterwards met, and such was Charles's terror of his elder brother that the place selected was a kind of barricade° upon a bridge near the chateau of Charron° over the river Brault,° in the centre° of which was erected a barricade° composed of bars of iron to prevent such a catastrophe as that which took place at the bridge of Montereau. The brothers met and parted however apparently in concord and amity, nor was it until some years later that the duke of Guienne, whose pretensions still kept his elder brother in alarm, died of poison administered to him by the abbé of St John d'Angély.° [98] He had all his life pretended the greatest fraternal love and regard for Charles of Guienne, although in his heart he never forgave the share which he took in the war of the public good. If we can believe° Brantôme,[99] the king's share in this crime was detected in a remarkable manner. Louis° was paying his devotions at the shrine of Notre Dame de Cléry,° whom he esteemed his good patroness. He did not observe that a fool who had belonged to his late brother stood so near as to overhear what the king said in his prayers. Being as superstitious as he was malignant, his orisons to Our Lady were of a kind very singular in their way, and Brantôme who tells the story assures us they were of the following tenor, much in the style of a child who soothes° its governess and tries to bribe her to conceal some petty delinquency.

---

* The following lines may serve as an imitation of these popular sarcasms:

> Master John Balue
> Has lost cry and hue
>   Of all he sees.

> His Holiness of Verdun,
> Not worth a single farthing,
>   Sits caged at his ease.[100]

"Ah my good Lady! my little mistress! my assured friend in whom I have my sole trust and confidence, I implore you to supplicate God for me and be advocate with him in my behalf to induce him to forgive me the death of my brother, whom I have caused to be poisoned by that wicked abbé of St John. I confess the truth to thee as to my good patroness and mistress; but on the other hand what could I have done? for you are well aware he did nothing but keep my whole kingdom in trouble. Cause me then to obtain my pardon, my dearest Lady, and you shall see what a rich reward I will give you."

The fool who overheard these singular devotions was not so crazy as not to retain the whole in his memory, and brought the story out before the whole world at dinner, reproaching the king with his brother's murder perpetrated by means of the abbé whom he had named. The fool who had possessed himself of this fatal secret was afterwards removed, lest he should come again upon the same dangerous topic. Some historians[101] have exculpated the memory of Louis from this diabolical crime and the odious hypocrisy which made it the subject of such devotion.° But although the death of the great by poison is one of the most common fictions of history, yet this fratricide and its consequences are so characteristic° of Louis XI that the charge is extremely probable, and highly credible.

Volume II

Chapter 1

The vacillation of the duke of Guienne in his choice of an appanage restored to Louis a considerable part of the advantage which he had lost at the treaty of Péronne,° and the rest was soon regained by the death of the duke of Guienne himself, poisoned as the age believed by the connivance of his brother. The duke languished for five or six months, a circumstance not then supposed incompatible with the power of poison, although a lady who was supposed to have partaken of the same fatal fruit did not survive above a few days.*

In the meantime King Louis was by every means in his power endeavouring to recover the ground which he had lost in his formal dispute with the house of Burgundy. He therefore resolved to seize the time as favourable to the recovery of the cities and towns upon the Somme which had been pledged to Burgundy and, though ransomed, had never been delivered up. Louis assembled the notables or principal persons of France at the city of Tours and engaged them in a train of hostile° proceedings against the duke of Burgundy, in which the king had previously assured himself of the alliance of the duke of Bretagne and his brother Monsieur of Guienne, as well as of the steady adhesion of the constable of St Pol.

The latter having already placed himself at the head of a considerable force made use of it in seizing upon the frontier town of St Quentin, one of the strongest places at present in debate between the king and the duke of Burgundy, and which he garrisoned with troops dependant upon himself and in his own pay, and which he long managed as at his own absolute disposal. Two others of the cautionary towns, Roye and Montdidier,° were also surrendered to French troops, and the duke, who had of late been himself effectually master of the conditions of peace, was now by the desertion of the dukes of Bretagne and Guienne, as also of the constable of France, in circumstances which were likely to oblige him to accept a peace of King Louis's dictating. Meanwhile such were the unfaithful habits of that time that the duke of Burgundy was privately informed that, providing he would agree to give his daughter, who was his sole heiress, in marriage to the duke of Guienne as had been formerly proposed, he

---

* The poison was administered in a large and beautiful peach divided by the abbot of John d'Angély, in consequence of eating one half of which Madame de Monseau° the duke's mistress died in a few days, although that prince himself survived until half a year had elapsed under a lingering disease. The monk was° laid hold of by the deceased duke's favourite minister, named the sieur de Lescun, who sent him to the duke of Bretagne, the ally of Charles, that he might be tried for the supposed crime. The process against this wretch would certainly have been urged to a conclusion had he not been slain in his prison by a flash of lightning (as was said) during his imprisonment. King Louis therefore put a stop to proceedings which could not perhaps have gone on without involving his own character.

should soon see his old allies return again to his side, and with them the greater part of Louis's own forces. Charles of Burgundy therefore, notwithstanding his stubborn temper, found himself obliged to temporize and apply in a very humble manner to Louis for peace, while on the other hand he intimated to the duke of Guienne his willingness to confer upon him his daughter as had been stipulated. In neither of these two inconsistent proposals was the duke probably in the least sincere; he probably desired only to gain time to intrigue with Edward IV of England, who had been by one of those sudden changes proper to the civil wars of England banished from the country, and his rival Henry VI placed in his stead. The duke of Burgundy by granting some small assistance to the exiled prince, who was his own brother-in-law, afforded him the means of recovering his kingdom and finally ridding himself both of Henry VI, his wife, and his son, and above all of the celebrated earl of Warwick, who having been long his favourite and partizan was now become his most dangerous enemy, and was at the head of the insurrection which expelled him from the throne. A counter-revolution almost immediately followed, in which Edward IV finally vanquished and slew the king-making earl of Warwick at the battle of Barnet and Margaret of Anjou at that of Tewkesbury,° which finally settled him on the English throne. When Edward IV was thus completely° reinstated in his kingdom, the duke of Burgundy began of new to treat with him upon the subject of continental politics, and to encourage him to make a landing in France with the purpose of reviving the pretensions° of England to various provinces of that kingdom. Edward, on the other hand, had no serious thoughts of engaging in a task which had proved too heavy both for Edward III and for Henry V, in both of whose reigns the° attempt had been made unsuccessfully, notwithstanding that the power of England was then unanimous within itself. But he had no doubt that to avoid a war which had been attended with so much evil and so much loss to the kingdom of France, Louis would be readily induced to pay a large sum of money which Edward's love of expensive pleasure would render very acceptable to him, and therefore he lent so far as that went a favourable ear to the duke of Burgundy's encouragement. He knew also that the° idea of a war with France would always be acceptable and popular with the bulk of the English nation. Thus therefore amidst the princes and others who entertained various views and interests for the settlement of so many interests, the ancient quarrel with England seemed once more to revive and threaten to add its various terrors to those of a war between France and Burgundy. The course of the various conferences and intrigues which took place was greatly accelerated by the death of the duke of Guienne, which province Louis immediately seized into his own hand, to revenge which encroachment the duke of Burgundy made an ineffectual attempt to seize upon the towns on the Somme, in which he was unsuccessful.

Duke Charles therefore, finding himself at present the weaker of the two disputants, began to listen to proposals on the part of Louis for the purpose of reducing the constable St Pol, whose affectation of independence, and of preserving by his own power a balance betwixt France and Burgundy, was odious as well as his conduct had been unfaithful to both the monarchs, so that Louis had some chance of being listened to when he suggested that both Burgundy and he had some reason in bringing St Pol to the death of a traitor and dividing° his forfeiture between them. But the duke of Burgundy, apparently thinking he had not yet enough of enemies upon his hands, and having great desire to make some acquisitions on the German frontier, engaged in a war with the emperor in which he besieged the town of Neuss.° [102] The consequence of this ill-timed enterprize was that, instead of having his forces in readiness° to conduct the English from their ships, he was found with his troops engaged in distant warfare, unable to give his brother-in-law the effectual support which he had promised to encourage him to invade France, while authors have hinted[103] that his men-at-arms in particular were so much broken down and jaded by hard work that he was ashamed they should be exhibited to his allies. When therefore Edward, in consequence of his treaty with Burgundy, and trusting to being joined by him with a large body of men-at-arms whose assistance was essential to the command, landed near Calais with a large army, he found that his ally the duke of Burgundy was engaged in an unnecessary war in Lorraine and did not make the least effort to join him with his forces.

It was indeed a part of Duke Charles's character to act upon projects which had their origin in his own head and were to be carried forward by his own unassisted plans and resources, without any accurate calculation of the means, which° at the moment of execution were found ill adapted to the end. His chief view was to shake himself clear of his vassalage to France and erect his territories of Burgundy from being a duchy into a kingdom; but although this was a natural desire on his part, or at least one which many princes would have entertained, he forgot that the suspicion attending his wishes would excite a general odium among the princes around him, and raise up unexpected opposition among neighbours whom his pride might despise, but whom his prudence should have compelled him to respect. The size and extent of Duke Charles's dominions made it indeed not unnatural that he should desire to raise himself to the rank of a crowned head, although considering that so artful a prince as Louis kept a perpetual watch upon his enterprises, husbanding his own resources till the time of the very struggle itself, and waiting until Duke Charles's rash undertakings exhausted his forces and wealth, it would have been most prudent to avoid making numerous enemies, especially in different quarters at once. Yet he embroiled himself in Germany and engaged° in this siege of Neuss° at the very time when he ought to have been ready with his heavy cavalry in readiness to assist° the king of England's invasion. He was especially rash in listening to Louis's insidious proposal for° the ruin of the constable St Pol, upon whose cooperation his treaty with Edward IV of England depended in a great measure. The constable had indeed come under an express obligation to deliver up some of the towns which he occupied to the king of England to serve for his winter quarters, and if this part° of the treaty with Edward IV had been kept it would have been some apology for the delay in the duke himself to join him with his men-at-arms, whereas the rumour° of a treaty between the king of France and the duke having for its object the destruction of St Pol was like to terrify from joining heart and head in accomplishing his treaty with England. But the news of the mischief designed against him was more apt to terrify the constable into indecision, as it actually did.

King Louis perceived the error of the duke of Burgundy's conduct, and with his usual acuteness foresaw° that if let alone he would destroy himself by his own courses, and lose all his objects by pretending to press too many to decision at the same time; nay, that the most certain way of pushing a temper like his to desperation, would be by affecting to give him friendly caution and useful advice, which he was certain would impel the duke to act in a way exactly contrary. Meanwhile the arrival of the king of England with his host was announced to the court of France by the medium of a herald claiming as usual the kingdom as the lawful inheritance of Edward IV of England in right of his predecessor and ancestor Edward III. Louis smiled good-humouredly when this was delivered to him, and having taken the herald into a more private place merely remarked that his brother of England had undertaken a rash adventure trusting to the assistance of two allies the duke of Burgundy and the constable of St Pol, both of whom would certainly soon desert him, in which case his brother would see his own advantage in making his peace with France, which° Louis hinted that he would find greatly to his interest in a pecuniary point of view. Thus he treated the defiance of the herald as being almost a jest, and at the same time he gave the messenger a present of three hundred pieces of gold; for his policy dictated a close and friendly intercourse° with all, however mean in rank, who were to have interference° in the treaty between him and Edward upon this or any future occasion, and acting with the same subtlety° which was his wont he caused his officers give to the English herald in public a gift more becoming his rank—thirty yards, namely, of crimson velvet—while in private he assured him of a gratuity of a thousand crowns providing he was assisting in bringing about a peace between the kings.

The original plan of Edward was to act in his invasion in conjunction with the duke of Bretagne, as Edward III had done with Duke John of Montfort who claimed that inheritance.[104] He also accounted upon the force of Burgundy, which as we have seen was engaged in the siege of Neuss,° and finally he expected to be warmly received by the constable St Pol, who had got possession of St Quentin and other frontier towns between France and Burgundy, and was besides married to a near relation of the queen of England's, and on King Edward IV's coming over had promised to put him in possession of some of the strongest of these places to serve the English troops for winter quarters. Of all these auxiliaries Edward IV was in one way or another disappointed, while Louis offered him such pecuniary advantages as might induce a prince who was fond of his ease and pleasure rather to rest satisfied with what advantages he could gain by treaty than to run the risk of such as could only be gained by arms.

The disappointment of the king of England's expectations took place thus. First the duke of Burgundy hurried indeed from the siege of Neuss° in order to meet King Edward so soon as he heard of his arrival upon the shore of France, but he brought with him no part of his forces—which according to some historians were too discreditable in order and appointments to make them fit to serve for men-at-arms to act with the gallant archers° whom Edward had brought over, expecting to be supplied by his ally with heavy cavalry—and therefore afforded the king none of the direct assistance stipulated. The duke however offered his aid in bringing forward the constable, who, like most persons that interfere betwixt two powerful parties, found himself now the object of suspicion both° to the king of France and to° Edward of England, and was afraid to decide either in the one way or the other. The duke of Burgundy had indeed promised to the king of England that the constable should surrender to him the town of St Quentin and other strong places which St Pol, desirous still to preserve a neutrality, now refused to do, and thereby drew upon himself the hatred of the king of England and duke of Burgundy, as he had already incurred by his duplicity the mortal resentment of King Louis.

Chapter 2

Thus Edward of England, disappointed in all the succours which he expected, might become disposed to seek some road out of an awkward° situation in which he could neither advance nor retreat; and it was a part of Louis's policy to take care to afford him a means of communication which should enable the king of France to sound his intentions, although it was not of a nature which should bind Louis in any advances he himself made. The stratagem, which was very different from the mode of thinking of the age, was so peculiarly fitted to the disposition of this unscrupulous prince that it is worth while to tell it here at some length.

A Frenchman of mean rank was returned° by the English to the French as being the first prisoner taken in the course of the war. This man was a Breton,[105] and King Louis had some suspicion of him. Nevertheless the enfranchised captive brought to him from the lords Howard and Stanley, favourites of the king of England, a friendly message. These English nobles had given the prisoner a piece of money, saying these words: "Recommend us to the good favour of the king your master if you can obtain speech of him."

On this message being delivered it occurred to the king that used skilfully° it might open a way for a private treaty with the king of England, without involving the interests of the duke of Burgundy or of the constable or requiring to be communicated either to the one or the other of them. He therefore called upon Commynes (who had transferred, as we have said, his services from the duke of Burgundy to Louis XI, by whom his wisdom was very highly esteemed) and directed him to find out a certain mean fellow whom he named, a valet de chambre° of the king's chamberlain M. des Halles,° and, speaking to him in secret, learn whether he had the courage to undertake to go to the camp of the English king in the disguise and with the pretended character of a herald, and to prepare him for such a masquerade. Commynes, when he had sought the man out, was surprised to see a person who had little either in his appearance or conversation which seemed to point him out as a person fit for representing such a character, and upon° the matter being first proposed to the valet de chambre° the man, whose name was Merindot, threw himself on his knees before Commynes, conceiving that in conferring such a dangerous commission his sentence of death was pronounced. But it was one peculiarity of the king that he studied particularly the character of the lower sort of people by whom he was surrounded, and was never at a loss to find someone disposed and qualified to play his part in such a contrivance as he now meditated.

Upon further conversation Commynes found the man qualified to represent the character, and not unwilling to undertake it upon° being promised a suitable reward. The banner of a trumpet was hastily made into the resemblance of a herald's coat of° arms, and a medallion such as was borne° by a herald was borrowed for the occasion, and thus Merindot, fully instructed in what he was to say, was dismissed in secret with directions to enquire when at the English camp for the lords Howard and Stanley,° whose message by the Breton prisoner argued some favour to King Louis which the king was desirous to cultivate at this emergency.°

On Merindot's arrival at the English camp° the king of England was at dinner, and the messenger was taken apart and entertained courteously till Edward had risen from table. He was then introduced and played his part with spirit and intelligence. He declared that his credentials were founded upon the desire of the king of France his master to remain at peace with England, which was proved by his never having been at war with her since he came to be king of France.

He stated that peace and a separate existence were for the interest of both kingdoms, and he apologised for the succours given by Louis to the earl of Warwick when that famous nobleman embraced the party of Lancaster, which had° been rather directed against the duke of Burgundy than against Edward IV. He also pointed out to the English monarch that the duke of Burgundy and his other allies had not stirred him to this invasion unless for the purpose of obtaining good terms on their own part from King Louis, and that therefore it ought not to interest the king of England in what manner these princes settled their own affairs with his brother sovereign, providing his own were advantageously managed. Matters, he added, were at a crisis when Louis would grant the best terms to the prince allied against him who should be first disposed to break up the confederates, and there was no just reason why the king of England should not desert the duke and constable as well as suffer himself to be deserted by them. He threw out also an intelligible hint that the king of France understood that Edward IV had been put to great expense for this armament, and that it might be necessary to compensate the hopes of such persons as expected to make money either by plunder or negotiation in the course of the war, which expenses the king of France had no objection to take upon himself in case of a private treaty being entered upon betwixt England and his kingdom. Lastly, this pretended herald proposed that commissioners should be appointed on both sides and should meet at either camp or at some neutral place between the armies. This message, which offered to the English king so easy and creditable a means of escaping from a situation which was likely to cost him great trouble and expense, was listened to willingly by Edward and his counsellors, and commissioners of rank were named for carrying on the rest of the negotiation. Merindot, returning successful to the encampment of Louis, was rewarded with a post in his native country, the Isle of Ré,° and a reward in money adequate to ensure his silence concerning his share in setting the treaty on foot, the king being greatly pleased with the mode in which he had played his part. This was indeed so dexterous that it is necessary to tell you why any trick should have been resorted to in a matter where plain dealing might have served the purpose as well and even better, and where a real herald would have carried on the treaty with less risk than was incurred by using the services of an impostor. We must however recollect first that it was not the custom of Louis XI, who was singular in his mode of thinking on many occasions, to have in his train or about his person heralds, pursuivants, or officers of that kind, who were in reality rather personages of idle pomp and formality than of real use, and nevertheless the time for sending a message of such a delicate nature was probably too pressing to admit sending for such an officer. Secondly, the purpose of the message might have miscarried, and a prince of Louis's natural temper would naturally then desire to have it in his power to disavow his messenger as a person whose words afforded no confidence, which the king° would not certainly have hesitated to do if Edward IV had received as an affront the proposal to buy off his invasion and sell his allies for a sum of money. Louis might in the same way have been prepared to parry the reproach of those among his own subjects who thought that he degraded his dignity by making such advantageous proposals to° the king of England, but who might rather enjoy putting a trick upon him by means of a false and imaginary° herald whose words might indeed deceive the king of England but could not bind the sovereign of France. Lastly, it is to be remembered that politicians who like King Louis become habitually addicted to trick and stratagem in their management of their affairs, lose the power, or at least the habit, of proceeding with openness and candour, even when such qualities could have best served their purpose. I have already shown you in several instances that it was a fault of Louis's character to act too often by cunning and artifice, even when upright and direct conduct would perhaps have best served his own interest, and of this you will find other instances before we finish the account of his reign. The account of this treaty with England is so curious as having° relation to the national character as well of our own country° as to the peculiarities of the king of France that we enter into it more particularly than would otherwise be necessary.

Chapter 3

King Louis during all this treaty with the English was particularly attentive to two circumstances: the one was to keep not only King Edward IV but the meanest archer in his army in good humour with him as a jovial and friendly host; the other was no less anxiety on his part to prevent any good understanding or renewal of amicable intercourse between the king of England and the constable of France, which might have defeated his purpose of a favourable peace with the former power. When the commissioners of England and France met for conferring on the preliminaries of a peace those of the former insisted upon some strong places being delivered to them, which unquestionably they desired to consider as a reestablishment of the English dominion within France, but to this condition the policy of Louis XI was positively determined not to give way. Flattery, precedence, everything which could secure the regard of the English and satisfy their vanity, he was most willing to concede to them, nor was he averse to purchase their retreat into their own country by means of considerable sums of money, large enough to supply not only the king for his public purposes and private extravagance but to glut the greed of his principal statesmen, to all of whom Louis XI made payment° of large sums as a present gratuity and added considerable pensions to the English courtiers of influence and rank for the future in order to secure their interest on the part of France, or in other words to bribe them to espouse the interests of France. But he had formed a determination not to yield up a single district, or even a town or strong place on the south side of the Channel,° well remembering the fatal effects produced by the English establishing a footing in France and making it the scene of perpetual wars. The dexterity of the French envoys, with the boundless profusion of their master's liberality, soon fixed on the heads of a treaty which might be acceptable to both parties, both being sincerely desirous of establishing a good understanding. The sum of money to be paid by France to England in ready coin was fixed at seventy-two thousand crowns; and an alliance between the kingdoms was to take place by means of the marriage of the eldest daughter of Edward of England with a prince of the blood royal of France;[106] a marriage afterwards prevented by her being united to Henry VII.

To gratify the English people, the revenues of the duchy of Guienne were assigned for this lady's support, but as they were declared redeemable for an annuity of fifty thousand crowns paid annually within the Tower of London the cession of territory did not therefore involve any contradiction of Louis's fixed principle° to give the English no permanent footing within the realm of France. Concessions were made respecting the commercial intercourse between the countries of considerable consequence to England, yet the apparent cession of Guienne might be represented in that light if it was° necessary to propitiate the Englishmen of the day, long accustomed to think of their French possessions as a part of the° natural dominions of their country.

When these proposals were reported to the French king's council many of the members were of opinion that the English were not serious in disposing themselves to accept of such terms of peace in place of carrying on a war which, like others on former occasions, might have proved very gainful to England and very dangerous to France. But Louis, who better knew King Edward's extravagance and love of pleasure, concluded that the king of England had gained his object, and expressed himself only anxious that his practices should be put beyond the chance of discovery or danger. It was agreed, although one would have thought that Péronne would have satisfied Louis of such interviews, that a personal meeting should take place between him and the king of England. Meantime it was resolved that money to furnish the great sums that had been stipulated was to be raised by all means possible, and the great officers present were given to understand that they must contribute to assist the king with such gifts and loans as were necessary to send the king of England and his army back to their own country,° protesting that upon no other terms would he make peace with them, and that especially he would never consent to their holding a village or hamlet within the kingdom of France.

All therefore consented to the terms agreed on as inferring much less danger, either in a war with England or giving them a firm establishment within the soil of France. The money was levied and paid as well to the king of England who lodged two nobles, Lord Howard and his grand equerry John Cheyne, as° security that he would fulfil the conditions of the treaty on his side. The money in the meantime was paid, and the English statesmen and courtiers received their private gratifications; among these the lord Hastings was remarkable for receiving with sufficient readiness two thousand crowns, a partial payment of the pension granted to him by Louis, but refused to grant a receipt to the person who paid it to him, saying such an acknowledgement should never be found in the French chancery; as if the disgrace had rested not in an English statesman being a pensioner of the king of France, but in his granting a receipt for the money which he did not hesitate to accept. The French historians[107] have explained Lord Hastings's conduct by supposing that he had received bribes from the duke of Burgundy also; but as something must be yielded to conjecture it is perhaps fairer to suppose that the proposed receipt was couched in terms which were offensive to the pride of the English nobleman.

Another trick, as it may be called, of King Louis was calculated to incense the duke of Burgundy against the constable of St Pol. This nobleman, whose perilous and double game we have already noticed, began now to fear that he would lose the favour of all parties, and therefore struggled on every side to obtain some protection by which he might pass safely through the storm. This was now directed fiercely against him when a part of the English host, having approached to receive one of the towns° promised for their winter quarters,[108] was received with a fire from it,° a breach of faith equally offensive to Edward and to the duke of Burgundy, for the latter plainly desired that the constable, in furnishing the king with winter quarters, should make him amends for his own breach of faith in not joining the English with the men-at-arms stipulated, whereas if the king of England's army could be detained in France during the whole winter, the purpose for which the war had been undertaken originally really might have been resumed in spring with success.

But by firing on the English troops the unfortunate constable had made his two late confederates his inveterate enemies, and it now only remained to make interest if possible with the king of France who entertained equal hatred against him, though he did not express it so loudly, and was in fact his most formidable enemy of the three sovereigns with whom the constable's versatility and repeated breach of faith had placed himself on such dangerous and precarious terms.

With a view to propitiate the king of France the constable detached to Louis's headquarters a gentleman of his household called Louis de Sainville° and his secretary named Jean Richer. They were° dispatched by him privately to lay their master at the feet of Louis, and by all possible means to make his peace with him whom he knew well to be the most deadly and inveterate of his enemies, especially since the constable had entered into treaty for delivering up the town of St Quentin to the English, although when pressed he refused to fulfil his treaty. This the constable's ambassadors endeavoured to mitigate by making a theatrical exhibition of the violent tone in which they said the duke of Burgundy had indulged against the English king. Sainville° it seems was a good mimic,° and could counterfeit to the life those violences of deportment which the duke of Burgundy's passions often induced him to exhibit. As it was Louis's principal desire to keep up the misunderstanding between St Pol and the duke of Burgundy, he took occasion to put the Burgundian ambassador M. de Contay in concealment behind a screen° [109] while he fetched into the apartment° Sainville° and Richer, the confidential messengers of St Pol. It was easy to put them, who were unaware of Contay's presence, into their former buffooning humour, and Sainville° swore the duke's oath by St George, stamped with his foot against the ground, and called Edward IV by the name of Blackburn, an archer to whom scandal had given the credit of being the king of England's father; and in short turned the duke into every species of ridicule.° Louis encouraged this by much laughter, and made the actors in the scene speak louder under pretence of being deaf, but in reality that Contay might hear distinctly how his master was treated with scorn and ridicule by persons of so little consequence as Sainville° and Richer. At length he dismissed them, telling them he would send them an answer to a proposal that the constable should be at liberty, without offending the king, to gratify the king of England by delivering up to him one or two insignificant villages in order that they might serve as winter quarters, such a licence being the expedient by which St Pol hoped with the consent of King Louis to seem° to satisfy his engagement to the king of England and the duke of Burgundy. But the king, though he temporized with St Pol, refused to give him a distinct answer to the curious proposal by which he hoped to satisfy all parties.

When the envoys of the constable were gone, the king called forth Contay, who came and was° scarcely able to contain himself with rage at the freedoms which he had heard from behind the screen taken with so great a prince as his master by persons of so little consequence as Richer and Sainville.° In this manner the king put a strain of personal hatred into the misunderstanding between the duke of Burgundy and the constable, which paved the way for the duke abandoning St Pol to the unsparing vengeance of Louis.

Meantime the duke of Burgundy, having heard of the treaty between Louis and Edward, suddenly and when least expected arrived in the camp of the latter king, though rather thinly attended. Edward felt some awkwardness in meeting with his ally, for he was conscious that in closing his quarrel with Louis upon the terms adjusted between them, he had violated his previous treaty with the duke of Burgundy, in consequence of which he had come over to France with a serious purpose of battle. The duke accordingly entered into a panegyric° upon the ancient° feats, sieges, and victories won by the English within the realm of France. He blamed the king's intention to enter into a truce, for he did not appear to be aware that the preliminaries were already adjusted, and declared° that he himself had formerly agreed to an alliance with the English, not that they had any need of assistance, but because he would have wished the kingdom of England to have recovered its losses, and that he would show that such was his intention, instead of becoming a party to any truce of the king of England's making, he would refuse any accommodation of the kind until three months had elapsed after the king of England had recrossed the sea. Edward, as may be supposed, took this language extremely ill, and the two brothers-in-law are not thought to have again met, either in friendship or otherwise.

In the meantime the king of France continued to observe the same policy towards the English and to extend his good reception of that nation's° troops to persons of the lowest rank in the service. Both parties approached towards the town of Amiens, and Louis, finding that the English troops according to their custom came in numbers to see the city, took care to have great quantities of food prepared, together with hogsheads of wine set abroach, and tables of which men who were renowned as good companions had charge and were instructed to act the good host to such English as came into the town. The English have at no time of their history been remarkable for a wish to decline good cheer when so gracefully offered, neither have they so much as other nations a sense° of that sort of retenue or moderation which is dictated by° artificial good breeding. They accepted with good will what was offered with hospitality, nor was it long before such great numbers thronged into the city of Amiens to assist in the merry doings going on there, until the apprehensions of the French nobility became seriously excited. The master of the cross-bows, a general officer of rank, attempted to communicate his apprehensions to the king, but Louis, who amid all his peculiarities was a strict observer of religious forms, and the time being the Eve of St Innocents, refused to interrupt his devotions. Early on the next morning Philip de Commynes, perceiving that there° were nearly to the amount of nine thousand English within the city, and there in great disorder, took the liberty of intruding personally upon the king's devotions, saying, "Notwithstanding this be the feast of the Innocents, it is necessary that I tell your majesty what I have to say. The English are come into the town in great numbers; they are all armed and none dare refuse them entrance into the houses for fear of disobliging them." The king, laying aside his devotions, sent Commynes and some others to speak to such English officers as they could see, and to obtain their help in preserving quiet; for every Englishman who was sent back more than twenty arrived in Amiens, and° in one tavern a hundred and eleven bills had been made out before nine in the morning. The house was already full of English archers, some sleeping, others singing, and all of them intoxicated.

Seeing this state of things, Philip de Commynes conceived that there was no danger intended, and the king ordered some two or three hundred men-at-arms to take arms within the quarters of their commanders, placing a sentinel at the door to prevent any Frenchman from sallying out and brawling with the English. King Edward, having heard of this, sent a message to Louis advising him to shut and guard the gates of the town and admit no Englishman into the place.

Louis answered in the character of the hospitable landlord that he wished to maintain order and quiet, that God forbid he, or any Frenchman by his orders, should prohibit an Englishman entrance, but if the king of England chose to send some of his own bodyguard of archers to admit or refuse those whom they pleased he was at freedom to do so. This expedient was resorted to as what could neither affront the English nor diminish the character of Louis's hospitality, of which he showed himself so jealous, and order was reestablished in the city of Amiens.

The meeting between the two sovereigns was next to take place with all the forms which had been observed on such occasions since the breach of faith at Montereau.

A place called Picquigny upon a bridge crossing the river Somme was fixed as a fitting place of meeting. The French king approached on the one side of the river through an open country, the English upon the other through a long and narrow causeway,° so that had not the intention on the part of Louis been fair and candid he might easily have taken an undue advantage. "Indeed," says the Flemish historian,[110] with a compliment to the English the value of which he seems scarce to have been sensible° of, "the English show little subtlety° on such occasions, and go only bluntly and clumsily to work. On the other hand you must take care not to af-front them and beware of their choleric and impatient temper." In fact it would seem that Commynes had already lived long enough with Louis XI to prefer a subtle and artificial character to one that was sincere, open, and candid.

The two princes met upon the bridge of Picquigny, where there was a palisade° constructed with iron bars resembling the cage in which lions are commonly transported. The bars were so close that a man could hardly put through his hand between them. The meeting however was friendly and fairly meant on both sides, and if it had been otherwise the resolution of one determined man like Tanneguy du Chastel could easily have rendered all these precautions nugatory. Louis observed the° same exterior of friendship and the same desire to gain his ends rather by the means of address, intrigue, and corruption than by those of violence. The meeting took place 29 August 1475. The king of France had with him eight hundred men-at-arms, and the whole of the English army was drawn up nearly within the sight of that of France. Each king was immediately attended by twelve of his nobility, and as an additional security against treachery two or three of each party were habited in the same dress with the king, and that of Louis, not° probably a very splendid one, was the same the king used to wear, while three or four of the English were richly attired in cloth of gold with a bonnet of black velvet on his head with a fleur-de-lys° composed of precious stones. He was a very handsome man, but now becoming a little too fat. As he approached within four or five feet of the barrier he took off his bonnet, and bent his knee till it was within half a foot of the earth in deference to the king of France. King Louis made also a low reverence and rested upon the barricade while he said, "Sir, my cousin, you are most welcome. There is no man in the world whom I have longed so° much to see as yourself, and praised be God that we meet on such friendly terms." The copies of the treaty were then exchanged, holding between them the relic° supposed to be a fragment of the wood of the true Cross, upon which they both swore to observe the treaty as agreed upon. The king of France, who understood well Edward's disposition, which inclined him to mirth and gallantry, now invited him in jest to favour° him with a visit at Paris, where he promised to "entertain him with the society of some pretty women," adding that he would assign him for his father confessor his own cousin the cardinal of Bourbon. This churchman was a prince of a gay and unreserved temper, not likely to fatigue the penitent with too much severity or too severe penance. This having passed over as a jest of the moment, the king asked Edward if the duke of Burgundy had the intention of being included in the truce between them? The king of England answered that he would give him a final offer of being included, and if he then refused he would leave Louis to settle the matter as he best could. The king of England then put the same question to Louis respecting the duke of Bretagne, expressing his interest in that prince, and desiring that Louis would not make war upon him, to whom he acknowledged himself very much indebted for the° mischances of his past life. Louis said nothing at the moment, but in two or three days he not only granted peace to the duke of Bretagne but named him his lieutenant° general throughout the kingdom. The kings then took a courteous leave of each other, and in returning to Amiens the king consulted with some of his confidential servants upon two things which had happened during the interview. The first of these was the readiness which King Edward had shown in accepting the invitation to Paris, which° he had himself thrown out as a matter of jest, and in which he could not be supposed serious. "This king," he said, "is a very handsome man and of an amorous disposition; should he come to Paris he is very like to meet with some coquette or another who will make it difficult for him to leave our capital, or at least easy to be recalled there, and we have already suffered enough by the residence of English kings within France. Again," he said, "I fear the king of England may be displeased with want of receiving a positive answer respecting the duke of Bretagne, and indeed we have learned upon more minute inquiry that if we shall make war on this prince, Edward is resolved to recross the sea in order to defend him." After this resolution had been made known Louis renounced all further thought of making war on Brittany and granted his admission to the truce in the generous and liberal manner which we have before mentioned.

The king of France had not only taken personal notice and said something civil to each of the English noblemen who had been present at the conference at Picquigny, but on° this occasion he neglected neither gifts nor promises to make friends° among the English statesmen. His finger was in every man's palm and his° mouth was in every man's ear, nor do we find any moralist so obstinate as to resist his pressing arguments. In addition to all these advances he also invited some of the highest rank of the English to sup with him at Amiens. Here the lord Howard took an opportunity, supposing himself doing a most acceptable thing to the English king, to whisper to Louis that he thought it was in his power, if his majesty consented, to induce the king of England to attend him as far as Amiens, or perhaps even to Paris itself in order to see the city and make good cheer. You may be assured that this offer of Lord Howard's was so far from being agreeable to Louis that it was the very thing of which he had expressed himself suspicious. He avoided returning an answer as well as he could and engaged himself in washing, while some of his more ready-witted counsellors, already aware of their master's real secret wishes in such a matter, and that he might have a° fair opportunity to escape from his invitation, objected to the king of England's visit that their master could not just now conveniently receive it owing to the necessity of his instantly assembling an army to march against the duke of Burgundy; so that danger was averted.

The impression still remained° upon the king of France's mind that the English might take it into suspicion that the good humour and respect with which they had been treated was only trick and malice upon his part. He knew the temper of the people, and that their resentment at thinking themselves imposed upon was fully equal to the credulity with which they might be deceived by a person so skilful° as himself.

An instance of this occurred in the case of a gentleman of Gascogny serving the king of England named Louis de Bretaylle.° This person, a man it seemed of acute sense, spoke to the historian Commynes against the truce which had been made, and said that the Englishmen had been over-reached in the negotiations upon the occasion, and being asked how many battles the king of England had gained in his own person, he answered that he had nine when he was present in his own person; and that he had never lost one except in the consequences of this negotiation, in which he had lost more honour than he had gained by his other nine victories. The king of France, informed that such language had passed, said (but using a more coarse° phrase)[111] that Louis de Bretaylle° was a mischievous° fellow whose tongue° must be stopped. Accordingly he began to pay the Gascon° gentleman every sort of attention and make him great offers of preferment if he would settle in his native country; finding him averse to do so he made him a present of a thousand crowns and promised preferment to some of his brothers, while Commynes recommended to Bretaylle° to contribute his best to maintain the good understanding between the two sovereigns.

In short the king himself retained no fear of anything so much as that he himself should be detected in making a jest of the English, and yet from the native shrewdness of his temper was unable to forbear from jests at their expense.

Upon one occasion he had permitted something to escape him touching the wine and presents which° he had sent the English host. He conceived no one was present but persons of his own council, but as he turned round suddenly he saw a wine-merchant who settled in England, and instantly became alarmed lest he should carry his words of raillery at° the expense of the lords and gentry of that nation. He quickly found it was in his power to silence this person by granting him a passport for a certain quantity of wine which he was desirous° of exporting and some other favourable terms, which induced the merchant to settle in his own country and of course took away from him all desire to speak on any subject on which Louis was desirous he should be silent. These instances paint to us curiously and minutely the subtle° character of this singular monarch.

Chapter 4

The truce of ten years being fixed between England and France, the English began to move back towards Calais,° and the constable St Pol became still more distressed in his mind when he considered his various intrigues with the three powerful princes of France, England, and Burgundy, with every one of whom he had contrived to break faith, and of course to make them all his enemies. Louis of France in particular was determined that he should not escape from their joint vengeance, yet he wrote to him in the same deceitful manner as formerly, mentioning that the king as well as the English and the duke of Burgundy had great occasion for such a head as the constable's to be present at their conferences. He explained this by saying to the Burgundian Contay° and the English Lord Howard: "You will please to observe that I do not wish for his body, but on the contrary, providing the head was at our meeting I should wish the trunk to remain where it now is."

But even now when all seemed in the way of being accomplished as Louis's policy desired, a dissension occurred, which if carried to a further extent might even yet have been the cause of breaking the treaty. The king, detained by his affairs, and particularly by his desire to patch up a temporary truce with the duke of Burgundy which might at least induce to the departure of the English, came to reside at Laon on the frontiers of Flanders. Here they found the chancellor of Burgundy with other ambassadors from that prince and a strong military escort of men-at-arms and other soldiers very well and splendidly equipped.° Some Englishmen of high rank also remained with the king of France as hostages for the king of England keeping the conditions on his side for which the French king had advanced a sum equal to seventy thousand crowns.

Upon seeing this Burgundian soldiery in such gallant array, one of the English noblemen, from whose eyes the dimness suddenly departed, spoke publicly in hearing of the king of France's train: "Had we seen on our arrival in France such men as these, it is very probable we should not have been in such a hurry to return to England." The viscount° of Narbonne, a French prince of the blood, heard this expression and thought the honour of his country required an answer. "Are you so simple as ever to think that the duke of Burgundy has not plenty of such soldiers as these? He had only dispersed them to refresh themselves, and if he had seen you really desirous of battle he would soon have collected them. But you had such good will to return that a few pipes of wine and a pension from the king of France was sufficient to send you back to your own country." The Englishman grew angry, and replied with vehemence: "It is then true what most of us have suspected, and you have been laughing at us all along. That money paid to us by the king of France which you call *pension* we call *tribute,* and by St George if you enter into debate upon that subject you will find it no difficult matter to bring us all back again to this side of the Channel." Some of the more prudent of the French counsellors[112] here interposed, and turned into jest a discussion which threatened serious consequences. The English nobles however could not digest the affront, and one of them dropped° a hint of it to the king, who was exceedingly angry at the viscount° of Narbonne for the speech he had made, and was well pleased at having the matter hushed up and forgotten.

Meantime his treaty went forward between France and° the duke of Burgundy, and indeed Louis, who saw that obstinate prince daily involving himself further and further in enterprises beyond even his immense strength, was sensible there was little necessary but to leave him to his own obstinacy, and suffer° him to waste the strength of his kingdom in contesting with the strength of the German empire and with the obstinate courage of the Helvetian league, with both of which he was engaged in hostilities which were both meaningless and dangerous, while he neglected France, which circumstances rendered his mortal enemy, and which possessed in a much more remarkable degree both the disposition and power to injure him. Louis therefore found no great difficulty in accommodating his matters for a general truce with Charles of Burgundy, while at the same time he settled with him the fate of the constable St Pol who had given both princes so much offence by affecting to dictate between them. The tragedy of this remarkable person was the next which was to be acted on the changeful stage of the Low Countries, and it may be here briefly said that, although Louis was only judged to have acted according to his own vindictive nature, yet the share which the duke Charles took on the occasion was accounted much less consistent with a temper which, though blunt, fierce, and violent, had never until now been accounted base, avaricious,° or treacherous.

The constable, rendered desperate by the consciousness of having made so many powerful enemies, chose rather to surrender himself into the hands of the duke of Burgundy. With° this purpose he took his departure from St Quentin, where he had° himself reigned in some degree as an independent prince, and retreated to Mons in the territories of Burgundy. He was delivered up by the chancellor of Burgundy and seigneur de Humbercourt, both personal enemies of St Pol, who acting under the duke's orders put the unfortunate victim of ambition into the hands of the king. He was subjected to a short trial, in which his treachery and versatility furnished speedy means of subjecting him to condemnation. The chancellor of France,[113] president of the commission by which he was tried, addressed him in these respectful terms: "Monsieur de St Pol, you have been hitherto always accounted one of the boldest knights of this kingdom; you must not lose that character in the closing scene which you have this day to go through." He then read the sentence of instant decapitation. "It is a severe judgement," said the constable; "I hope God will support me in submitting to it."

He was accordingly transported from the judgement hall to the scaffold, where his head was struck from his body. Having been washed by the executioner in a pail of water, it was deliberately exhibited at the four corners of the scaffold with the usual publication that this was the head of a traitor. The judgement he underwent with characteristic intrepidity, and this was the end of a powerful nobleman who had held as independent proprietor several frontier towns and strong places upon the frontiers of the kingdom, and who possessed the command of four hundred men-at-arms regularly paid by the king of France yet acting under the constable's exclusive direction, often against the monarch by whom they were paid. What made the duke of Burgundy's share in this tragedy appear worse was the king abandoning to him the forfeiture of the unfortunate criminal, so that all men imputed his delivering him up to avarice and rapacity, which was held to be a meaner motive than that of revenge or malice to which Louis XI's part of the same tragedy was ascribed.

In the meantime Charles duke of Burgundy, of whom we have spoken so much in this history, engaged in a train of hostilities which he persevered in with the rashness and obstinacy proper to his character until° they were closed by his own death and the downfall of his house. It is not our present object to detail these events so minutely as has hitherto been our practice with respect to former incidents because they belong rather to the history of Switzerland and Germany than that of France. Hitherto the duke's ambitious views had been rather successful; he had conquered the whole duchy of Lorraine, had received from Louis the towns of St Quentin, Ham, and Bohain,° and had enriched his treasury with all the moveable effects of the constable of St Pol. But along with these advantages his army had been very much fatigued and diminished, and his reliance on his own natural subjects had become much less than formerly, so that his resources for recruiting were chiefly by taking into his pay a number of German and especially Italian men-at-arms, whose faith it was too late found was not° much to be relied on. At the head of an army so composed, comprehending one of the finest parks of artillery in Europe, he advanced to the eastward, and having adopted an idle quarrel with the warlike and independent Swiss, the allied cantons sent an embassy to deprecate his displeasure and to offer an alliance which would have been advantageous for both parties.

They undertook to afford him the service of six thousand men at a very moderate payment, and particularly against the king of France himself if so required to do. They° remonstrated that their wealth consisted only in men,° and that they would be more useful as faithful allies than as enemies whose defeat might afford plunder, since there was more silver on the bridles and stirrup-irons of the Burgundians than° was in their host in

19 DECEMBER° 1475

any shape whatever. But the duke of Burgundy was excluded from this advantage by the superior dexterity of Louis of France, who had long preserved relations with the Swiss cantons, and by the rashness of Charles, who despised these states as consisting only of shepherds and peasantry, whose alliance he held in contempt. He rejected therefore the offers and even entreaties of the Swiss, although that nation was already distinguished by the opposition which it had made to the aristocratic nobles of Austria, and were doomed to raise their reputation still higher at Duke Charles's own expense. Proceeding thus rashly, the duke laid siege to a place called Granson,[114] which a Swiss army advanced to relieve.° The duke took the town nevertheless, and cruelly executed a considerable part of the garrison. He then proceeded to move against the Swiss army of relief which was still in the gorges of the mountains above the place. He engaged them without much precaution, and at a time when they were infuriated on account of his treatment of the garrison of Granson. To his own extreme surprise° he was defeated considerably; his camp, wardrobe,° and jewels fell into the possession of the rugged mountaineers, who did not even know the value of jewels which were then accounted the choicest in Europe. In this action the duke lost not only his camp,° his artillery, his tents, and his baggage, but the reputation of good fortune which he had hitherto enjoyed; for he had until now gained either the honour or the credit of every enterprize in which he had engaged. He was now on the contrary obliged to send ambassadors to King Louis requesting him not to take the advantage of this defeat to break the truce which he had lately agreed to. Although Louis was sufficiently sensible of the advantage at present presented to him, yet he conceived the duke was in a way of ruining himself without his taking an immediate share in the war, and of course rather chose the task of overlooking than of assisting in his destruction. He contented himself with supplying the Swiss with money and using other means of inflaming the war without expressly joining in it.

In this situation of things the duke assembled so large an army that he thought he might again hazard a second battle, and with this intention advanced towards the small town of Morat; here he was again defeated by *22 JUNE°* the Swiss, who encountered him with the greatest courage. He fled as far *1476* as his native dominions of Burgundy, and so many were slain upon the spot as filled with their bones a chapel built near the field of battle, where° they were to be seen at no distant period, bearing° the proud inscription that Duke Charles of Burgundy had left behind him on that field of battle this monument of his army.

This perseverance in ill-judged measures being, as is natural, followed by a continuance of the same bad fortune, the *Bold,* or rather the *Rash,* duke of Burgundy now showed a disposition to sink under the repeated misfortunes which he had so rashly encountered. He became careless of his dress, suffered his beard to grow long, and assumed all the external appearance of discountenance and despair.° His diet too was changed as well as his manners, and everything about him announced mortification and the depth of sorrow. As he was naturally of a warm temperament he used° to drink the weaker sorts° of wine, and those much tempered° with water, instead of which he was obliged to use frequent draughts of strong wine unalloyed by any mixture of that element.° Reanimated at last by the exertions of some faithful servants when six weeks had elapsed he began again to take arms for the purpose of having a band of English in his pay, by whom the town of Nancy was defended against the duke of Lorraine and who were° now reduced nearly to extremity° their commander having been killed by a chance shot. The host of the duke of Burgundy was not great upon this last occasion, yet it comprehended more soldiers than were prepared to serve their master loyally. Among these there was an Italian adventurer called the count of Campo Baccio, or Campo Basso, who, having been in a state of great poverty and taken into the duke of Burgundy's service with a great appointment, was nevertheless so ungrateful as to plan his master's defeat and death, and repeatedly offered to put him into the hands of Louis. The reason of this ingrateful villain's treachery is not positively known, but it is said (and the thing is not unlikely) to have been excited° by a blow which the Italian received from the duke in one of the extravagant fits of passion to which the prince° was subject. It is said that the king of France in an unusual fit of generosity communicated to Charles of Burgundy the proposed treason of his officer, but Charles refused to pay attention to the communication, saying that if the information had been real it was inconsistent with King Louis's well-known character to warn him of it. Whether indeed a trait so little agreeing with Louis's character was actually well founded or not we have no certain means of knowing, yet so° winding and indirect were the politics of Louis that he is not unlikely to have given the warning under a conviction that the duke would not believe° it as coming from him, and historians seem generally° agreed in the use of treachery being employed in the *last scene* of this great prince's life.

Charles hastened, as we have said, at the head of a small army scarce amounting to four thousand men in number to relieve° the town of Nancy, which however was compelled to surrender before his approach. The governor had° been killed by a chance cannon° shot, and the garrison having suffered great want of provision were now become desirous of surrender. Charles, with the obstinacy which always characterised him, resolved° that he would lay siege to and recover the town before the duke of Lorraine, who was in the field at the head of a considerable army with a strong auxiliary force of Switzers, could possibly accomplish its relief. No advice of the duke's most faithful servants could dissuade° him from this dangerous enterprise, nor prevail upon him instead to withdraw to some distance from the town of Nancy until his army should be recruited and recover the terror which consecutive defeats seldom fail to inspire into a body of forces. The duke continued obstinately determined to press the siege, though in the winter season and with an army° of superior numbers hanging° in the neighbourhood watching every opportunity to raise the siege. At the same time his own troops were few in number, ill armed, ill paid, affected with many maladies, discontented as is usual in adversity, and having among them the traitor Campo Basso, whose plans comprehended the final defeat and murder of Duke Charles. On the other hand the young duke of Lorraine was at the head of an army which had hitherto been paid partly by the king of France, but who was likely soon to tire of undertaking that part of the war.

The duke of Burgundy having held a council, which was not often his custom, most of his servants were of opinion that he should retire to a strong position in the neighbourhood and suffer the duke of Lorraine to victual Nancy, after which they doubted not that he would be obliged to disperse his army for want of money. The duke of Burgundy however adhered to his opinion and remained at the siege, it being then 5 January° in the year 1477,° and he having taken his oath to enter the city before the festival of Epiphany on the sixth day of January, the° traitor Campo Basso deserted his post assigned him on the defences of the duke of Burgundy's camp and marched out with about eight score men-at-arms with whom he went straight to the duke of Lorraine's position and was astonished to be refused entrance there by the honest Germans, who declared they would not permit traitors to join in their ranks. Thus repulsed, Campo Basso and his band placed themselves in the neighbourhood of Condé where they hoped they might lie° in the road of the duke of Burgundy's retreat, when they would have an opportunity of executing their full intentions against him by being in the road by which he must attempt his retreat if routed as seemed most likely. Upon 5 January as had been expected the duke of Lorraine made such an attack upon the Burgundian army which lay before Nancy that though the slaughter was but small the rout was complete, and after he had as usual distinguished himself by° the most desperate exertions of valour Duke Charles was° at length borne° away by a torrent of fugitives and finally was himself beat down or fell from his horse with so many wounds as showed that some traitors had been round° him at the fatal moment. His body was so much disfigured as to be only known by his nearest attendants. Whether he actually fell by treachery or not cannot be well judged, but some of his personal jewels were afterwards disposed of at a smaller price than that which° any man who knew his person and suspected their value would have been likely to have demanded.

Charles of Burgundy left only one child, a daughter, whose alliance had been a sort of bait which he had held out to the different princes to whose ambition at various times the match had been a temptation. It was remarked by many that notwithstanding his rashness he never failed in obtaining the victory, or at least the advantage, in every undertaking until the execution of the constable St Pol, after which he was prosecuted° unrelentingly by a train of bad fortune which followed him like the judgement of heaven upon his revengeful and treacherous conduct towards that nobleman. It is certain that he fought with the utmost valour. The historian Duclos[115] says that, instead of being killed by Campo Basso and his Italian assassins, he° was closely pursued by a knight called Claude Blomont,° the seneschal of St Dié, to whom he called for quarter, but Blomont° being rather deaf and not understanding what he said threw the duke to earth with his lance and was trod° to death amidst the general rout. His dead body was found frozen to the earth in the morass where he had died. His jaw was split by a halbert, and two pikes had traversed his thighs from side to side. Notwithstanding the finding of his dead body, recognised by his physician, his chaplain, and the gentlemen of his bedchamber, a cloud fell over the particulars of his death, and like that of many other great persons his escape and return were for a long time believed possible if it was not hoped for by his former subjects. Nevertheless the body supposed to be his was transported to Nancy and laid in state in an apartment hung with mourning. René duke of Lorraine paid the funereal honours to his enemy himself, singularly attired in a golden beard reaching to his middle, and taking the dead corpse by the hand addressed in the following affecting manner his deceased enemy: "God rest thy soul; thou hast given us much trouble and grief."° With the life of Duke Charles of Burgundy fell the great fabric of power which had been reared by his family after their having been for a century by far the greatest house in Europe which had not attained the rank of royalty, and superior in real worth and power to many who had attained even that rank of royal distinction.*

---

* The common people have at times shown themselves unwilling to believe° in the death of remarkable men, even where the circumstances are better known and more public° than those of Charles's death at the battle of Nancy. The Maid of Orleans who was publicly° executed, Sebastian king of Portugal° killed in the defeat of Arcila,° [116] and James IV of Scotland who was killed at the battle of Flodden Field° were all believed by the vulgar to have escaped from their supposed fate and were fondly° expected to return to their native country.

Chapter 5

The death of the duke of Burgundy in the battle of Nancy struck a mighty government which had long ranked high in the European republic° out of the map of that most civilized quarter of the world. It must be remembered, says the ingenious Sir Nathaniel Wraxall in a valuable précis of the history of France,[117] that at the accession of Louis XI neither Bretagne, Provence, Franche-Comté,° Lorraine, Burgundy, nor even the whole of Picardy° was included in the French monarchy, besides that the province of Berry constituted the personal establishment of Charles duke of Berry, Louis's brother. After these° numerous defalcations France, though larger in point of extent, can hardly be esteemed as containing more resources or producing a greater revenue to its sovereign than Charles, who reigned uninterruptedly from within a few leagues of Lyons south nearly to the gates of Emden° north. It required all the rashness and violence of character which distinguished this misguided prince to pull down a fabric° so vast and so strongly cemented.

According to the general law of descent in France the immense estates of Burgundy ought to have descended to the young duchess, the heiress of her father, to° which fiefs the Salic° law was not held to apply. Louis gave out that he intended° to match this young lady, who was in the twenty-first° year of her age, with his son the dauphin, who was only seven. Instead of this unsuitable match the king had better have consulted° his own selfish politics by marrying the young lady to his own nearest relation the count° of Angoulême, who was the only nobleman of his family by whom so great a match could have been formed. Neither would the princess's feeling in her orphan state have formed° an obstacle. The funds of Burgundy were exhausted, its armies destroyed, its councils broken. The safest way was deemed to submit herself entirely to the direction of France, and to beseech humbly and almost urgently that her patrimonial territories might be united once more with France by her own marriage with a French prince, the choice of whom she submitted almost implicitly to her lord paramount Louis XI. One would have thought that a consummation° which placed at this artful prince's almost entire disposal a power which, while it existed, formed the torment and dread of his whole life would hardly have been neglected by so politic° a monarch. Accordingly Louis received the news of his rival's defeat and death as if it had been a prophetic communication from heaven, and he had deemed it a favour fit to be acknowledged with splendid donations to heaven.[118]

But the crown of France itself was not so immediately enlarged in power and wealth as the selfish avarice of the king who wore it desired that it should be.

Upon receiving the news of the duke's death Louis expressed himself extravagantly joyful, and made a vow that he would execute in silver a railing or enclosure of the church which existed in brazen metal, the accomplishment of which vow cost him a hundred thousand crowns. This was meant to show that he was grateful to heaven for the prospect of advantage afforded him and meant to use it to the utmost of his power. Instead therefore of directing the choice of the infanta or princess of Burgundy in marriage he considered it as preferable to break the power of that house rather than again to reestablish it in its full authority. He would not therefore hear of the marriage of the count d'Angoulême,° or any other dependant of France whomsoever, with the princess of Burgundy, and studied to detach from her estates as much territory as he could under various pretences add to his own. He performed these feats of acquisition and spoliation partly owing to the intrigues which he had long set on foot with the subjects of Burgundy, great part of whom could not forget that they had been at one time subjects of France, and partly owing to the exhausted state of that province, which° the insane obstinacy of Charles the Bold had by three successive and desperate defeats drained of men and money and reduced to a state of imbecility.

The princess, despairing of the accomplishment of any match so agreeable to Louis as to induce him to spare any part of her dominions that° lay within his grasp, resolved at least to make such a choice as might preserve to herself those territories which lay most contiguous to the German empire, and in which the intrigues of Louis found fewest listeners. She therefore made her choice accordingly. In the meantime, before she could execute her purpose, Louis had placed under his own allegiance the towns upon the Somme which had been so long the subject of contention between° him and the duke of Burgundy, together with the greater part of Burgundy itself and of Artois, the knights and nobles of which countries saw an obvious advantage in becoming vassals of a king so powerful, and who was renowned for his policy, instead of a prince who had brought his dominions into such a wretched state by his rashness. Philip de Commynes° therefore, and other Burgundians whom Louis had taken into his own service, were employed (with the power of disposing of large sums of money) to urge the submission of the towns and castles to Louis, and were generally successful. The princess, seeing her dominions thus melt away, judged herself compelled to make a match with Maximilian of Austria, son of the emperor and afterwards emperor himself. He was a poor-spirited prince, dominated by a spirit of petty avarice—not like that of Louis, which, sufficiently sordid when he gave way to it, was usually made by him to give place to any real object, while that of the German was but a mere dread of expending money even for purposes the most necessary and advantageous; yet to this prince, mean-spirited as he was, those parts of the dominions of the late duke of Burgundy were naturally attached which belonged rather to Germany than to France.

These German portions also might have fallen to Louis's share if he had chosen well-adopted means of conducting his intrigues amongst them; but the king of France's dislike of persons of gentlemanly feelings and of noble rank led him (although he employed in some cases, as we have noticed, Commynes, Crèvecoeur, and men of rank as well as talent) yet his chosen agents were usually men of mean birth possessing no talents whatever except a low cunning and unscrupulous obedience to the king's instructions. The celebrated Olivier Dain,° or Diable, was one of those obscure agents whom he used as his channel of communication with the citizens of Ghent and other principal towns in Flanders.

It is seldom however that men who are themselves of low birth and rank are proper agents to deal with a popular party, who are generally sufficiently partakers of the common feelings concerning rank as to think themselves ill treated in the choice of such envoys. Such agents indeed were so far successful in their mission that they were able in the king of France's name to stir° up the people of Ghent to insurrection against the young princess and beheaded two of her favourites—De Humbercourt, often mentioned, and Hugonet° the chancellor of Burgundy, for whom the infanta in vain personally entreated° the rude populace, though she appeared among them in mourning robes and condescended to request the lives of her faithful servants. Though° Olivier Dain° was successful in thus far contributing to a more melancholy tragedy, yet when they began to claim more openly the credit due to royal emissaries the Flemish citizens, far from putting themselves into the hands of Dain,° who had no ostensible situation save that of the king's barber, and whom° they did not judge of rank or consequence sufficient to enter into their court house, drove° him out of the city of Ghent with disgrace.

Meanwhile, notwithstanding some miscarriages, the intrigues of Louis in the estates belonging to his late rival were so successful as to place him nearly in half the possessions which had once made Charles of Burgundy so formidable in point of power.

Louis was called upon to attend to the motion of a rebel whom in his father's time he had been entrusted° with the task of subduing, and who was now again nourishing the same rebellious projects, and indeed may justly be considered° as a criminal stained with much guilt, but who nevertheless was proceeded against by the king so cruelly as made him a universal object of compassion. This was Jacques° d'Armagnac duke of Nemours, against whom the king proceeded with great severity. Having obtained possession of his person by surrender of the strong castle of Carlat, where the duke resided under the most solemn promises of his personal safety, the king had him conveyed hastily to Paris and committed to the custody of the Bastille,° where he was for some time shut up and put to the torture. The instructions of the king still exist in which these inhuman directions are given, and every indulgence to the prisoner is strictly prohibited. The unfortunate duke, after such cruel preparations, was brought to trial before a commission who lothly and reluctantly con-

demned him, when in fact the real crime was his share in the war of the
public good, an offence for which the duke of Burgundy's death now permitted Louis to exact a vengeance which he had never forgotten, though
it had for a time slept. The unfortunate duke of Nemours was after condemnation transported from the hall of justice to the scaffold upon a horse
caparisoned with black, and by an inhuman refinement of barbarity his
two children, too young to have partaken in his guilt, were placed beneath
the scaffold that they might be stained with their father's blood as it
poured from above through the seams of the planks which floored the
scaffold. This is one very striking instance of the odious cruelty of this
prince, who appears to have delighted in hearing with his own ears the
exclamations and cries of those who were subjected to torture; nor could
the opportunity of such gratification be uncommon, since Commynes in-
forms us that no less than four thousand persons were put to death during
his reign by private modes of death, or expired under the torture without
the ceremony of any form of legal trial whatsoever.[119]

The despotic power also of which this tyrant possessed himself was so
exercised as to extract from his people great sums of taxes, the payment of
which was enforced with the most strict regularity. His barber Olivier° Le
Diable in serving his master for the purpose of these exactions rendered
himself generally odious to his countrymen, and his demerits were not
forgotten when his patron died. Implacable cruelty therefore and grasping
avarice were the master passions of this extraordinary prince. No length of
time obliterated an offence from his recollection, and no sense of generosity could induce him to relax any demand upon his subjects which could
by any means be made effectual, and his wisdom, which in other respects
is worthy of praise, could never see how very much his character suffered
among his subjects by such indulgence of his rapacity and inhumanity.

About the year 1477° the king was embarrassed with a war with the
archduke Maximilian, whom his marriage had placed towards him in
some respects in the situation of Charles his deceased father-in-law. It is
true the state both of those French possessions of Burgundy and Artois on
the one hand, and the Flemish provinces on the other, recommended to
both princes rather to put what each enjoyed into secure possession than
to think of disturbing each other's dominions; their quarrels therefore
were closed by a truce which was to endure for a year.

In the meantime Louis became again afraid that the English, whose retreat to their own country he had procured at such expense, should now
begin to seek an opportunity for meddling with his affairs. It was scarce
possible for Edward IV to° forget that he was the only near relation of the
duchess,[120] being her mother's brother, and that the claim upon the French
crown so gloriously, although so dearly, enforced by his predecessors was
still a favourite object of his subjects of England. King Louis had hitherto
stifled° those recollections, supplying Edward underhand with° considerable
sums of money, which the king of England had applied° to his pleasures,

while there were now and then moments in which the naturally martial spirit of Edward seemed to threaten to wake into activity.° At length Louis 1478 engaged in a formal treaty which was to last a hundred years and constitute an alliance both offensive and defensive. During all° this time an annuity of fifty thousand livres was° to be paid by the king of France and his successors to him of England and his successors. He stipulated also once more that the oldest daughter should wed with the dauphin in fulfilment° of the treaty of Picquigny. This last part of the bargain probably drew the king of England's approbation of the whole. In the meantime the war between Louis and Maximilian again broke out in the battle of Guinegate,° in which neither the French° nor Flemings had much reason to boast of success. The fiery chivalry of France defeated the cavalry of Maximilian, who were inferior to them in° number, courage, and discipline. On the other hand the Flemish infantry with their archduke Maximilian at their head attacked the franc° archers of the French, who had already fallen into disorder with a view to pillage, and obtained a complete victory in that point. Both princes were so much incensed at this dubious issue of the conflict that they executed the prisoners that were taken on either side; but in spite of this exasperation and that attending a naval battle gained by the French the truce betwixt the sovereigns was again closed by the mediation of the pope. The influence of the pontiff's envoy was so considerable that he obtained from Louis, notwithstanding his unforgiving temper, the pardon and liberation of Cardinal Balue, who had languished in an iron cage ever since Louis's dangerous interview with Duke Charles in the town of Péronne in 1468.

The consequence of the battle of Guinegate° now began to show itself, though a considerable time after it had been fought, for the resolutions of Louis were generally taken with deliberation and executed with steadiness. At present, disgusted at the behaviour of the French archers who were raised by the villages, the king reduced that species of force entirely and levied in their stead ten thousand hired Swiss and ten thousand French infantry, who were regularly supplied with pay which the exactions of Louis, as well as his saving temper, enabled him to supply with regularity. In the meantime fortune, which certainly did not favour this prince in the early part of his reign, became very propitious to his latter wishes. The archduchess Mary, heiress of Charles the Bold and wife of Maximilian,° was killed by a fall from her horse while hunting, or rather died in consequence of refusing masculine assistance in setting the thighbone which was fractured by the fall. Louis was overjoyed at this accident, and by his intrigues with the people of Ghent he obliged the archduke to consent to the marriage of the princess Margaret, his only daughter by the late archduchess and heiress of all her mother's fortune which had not been already devoured by Louis himself, to his own son the dauphin, whom two years before he had pledged to marry the daughter of Edward IV. But he was well aware that the health of the king of England rendered him incapable of doing more than expressing his displeasure in words: accordingly he had only time to declare his resolution to make war upon Louis as a false and perfidious prince when he was removed by a stroke of apoplexy, and by his death the last natural relation of the house of Burgundy was removed far from the possibility of protecting its orphan. Fortune however was impartial, and did not grant to the intriguer Louis any exemption from the lot of humanity which had been dealt to the king° of England.

The health of Louis had for some years been failing, and he had sustained at least one shock of an apoplectic nature. As early as 1481 the king had sustained two shocks of this disorder, supposed to be brought on by too much thought and application to business, as the same disorder in the case of Edward IV had undoubtedly its rise in a voluptuous life and too great indulgence in what is deemed the pleasures of the world. So many and so various are the paths which lead° men to the same general termination, the grave.

Nothing is more remarkable than the extreme cowardice with which Louis XI regarded the last inevitable termination of mortality. At all periods of his life he had been addicted to pilgrimages, devotional gifts, vows, and such species of composition as superstition supposes it is possible to make with offended heaven. You cannot have forgot the remarkable prayer which he made to the Virgin Mary to induce her to become intercessor for his pardon for his accession to the murder of his brother Charles of Guienne. Another extraordinary instance of devotion was when he seized upon Boulogne, which county he solemnly conferred upon the Virgin Mary and invested her, or the priests who should represent her, with every circumstance of personal pomp which could be claimed by a favourite noble whom the king delighted to honour. Now when he could not disguise from himself the increase of his malady he endeavoured to drown it in such pleasures as his age and infirmity might yet permit him to enjoy, or rather he was disposed that his subjects should believe that he was engrossed in the pleasures of this world while he was thinking with terror upon his approaching end.

He had been at great expense in repairing and rebuilding the castle of Plessis-Lès-Tours, which he enlarged and improved, but in a manner partaking so much of his dark, fierce, and suspicious temper of mind that it had much more the air of a state prison than that of a royal chateau of pleasure. It was surrounded by several circuits of high walls bearing on the top of each rows of towers or turrets composed of spikes made of iron gratings, where the sentinels of the Scotch Guards were mounted with strict injunction to shoot everyone who approached without the regular sign, and other defences of a fearful and ominous nature. Other towers contained dungeons and torture chambers, and others° vaulted apartments for including the iron cages in which some state criminals against whom Louis had particular antipathy were doomed to linger out a painful existence. It is remarkable that when the king travelled these cages with their unfortunate inhabitants were always dragged in his train as if they had contained wild beasts instead of human creatures, and as if the owner had been jealous of his menagerie and would not part with them out of his° sight. Lastly, that the outside of the castle might equal the interior in its patibulary aspect, gibbets dispersed through the park exhibited the bodies and quarters of banditti who had infested the high roads, offenders against the game, and above all offenders against the state, on which subject the laws were so severe as to make it criminal even to hear of such projects without discovering them to a magistrate.

Such being the buildings and ornaments best suited to the king's disposition which adorned Plessis-Lès-Tours and the other royal residences of Louis XI, there were others of a nature strangely contrasted, and which must have mixed with a very singular effect amongst all those preparations for embittering and shortening life. All the young people in the neighbourhood for example, especially handsome maidens and youths of grace and activity, were obliged to attend solemn dances and other active sports on which the old king used sometimes to look from the balcony. His withered cheek and blighted strength strangely contrasted° with the appearance of those around him and the gay, rich, and youthful dress which, contrary to the custom of his better days, it was his pleasure to wear amid disease and the decrepitude of age. This spectre of a monarch, although he was occasionally visible to the spectators or performers of these village sports, always withdrew the instant he observed that the signs of mortality on his physiognomy attracted the attention of any spectator in the group.° Another art which he resorted to to disguise from the public the signs of mortality on his face and person was an affectation of anxious interest and curiosity concerning strange animals, pictures, statues, and other curiosities of art and nature. Louis had an internal consciousness that he was not beloved by the great persons of his kingdom, nor, to speak truth, by many of the small, and therefore° it was that he used the most extraordinary means of defence against treason, mingling always with his suspicions an intimation of a private contentment and interest in life, which if ever he had enjoyed it must have long vanished.

We have often had to notice the king's strong faith in the superstitions of his church, which he intimated in a thousand ways without once accompanying it with a single word of repentance for sins of which he endeavoured to avert the effects by the grossest practice of superstition.

He sent to the cathedral of Rheims, for example, for the holy vial of oil with which the kings of France are anointed at their coronation, and over which St Peter is said himself to have performed divine service.[121] The sacred vial containing the ointment was brought at his desire from Rheims to his sick apartment° at Plessis-Lès-Tours, and it was his idea to be anointed in his dying moments with the same holy substance with which he had been consecrated as a sovereign.

The Grand Seignior also, or Turkish emperor, readily humoured this powerful king by sending him a box of supposed relicts taken from the Christians, on which it may be supposed he himself set no personal value. Other means he had recourse to to avert the terrible hour which he dreaded so much. An Italian saint, either impostor or enthusiast, had made himself famous through the Catholic world by the name of the "holy man of Calabria,"[122] and was supposed to° have tasted during the greater part of his life neither flesh nor fish, eggs nor food made of milk. He lived beneath a rock, and was with difficulty, and not without the pope's express orders, prevailed upon to come to France, even though he obtained the permission of the pope and the leave of the king of Naples and Sicily. There was one singularity in the manner in which Louis used the intercessions of this Italian hermit and other holy men. He was pressing to have their prayers for his bodily recovery and personal health, but when anything was said of prayer for the sufferer's sincere repentance and for heaven's pardon of his sins he desired such petitions to be omitted, saying it was policy not to ask too many things at once, and that if his bodily health was restored it would be time enough to importune heaven about the pardon of his crimes.

There is a report equally silly and incomparably more atrocious than any we have yet said. A bath was prepared for this royal patient composed of the warm blood of infants, the effect of which was to refresh the blood of the old decayed man, soften its crudities, and restore its circulation. But we dare not believe° this of man born of a woman, even if that man be Louis XI.

Meantime, in applying to all modes of devotion, and purchasing them at as high prices as if they were really objects which could be bought and sold, the king did not neglect such assistance as could be afforded by the professors of medicine. A person of the name of Coictier,° high in renown for medicine,° maintained a species of authority over him, which, considering the person whom it was exercised over, constituted° a very dangerous game. He exacted an enormous sum by way of annual stipend, and when he found the king's munificence did not flow perfectly readily he used to break forth into threats and reproaches against the patient for his ingratitude. "I know," he said, "that you internally hate me, and would willingly rid yourself of me as you have done of others who have served you to the best of their power. But take care, for you shall not outlive for a fortnight the day that you dismiss me from attending upon you." The trembling tyrant heard this denunciation with perfect faith, and his fears secured to this man, who was probably no more than an impudent empiric, a remuneration° which no sense of justice could have rung from the dying miser.

While Louis thus gave way to fears which proved too strong even for his avarice, he still endeavoured to support the reputation of health in the eyes of the world, and was perpetually engaged in such alterations in his household as made him be talked of in the world abroad, although he was visible to few or none except the archers of his guard. Of these, four hundred men nightly mounted guard, and if he remembered that the last years of his father Charles VIII were embittered by his own tampering among the soldiers of the same corps it must have added many a pang to those which he sustained. It is certain that he was suspicious of his nearest relations, particularly of the dauphin, a boy whom he had brought up very° ill, for fear that if well educated he might become a tool in the hands of some discontented nobles to be used for bringing his own reign to a period.

Of all his family Anne of Beaujeu, his second daughter, and her husband had alone the privilege° of visiting him and paying respects to him without form, as it was in her hands that° he designed to deposit the regency in case of his own death.

He had a jealousy even of his son the young dauphin, which was probably owing to the trouble which he gave to his own father when he himself had scarce attained the age of thirteen, and afraid probably of his son being engaged in such a practice. Meantime in the year 1483 he sent for this young prince, whose education had been singularly neglected, at whose ignorance, though it was according to his own instructions, Louis seemed shocked and surprized. He for the first time in his life went into a set of detailed instructions to this young man, and pointed out to him the faults in policy of which he had himself been° guilty upon his accession to the crown. He commanded him to cherish the princes of the blood, to act by the advice of the wisest counsellors, to obey the established laws, and to diminish the extravagant imposts which he had himself laid upon the people. In this interview Louis exhausted his last temporal duty, and his confessor became sensible that it became his special duty to warn the dying king that his existence on earth was near a close, but in his terror of encountering the terrors of mortality he had extorted from those around him at some former period a solemn promise that they would not appal him by communicating the fatal intelligence of his approaching end; all therefore beheld in silence the approach of the king of terrors to the dying monarch of France. At length Olivier Dain,° or Le Diable, a man from whose bad character no voluntary piece of good service was to have been expected, especially of a disinterested kind, adventured nevertheless to perform the office of monitor upon this difficult occasion. "It is my duty," he said, "to tell your majesty that you must lay aside all thought of help, either in this holy man ('the Hermit of Calabria') or in any other mortal, for your last hour upon earth is fast approaching." The king heard the news with unexpected composure. "You may," he said, "be mistaken, and the compassion of heaven may yet prolong my life." After this he again turned him to the instructions which he was to leave behind him, and it is remarkable that most of his directions were at variance with his own practice. He recommended to his successor to pursue no hostilities against the duke of Bretagne, and to lay aside all thoughts of regaining Calais from the

English, two projects which had certainly occupied his own thoughts for some years, and had he been granted the power of framing any wish on his deathbed there is little doubt that these achievements would have been his principal objects. It is probable that he wished to impress upon those around him, and even to impose on heaven itself, a belief that he was renouncing upon his deathbed those schemes of ambition which if he had lived he would certainly have prosecuted. He laid aside the vain terror by which he was agitated, coolly directed the ceremonial of his own funeral, and died 30 August 1483, preserving to the last his faculties, and leaving the memory of a reign useful to his country by the almost final expulsion of the English, and the union of Burgundy, Artois, and Provence with the rest of the kingdom of France. His talents were great, but we are scarcely entitled to say that he possessed any virtues at all: for the good which he did flowed naturally from the exercise of his good sense° and his comprehension of the most useful objects of pursuit, which led him in the same direction to which another would have been guided by inclination to do that which is good and a love of virtue.

Chapter 6

When the reins of state were quitted° by the dying hands of Louis his family, although strong in point of numbers, was yet weak in masculine talent. Charles° the dauphin had been bred up in mean obscurity and left ignorant of all that a prince of his rank ought to have known, the jealous fears of his father having made even this poor child an object of suspicion and left his education basely imperfect. Two daughters, both arrived at woman's age, had been for some time settled in the marriage state with° their own nearest relations. The eldest, the princess Joan,° was wedded to the dauphin's nearest male relation, and was heir of the crown on his failure: this duke of Orleans was grandson of him who was assassinated° in the reign of Charles VI on the bridge of Montereau° sur Yonne by contrivance of the duke of Burgundy, he himself therefore the heir apparent of the kingdom and married as we have said to the eldest daughter of Louis XI. The duke of Orleans might easily have aspired to the regency of France and the direction of the young king's education, but such had by no means been the purpose of Louis in wedding his eldest daughter to the duke of Orleans.

The princess Joan was a good, mild, and accomplished woman, but unhappily not only plain in her features but somewhat deformed in her person, and in compelling the duke of Orleans to unite himself with her it was the intention of Louis XI that the house of Orleans, now vested in a last representative, should at least form a marriage which should have every chance of being without family, and affording the duke therefore no temptation to nourish any scheme respecting the succession to the crown, since he was to be destitute of heirs to whom to transmit it. Accordingly the prince, though he dared not refuse the king's eldest daughter, yet never lived with her as his wife nor was kind to her, nor had they any family. The purpose of the wily Louis XI in condemning his nearest collateral male relation to a sort of wedlock which was equal to celibacy was to remove him as far as possible from all charge of the king's person upon his accession, which duty he intended should devolve upon his youngest daughter called Anne de Beaujeu, and with regard to whom he had always expressed a strong partiality as displaying talents in some degree resembling his own, and whom he had instructed with great care with the secret purpose of confiding to her the government of the state during the minority of her brother Prince Charles the dauphin. His reasons for preferring° his younger daughter to the regency was that the Lady° of Beaujeu could form no ambitious projects upon the government, as neither in her own person nor in that of her husband did there exist the least title of claim to the crown; for the sieur de Beaujeu with whom her father's policy had wedded her was indeed descended from the royal family, but in a distant and collateral line and by a remote descent. We must also suppose that the Lady of Beaujeu had already exhibited to her father the extraordinary talents for government which she possessed and which, besides being accompanied by a virtuous principle (to which Louis XI was a stranger), were in respect of judgement and decision nearly equal to his own.

The Lady° of Beaujeu entered upon the task assigned to her by her father's will without the least opposition from anyone, and as regent of the kingdom was honoured by the title of *Madam,* emblematical° of supreme power. The prince her brother had been always educated at the remote castle of Amboise, and willingly submitted to the influence of a sister under whose direction he had been brought up.

In the meantime the Lady of Beaujeu took a course with the wealthy and unscrupulous favourites of the late monarch, which as usual with the unpopular set of persons, favourites who have lost their protector, was highly popular. Olivier Le Dain,° assuming the title of compte de Deulant, whose exorbitant° wealth bore witness to the extent of his oppressions, was° condemned for adultery and murder. Another favourite of the late king called John Doyat° was condemned to a cruel punishment which he underwent with singular fortitude. He was scourged through the streets of Paris and had his right ear cut off; was then remitted to his native village of Montferrand situated in Auvergne, of which province he had been governor, and was there again scourged through the streets and had his other ear cut off; but while this cruel punishment was imposed the criminal endured all its severity without permitting the secret to escape him in what manner he had disposed of his wealth, and thus secured it for his own enjoyment when he retired to obscurity.

Coictier° too, the physician° whose insolence to King Louis XI on his deathbed we have already noticed, was also punished, with a fine, which however was a moderate one in comparison to the immense wealth which he had acquired in the king's service, and which he was permitted to enjoy without further investigation in safe privacy.

While Anne de Beaujeu thus gained popularity by visiting the crimes of those who had abused the confidence of the late monarch or had been the willing agent of his crimes, the duke of Orleans made several efforts, both by intrigues and even denunciations of hostility, to gain some greater share of the administration of France than what his late father-in-law had assigned to him. He easily found a party in the states of the kingdom, and so general was the custom of giving the next adult the charge of the government during the minority of a young king that perhaps the duke of Orleans's youth (being only twenty years of age) was the chief argument,° united to the merits of the Lady of Beaujeu, who was allowed to display her father's talents, though she exhibited better principles, which moved the most of estates in her favour. As time moved on however the objection lost its force, and the affairs of the province of Bretagne assumed such an aspect as rivetted the attention of both the candidates for power in the ministration of France upon the matters of that province.

Brittany it will be remembered was the only subsisting great fief of the crown of France, Louis XI not having succeeded in uniting it to° the crown at the time of his death, and though that monarch had warned his successor to abstain from troubling the government of the duke of Bretagne, his daughter the Lady of Beaujeu thought it right rather to follow her father's policy than the more cautious and scrupulous instructions he had expressed upon his dying bed. The duke of Orleans on the other hand, as the only means remaining to vindicate his rights, resolved to watch an opportunity to make common cause with Francis duke of Bretagne, and to baffle the regent's intention of swallowing up in the monarchy of France this last of the independent fiefs.

Francis II, the prince in possession of Bretagne, a weak character, had,° greatly to the displeasure of his nobles, made° a favourite of a person of low rank named Peter Landais, whom he had raised to the rank of his prime minister and universal favourite. The nobles of Brittany were just about to quarrel with their duke on account of his favour to this man, and had indeed implored the assistance of France as the lord paramount, which the lady regent stood prepared to grant them with the view of finally bringing about the forfeiture of the dukedom of Brittany, when a domestic quarrel precipitated her intentions as well as those of the duke of Orleans.

While the court was residing at the castle of Melun the king and his sister the regent were looking at a game at tennis when there occurred a disputed stroke between the duke of Orleans and the other party who was playing. The Lady of Beaujeu had no hesitation to give an award against the duke, on which he exclaimed aloud that whoever° had decided that stroke against him, if a man, had lied, and if a woman, was a person of no character. Recollecting the consequences of such an affront given to a lady of that rank, and naturally afraid of the consequences, he fled° to his castle of Beaugency,° but he presently after found himself obliged to surrender to the French troops by whom he was besieged and to submit entirely to Madame de Beaujeu, aware of his intrigues with Bretagne. He next received orders instantly to attend the maréchal° Gié to bring him to court, where he was deprived of almost the only appointment he possessed, that is° the government of the Isle of Paris. The noble prisoner, alarmed at this severity and at° the advantage which might be taken against him for having allied himself with the duke of Bretagne, and afraid° of the issue of his intrigues, made his escape from the guards by whom he was surrounded and found his way at length to Bretagne, where the duke of that province received him with open arms, promised him his eldest daughter in marriage, and agreed with him on every point in which they could strengthen each other's interest. The French government pushed a strong army into

Bretagne with a view to pursue the policy of the Lady of Beaujeu by an-
nexing that fief to the crown. The lieutenant general of these French
troops was the seignior de La Trémoille. After various political and military
operations between the French troops on the one hand° and those willing
to defend Bretagne on the other, John of Châlons,° [123] called the eighth
prince of Orange, embraced the same cause, and both he and the duke of
Orleans incurred the same misfortune.

A sharp engagement took place at St Aubin du Cormier, in which the
duke of Orleans and the prince of Orange, who were the very soul of the
league among the Bretons who had endeavoured° to associate themselves
for the defence of their national independence, were made prisoners after
fighting bravely,[124] and were a little alarmed at the treatment they might
receive—Orleans especially so, for there were pretexts at least for treating
him as a traitor since he was taken fighting against the regular French government. In the evening after the battle these two distinguished prisoners
were invited to supper in the tent of the victor general Monsieur de La
Trémoille. Some French officers of less rank taken in the army of Bretagne
were also of the party. At the moment of the dessert° being served two
Franciscan friars were introduced in the garb of their order. As the purpose of these religious men was probably to prepare some of the party for
immediate death Orleans and Orange° looked on each other, apprehending that their death-hour was come. But La Trémoille hastened to break
the melancholy silence by explaining this apparition. "Princes," he said to
the duke of Orleans and the prince of Orange, "I have no right to judge
you, nor if I had would I venture to make use of it. The king alone must
in person decide your fate. But for you officers who have broke through
the laws of military discipline and broken your oaths to Charles VIII you
must prepare for immediate death, and these holy men will if you think
proper unburthen your consciences." Accordingly they confessed themselves to the Franciscans and suffered instant death. The prince of Orange
was sent to one prison, the duke of Orleans to another called La Sablé
where he was under keeping of an officer more devoted to the Lady of
Beaujeu than to the king himself. He was afterwards sent to Bourges and
Lusignan,[125] and was shut up at least during the night in one of those°
tremendous iron cages devised by Louis XI.

The terror and agony which the duke of Bretagne sustained in consequence of the defeat and dangerous captivity of his principal allies was
such that,° aided as it was by the effects of a fall from his horse, he died a
short time after the battle of St Aubin. Shortly after, the Lady of Beaujeu
began to act with severity against those who had° joined in the conspir-
acy° of the duke of Orleans. The celebrated Count Dunois was found
guilty of treason, and the parliament of Paris declared his property confiscated. The celebrated Philip de Commynes° was also fined in one-
fourth of his subsistence and sustained a severe imprisonment during
which he also obtained a personal acquaintance with the cages devised

by his master Louis XI, of which he has left so striking a description.

Many intercessions were made for the unfortunate duke of Orleans, and one of the most zealous and affectionate intercessors° was the princess Joan his wife, though conscious she was not beloved by him and married to him rather as a victim to Louis XI's policy than as a person whom he could love and esteem. She had the more merit in these interferences because her husband's ambitious plan of wedding with the princess of Bretagne was founded° on his hope of getting a divorce from herself on the grounds the most offensive perhaps to a female, that is upon charges against her of personal plainness and imperfections.

But though Orleans's own imprisonment was kindly softened by the mediation, yet the rigours inflicted on his friends° began to be diminished. The famous George of Amboise, bishop of Montauban, and the bishop of Puy[126] were enlarged from the state prisons in which they had been detained on the charge of countenancing his intrigues.

In the meanwhile the German prince Maximilian, having a strong party among the Breton nobility, was so far preferred to his rivals as to celebrate in private a marriage in which his ambassadors represented the absent bridegroom.[127] This marriage by proxy was kept a close secret until the death of the princess Anne's only sister Isabella, when it became public.

The friends° of the duke of Orleans now redoubled their instances for his liberty, and his wife Joan,° throwing herself at the feet of her brother the king arrayed° in deep mourning, entreated° for his pardon, and she hinted° that her husband knew the interest which the king took in Anne of Bretagne and was willing to subdue his own pretensions to the inclinations of his sovereign, and that° he still had partizans in Bretagne whose good offices might be useful in assisting to cancel the marriage between Maximilian° and the princess of Brittany. "Sister my darling," answered the king to this affecting entreaty,° "you shall receive back the husband whose loss of liberty causes your distress, and heaven grant you may never repeat what you are now doing in his behalf." These expressions the king used as entertaining the belief that the duke of Orleans, if° he could ever find an opportunity, would not omit to pursue his divorce with his affectionate but very plain wife the princess Joan. Accordingly he was persuaded to put an end to the prince's suit and make° the deliverance of the duke of Orleans the first deed which should mark the assumption of the regal power into his own hand. Having° delivered him, as much to his surprise as his joy, from the state prison of Bourges where he was imprisoned for the time, the two young princes swore eternal friendship and kept it better on both sides than was always the case with such sudden engagements. In particular° the duke of Orleans willingly agreed to sacrifice to the king any inclination which he himself entertained for Anne of Bretagne.

This exertion on the part of the king of personal authority was a virtual end of Anne of Beaujeu's regency, yet the good-natured king made a sort of apology, and therefore no breach ensued between him and his sister.

Anne of Bretagne cannot be supposed insensible to the superior advantages which the match with France possessed over every other which had been proposed to her. But then in respect of delicacy she might suppose herself fettered by the ceremony which Maximilian had passed through with her, though by proxy only. At length Maximilian showed himself so cold and indifferent a suitor that his bride became ashamed to be forward in desiring a marriage which he, the bridegroom himself, seemed° so slow in urging forward, and chose° the match with France as that which promised the most quiet settlement of her states. The compte de Dunois assisted with his persuasions, until at length she consented to give her hand to the king of France. She retained an affectionate partiality for her native subjects, of whom she kept a bodyguard of one hundred men in constant attendance on her person.

The king's own personal interference in the freedom of the duke of Orleans might be said to close the regency of the Lady Anne of Beaujeu, although she seems entirely to have retained her brother Charles's firm affection and gratitude.

Chapter 7

The French nation welcomed° with joy a match which united it with° the kingdom Bretagne, the last province which remained divided from it as a grand separate fief. This disunion prevented the only chance of Bretagne saving her independence, which could not have been otherwise rescued except by the unanimity of the subjects. Maximilian, king of the Romans, who had been formerly the husband of Mary° of Burgundy, presented himself now as a suitor for the hand of an heiress very near as well endowed as the wife he had lost. He obtained the approbation of the greater part of the Bretagne estates, and if he had come in person to the court of the province there is little doubt but that he would have obtained possession of that fair and wealthy bride, and thus, though a prince of little merit in his own person or understanding, he would have had the good fortune to win in succession the hands of two young and lovely women, the richest heiresses in Europe. The preferred match came so far that the actual marriage was celebrated by proxy, for the avarice of the emperor made him reluctant to allow his son a sum of money necessary for the expenses upon the occasion.

This was the cause, as we have already hinted, of the total breach of the match, for the nobles of Bretagne were° divided among themselves upon° whom to bestow the hand of their princess, and in these circumstances her hand was applied for by Charles VIII, the young king of France, with a weight of influence which there was no power to counterbalance except that of England her ancient rival, which state had now undergone its last revolution occasioned by the War of the Roses. This was accomplished by means of the victory of Bosworth field which placed the crown on the head of Henry VII, where the Breton adventurers had a considerable share in the victory and of course a claim to the gratitude of Henry VII. That prince, though prudent and sagacious, was by no means either generous, chivalrous, or adventurous, and his politics inclined him to avoid reviving the great war with France, at the risk of leaving Bretagne to its fate. He sent indeed an army to Calais with which he threatened to advance into France° and decide the fate of Brittany by arms, but in reality he seems to have had no such intention,° and though with a different purpose he accepted, like Edward IV at the treaty of Picquigny, a large sum of money, intended however to fill his coffers and not to augment his expenses, he therefore led back his army and left the young princess of Brittany without the assistance of the only power by whom she might have been supported.

In this general dereliction of her cause the princess and a few faithful lords saw themselves obliged to yield to necessity. Maximilian was too cold a suitor to trust anything to his advancing in arms to the support of his claim, and the king of France's power was equally near at hand and irresistible. In this emergency the match with Maximilian was broke off, the more readily that the Flemings had about the same time sustained° a defeat from the French, and that with the young king Charles VIII was agreed to under such articles as amounted to a total separation° of the last grand fief of France that enjoyed independence.

As this was the last instance of the politics of Louis XI, so the measure was carried into effect by the Lady of Beaujeu, in whom alone survived a portion of that extraordinary prince's political wisdom and energy of character. Not the least spark of Louis's peculiar temper appeared in the person of his son; far from having his malignity or even his firmness of character, Charles VIII was one of the easiest and most flexible of characters, extremely good tempered and well disposed, without° possessing a single spark of that temper which induces a prince to form an opinion of his own interest and steadily to adhere to it. Such a character as that of Charles began to desire a change in government, which was the more expected because a party in the parliament espoused° the cause of that unfortunate prince the duke of Orleans, who had now been four years a prisoner and who had nevertheless a just title to be consulted in the affairs of the government.

The union of Bretagne with France removed the fears of internal war which had been so long threatened in case of any attempt to defend the independence of that province; but its union with France had given the latter kingdom a complete prospect of entire quiet and tranquillity.° But this prospect had no charms for the fiery young nobility of France, not even for the king himself or those whose interest was more immediately concerned, the° community of the kingdom. France had been in every respect, at every time of their history, and in every form which the nation has assumed, a people attached to war and to whom no feeling is so dear as the stimulus of national glory, to which she is always too ready to sacrifice moral justice and the rights of her neighbours as well as the interests of the country itself. The conversation of the old soldiers who were placed round the person of King Charles VIII° in youth had naturally inspired him with a bias towards military affairs, and the style of his reading, left greatly to his own choice on account of his neglected youth and the indulgence attached to a weak state of health, had the same tendency, and though the character did not very well assort with other parts of Charles's disposition, he was yet ambitious of the fame of a conqueror, or rather of a hero of romance; for there enters into the former character a strength of mind and power of decision which Charles never appears to have possessed, although sufficiently brave in his own person.

The state of Italy at this time showed such symptoms of discord as seemed to afford to a prince desirous of war an opportunity of signalising himself by arms. After the fall of the Roman empire that portion of it in which Rome had once reigned mistress of the world possessed indeed all the advantages which it might have required to have formed a single state flourishing under the most favourable auspices; the climate was beautiful, the soil rich and varied, the people naturally acute, talented, and possessing in the greatest perfection such relics° of ancient learning as had been left undestroyed by the tempestuous passions of the barbarians; but in spite of all those attributes which might have led a legislator to hope that the kingdom of Italy, like others, might find an internal point of adhesion which would make so favoured a province capable of recovering itself and arising after the general fall of civilisation, there were unhappily reasons which prevented the fragments into which it was broken by the shock from being reunited into any social body which could pretend to represent Italy in a united state, defined by natural limits and forming a single country governed by a single common interest. The physical shape of a peninsula like Italy formed an objection to the parts into which it was divided constituting the separate portions of a single whole. The top and toe of the *boot,* as geographers have fancifully named Italy, and the position of the Appennines° which divide the country laterally and greatly impede the communication of one province with another, prevents that community of manners and community of interests from taking place betwixt northern and southern, eastern and western Italy which is essential to provinces designed to form part of the same state, and they have always arranged themselves therefore under different governments, independent° of each other, and different both in customs and in laws. Accordingly° the history of Italy had been since the fall of Rome the history of a series of petty republics perpetually convulsed either by war each within itself or with each other; a° field of combat also which strangers, the Greeks and Normans, the Saracens, and whoever contended for military eminence, were accustomed to consider as their appropriate field of battle.

The ingenuity of the inhabitants and their acquirements were unfavourable for constituting large states, for although a rude nation may be easily formed into a kingdom, which is the most simple and intelligible form of government which exists, yet it becomes impossible for a hundred or two of petty towns or provinces to mould their general principles of government into the form of a single extensive republic, and the very circumstance of their being an ingenious and acute people, setting a fanciful value upon their peculiar laws and rights, makes them less capable of amalgamating into one general form of government. Whether we have assigned a true reason for the division of Italy into hostile states and the constant wars which they carried on with each other, the case is no less certain that such a division did exist, and that the country was at no time more divided than when its domestic discords invited the French to take the chance of conquering it.

I have already mentioned to you that the king of France was the unquestionable inheritor of all those claims in virtue of which the house of Anjou had long furnished kings to Naples, Sicily, and the Calabrias. They were now superseded° in their right by the house of Aragon. Ferdinand I of Naples was now upon the throne, an aged monarch who° felt he was possessed of no strength to enter into war and was° willing to deprecate a contest with the power of France almost upon any terms. At the same time he felt the disgrace of submitting tamely to the aggression of the invader and employed churchmen about the king's person, whom he bribed highly, who recommended to the king of France as matter of conscience to restore the two border counties of Roussillon and Cerdagne, of which Louis had obtained a mortgage. He did not even stipulate the restitution of the money for which these counties stood pledged, but contented himself with stipulating that the three hundred thousand crowns for which they stood pledged should be remitted to King Ferdinand on the faith that he would promise not to make war upon France nor support any other sovereign who did so. By this engagement[128] the king of France hoped to prevent an alliance between Ferdinand of Sicily and the German prince Maximilian who had been plundered of more than half his fortune by the devices of Louis himself. He had accordingly patched up a reconciliation between the king of France and the house of Austria, and hoped therefore to find an opportunity of bending his whole strength to his favourite enterprise of the invasion of Italy.

The person by whom the king was chiefly persuaded to this distant and impolitic expedition was the notorious Ludovico° Sforza, called from the darkness of his complexion *The Moor*. This wicked man had seized upon the principal power of the duchy of Milan, which he administered in the name of John Galeazzo,° his nephew and son of his elder brother. This temporary administration he proposed to convert into the full sovereignty so soon as the state of Italy should be so disturbed as to permit him to perfect his usurpation without attracting too much attention.

For this reason he urged Charles VIII (a young, unexperienced, and not a very able sovereign) to the invasion of Italy, although in doing so he asserted a very doubtful right to a kingdom at a great distance from his own and engaged in a war which he had few troops and less treasure to carry on in a manner required for success.

Accordingly Charles refused an offer made to him by Ferdinand I,° reigning king of Naples, proposing to him to do homage for his kingdom and grant to King Charles an annuity of fifty thousand crowns with other proposals of the most submissive nature, from which, had they been effectually performed, the young king must have reaped to a certainty much greater advantages than what he could have expected from the perilous and dubious expedition which he meditated. Having persisted in his purpose the French king appointed Peter duke of Bourbon, husband of the Lady of Beaujeu, regent in his place, although that nobleman as well as his wife was extremely anxious to dissuade° him from the expedition.

The king involved in this fatal attempt almost the whole disposable forces of France. His° naval forces were commanded by the duke of Orleans, his relation, and his army, consisting of about six thousand horse and twelve thousand infantry, who had their van led by Robert Stuart lord of Aubigny, were personally° endowed with the highest valour and the power of doing as much as could have been expected from the same number of any other men in the world. But the king was very ill provided with money to supply the wants and subsistence of his army while marching from Lombardy to Naples. For this purpose he borrowed the duchess of Savoy's jewels when he arrived at Turin, and those of the marchioness of Montferrat,° of which precarious resources of the war two or three petty loans from merchants and bankers were the only pecuniary aid which he found it possible to raise.

Charles was also stopped° at the town of Asti in Lombardy° by an attack of the smallpox, in which disease he had nearly closed both his expedition and his life just as he arrived in Italy. When advancing into the Milanese territory he found the lawful duke John Galeazzo° dying of poison administered, as no one questioned, by his uncle the usurper Ludovico° Sforza. It does not appear that he afforded Charles more assistance to make out some of his loans, and the king of France is universally blamed for not inflicting punishment on° this bold bad man who had just committed so execrable a crime while the king of France stained himself with some disgrace by his alliance with so unscrupulous an adviser. All Italy was convulsed by the news that Charles VIII had actually commenced his expedition. He had entered Florence[129] as a conqueror and in complete armour, his visor being closed and his lance couched, and had proposed the establishment of a free republic in that city as well as Pisa and Siena,° in which places he was received with enthusiasm.

The king's next most implacable enemy was Pope Alexander VI, whom Catholics themselves describe as a man without faith, a prince without mercy, and a pontiff without religion.[130] He was remarkable for having formed an alliance with the Turkish emperor Bajazet, by which he undertook to keep the sultan's brother Zizim close prisoner, being rather an edifying treaty betwixt the great Turk and this pontiff, and not much to the credit of Christianity. Hearing of Charles's approach Pope Alexander retreated into the castle of St Angelo, which is a citadel of Rome, and left the gates of the city itself open and the walls undefended. The French army entered by torchlight with colours spread and in array of battle, the king himself being at their head.[131] He was urged by the pope's enemies to storm the castle, take the pontiff prisoner, and depose him from his holy office; but contented with having occupied Rome as a conqueror, Charles moved southwards without coming to farther extremities.

Meantime strange changes had taken place in that city.[132] Ferdinand I had died° of a disorder apparently in the nerves caused by grief and fear a short time before Charles VIII set out upon his expedition against Italy, and out of grief for not having been able to avert that calamity. His son Alphonso° II who succeeded to the vacant throne, conscious of his own unpopularity and terrified at the approach of the French, seems to have been seized with a nervous disorder like that of his father, which presented the enemy's battalions to him while they were yet sixty leagues distant. He° exclaimed repeatedly "France! France!" while he only gazed on the alarmed citizens. He° sent his son Ferdinand II duke of Calabria to offer some opposition to the invaders, but on his return without having accomplished that object the alarm of Alphonso increased so much that he resigned the crown to his son and embarked with a few jewels and a small sum of money, not forgetting an ample stock of the best wine and a collection of flower seeds for his garden of which he was a great cultivator, and with such provision for the amusement of his future days he retired to a convent in the town of Messina.° Too much of care and sorrow attended him into his retreat to admit its operating to restore his° health, and he died within a year after betaking himself to this retreat where he had made provision to indulge his favourite tastes of good living and of gardening. It appears the less wonderful that this Neapolitan prince should have failed in his attempt to occupy the throne which Ferdinand yielded up to him.

It is true the soldiers easily were engaged in constant war with each other, but these were not carried on according to the mode of France, England, and Germany, nor were the soldiers raised in the same way or subject to the same laws or military discipline. They were formed of a set of professional soldiers who were included° in various bands under leaders called conductors or condottieri; these men were very like the free adventurers under the French and English leaders of Edward III's time and Charles VII's,° who scarcely reckoned themselves attached to one kingdom more than another, but the same species of troops in Italy were far from possessing the same sort of military spirit which animated their northern and more warlike brethren.

The soldiers of every condottiere° were his stock in trade, his property, the means by which he maintained his reputation and carried on his profession; of course it was the business of the leader to expose his men as little as possible in scenes of slaughter, and indeed the evil which combatants° of this sort chose to do to each other was to make prisoners° by the ransoms of whom they might acquire riches. The artillery might have varied this accidental mode of making war, but there was a species of rule that the guns on either hand should not fire upon each other,[133] so that unless it was by some unhappy accident a death by chance shot was of rare occurrence. The famous philosopher Machiavelli° mentions under the name of two great battles the scuffles as they might be called of Castrocaro° and Anghiari. In the first of those, which was rather remarkable for its length and obstinacy, there was no one whatever either killed or wounded. The second, or battle of Anghiari, was saddened by the death of a single man-at-arms who, having fallen from his horse, was trodden to death by a squadron of horsemen who rode over him, a kind of death which struck great horror into the companions of this unhappy cavalier.° From this we may conclude that the very quality of bloodshed was in a manner banished from Italian warfare. A town or prince who went to war with another hired the most renowned and powerful leader of these troops. He came with a body of which the officers bore the terrible names of *Iron-arm, Cleave-steel,* and similar epithets contrived to express terror, who thought they discharged their duty if they made a semblance of fighting rather resembling a combat upon the stage than an encounter of real warriors in any other country than Italy.

Attachment to the sovereign the condottiere° could have none, and as little interest in the cause for which he fought. He was only concerned so far as to give the merchants he traded with a fair pennyworth of such military valour as he and his Myrmidons generally dealt in; and if he was a man of prudence he was bound at the same time to take care of the lives and limbs of his followers, as well for his own sake as for theirs.

It may be guessed with what horror these prudent and moderate-tempered Italian cavaliers beheld the onset of the knights of France, who rushed upon them with sharp swords and grinded lances, and sought to distinguish themselves by that close conflict in which life was willingly exchanged against the hope of victory. "It was new thing," says an Italian historian Guicciardini, "and full of the greatest terror to the Italians, to behold battles no longer presented in a theatrical manner by mere representations of war, but mixed with headlong charges and having both sides inspired by the resolution hitherto unknown to the combatants° to conquer or die."[134]

It is also certain that the French had great advantage in the artillery department; since about the end of the fifteenth century, which is the time we describe, that formidable arm has always had a main effect in deciding warfare. The French already used artillery of bronze° transported by horses, while the Italians were unfurnished with any excepting iron guns which were painfully and awkwardly° transported by cattle; such were the advantages which the French possessed in a warfare with the Italians, who had by a species of premature civilization become as superior in the art of politics as the French in that of war, and capable of overcoming in the long run the fiery valour of those warriors from beyond the Alps, whom in the field of battle they had found so unsparing either of the blood of others or of their own.

In the meantime Charles VIII, overrunning Rome in his passage, advanced to the Neapolitan territory and found that Alphonso had betaken himself as we have stated, leaving the crown to his youthful son Ferdinand, who appears to have had more spirit to defend it than either the father or grandfather that had preceded him. The young prince flew to the frontier, but being defeated in an engagement a general disaffection seems to have seized on his subjects, and such had been the unpopularity of his grandfather King Ferdinand I and of his father King Alphonso that it became evident that the people of Naples, as well as Marano,° Aversa, and other parts of the kingdom, intimated an obvious intention to receive the French as liberators and not as invaders. Ferdinand II made some impression on the multitude by the terms in which he released them from their oath and fealty to himself, but he did not escape the common fate of those princes who appeal to the compassion of the populace when their good luck appears to have abandoned them. The rabble presently assumed the form of an insurrection and began in his presence to plunder his palace, and rendered it necessary for him to go on board one or two galleys having his Uncle Frederick, his grandmother the widow of Ferdinand I, and her daughter Joan,° with a few attendants in his train. He often looked back upon Naples and quoted aloud the verse from the Psalmist, "Unless the Lord doth keep the fortress the watchman loses his pains."[135] He saved himself and his followers by disembarking on the little island of Ischia, of which he took possession.

The very next day a deputation from Naples carried the keys of the city to Aversa which Charles that day took possession of, and offered° him possession of the metropolis. Charles eagerly marched upon Naples, the castles or citadels of which made little resistance. The treasures of the kings of Naples were all deposited in the citadel, and it took eight days to remove them by dint of carts and labourers.

The castle of Dell'Ovo° surrendered shortly afterwards,[136] and Charles VIII refused with scorn an offer on the part of Frederick, the uncle of the reigning prince, to surrender all the other provinces if the French king would only leave his nephew in possession of Calabria. But Charles VIII was so delighted with the beauty and wealth of the kingdom which he had gained so easily that the only compensation he would offer to the dethroned prince was a retreat in France.

Charles meantime took possession of a royal residence which had been founded and decorated by Alphonso, a professed admirer of good wine and apparently a man of taste for the beauties of nature as well as its pleasures. The following description of this royal retreat by a contemporary° author gives a curious idea of the luxury and industry of this wealthy country about the year 1495. "The buildings composed several suites° of apartments where they had assembled the most valuable specimens of refined luxury, together with vast galleries ornamented with statues of marble and alabaster, the taste for which had begun to revive after example of the Classical sculpture. These edifices were surrounded by delicious gardens exhibiting in one place an extent of the most verdant turf, in another long tufted alleys where a multitude of rivulets and of fountains maintained the coolness of the air. A regular stone wall formed a park more spacious," says the Frenchman,[137] "than that of Vincennes.° This again was subdivided into inclosures destined for particular objects of rural economy and various kinds of cultivation. Here were inclosures where they brought up foreign animals which were objects of curiosity; here were also aviaries containing the most rare birds, paddocks which maintained breeds of most excellent horses, and ovens in which according to the oriental method thousands of eggs were hatched. The olive tree, the orange, the pomegranate, the fig, and the date, had each immense parterres for their cultivation. A quarter was particularly dedicated to the cultivation of roses," probably for the purpose of extracting the perfume now termed ottar of roses, for the author adds: "for they produce a perfume almost as perfect as those of Arabia. The park also contained upon its sloping banks a vineyard whose grapes produced a wine of the kind called Muscat of most exquisite quality; lastly, in the middle of the park an artificial fountain threw up its living treasures into the air, the supply of which was sufficient if required to supply all Naples with that element, so delicious in a warm climate and so necessary in all. In fine," says the contemporary° historian in finishing his picture, "the place was altogether a terrestial paradise";° nor was there any want of the fairest specimens of that sex by whose means the earthly paradise was lost. The most beautiful *specimen* of the charmers of Naples contended which should best diversify the pleasures of a victor monarch who was only twenty-five years of age.

The duchess of Malfi, one of the finest women of Naples, gave the king a new and unusual pleasure by mounting in his presence an unbroken horse and putting the fiery animal through the various paces of the menage with equal grace and dexterity. Others strove to gain his attention by a like display of their charms, and they were so successful as to inspire him with the brightest dreams of becoming conqueror of the great Turk and emperor of the east at a time when the powers of Italy had united to deprive him of that kingdom of Naples of which he had with so much ease appeared to become temporary master. Letters from his ambassador Philip de Commynes now acquainted him with intelligence that placed the affairs which had lately seemed so promising in a light which was alike disastrous and doubtful. Ere however such news was received Charles° VIII enjoyed one day of triumph. He entered into Naples in solemn triumph,° clothed with an imperial mantle and holding in one hand a sceptre and in the other a golden globe, both well-known emblems of imperial dignity; surrounded by his paladins, as if sustaining the part of Charlemagne in a romance, he paced through the streets of Naples, and arriving° at the cathedral of St Januarius he swore upon the phial containing the blood of that martyr to defend the rights and privileges of the city of Naples. The multitude who pressed round him answered the protestations of Charles with shouts of devotion, while the ladies crowding around the high-spirited and ambitious young prince entreated from his hand the honour of knighthood for their sons. It was a moment doubtless of triumphant feeling, to which in a day or two was substituted intelligence which not only awakened Charles from his golden dream concerning the eastern empire but made it very doubtful how far he might be able to make a safe retreat from his short-lived conquest of Naples.

The grand master D'Aubusson° of the Order of Rhodes[138] had been gained over by the pope with the promotion belonging to the hat of a cardinal. An archbishop of Durazzo employed as an agent to purchase arms for the use of the Grecians and Albanians against the Turks was arrested at Venice and all his papers sent to Bajazet,° who put a stop to the conspiracy (which amounted to a second crusade) by putting to death forty thousand Christians. The death of Zizim, not without suspicion of poison administered by Pope Alexander, put an end to any hopes which could be founded upon that prince's claim for disputing the empire with Bajazet.° In short the vain hopes in which the French monarch had engaged so rashly appeared in their proper light of a morning dream when the sleeper is awakened. But this was not the worst of Charles's situation; a league of the greatest powers of Europe having Pope Alexander VI for its head, with the republic of Venice, the emperor Maximilian, his son the archduke Philip, Ferdinand king of Aragon, and even the villainous and ungrateful Ludovico Sforza, joined the confederacy against Charles, whose invasion he had been the very first to encourage. Each of these confederates had his part assigned in the ensuing campaign. Ludovico Sforza undertook to besiege the duke of Orleans, who had been left at Asti° in the north of Italy with the rearguard of the French army, who wrote to the duke of Bourbon if possible to cause a band of Swiss to be enlisted for keeping his communication open with France, and to sell, mortgage, or pawn any property belonging either to the duke of Bourbon or himself for contenting such a reinforcement, whose approach was absolutely necessary for the safety of the king or his army while Ludovico° thus besieged the duke of Orleans in order to cut off Charles's retreat. It° was agreed that the Venetians° with forty thousand men should wait for the French king on the descent of the Appennines,° while Ferdinand of Aragon, nearly connected by blood with Ferdinand II the expatriated king of Sicily, should enter the Mediterranean° with a fleet and an army to disturb Charles in possession of Naples and his new conquests. To make the attack on France still more general Maximilian undertook to move from Flanders upon Champagne° at the head of an invading army, and the allies trusted that Henry VII of England could be tempted to cross the sea and land in Picardy° in renewal of the ancient quarrel between France and England.

Such was the scheme of the league of Venice which was as well calculated as any confederacy could well be for achieving the ruin of the young king of France. Like all other such plans however it depended not only upon the power which each party possessed of playing his part in the war, but upon the way in° which Fortune might determine the gale of interest in their favour and of consequence their own inclination to observe their treaty.

Charles VIII, determined° by the prospects around him to return to his native country, endeavoured however to make as light as possible of the dangers which at first he treated as impossible, and which even now he was not disposed to take into serious consideration. His nobility also, who had to press upon him a repayment or recompense of the sums which they had expended in his service, were gratified with grants of the governments of towns and provinces, of offices, and even of victuals and ammunition,° all which the king from his natural kindness and generosity granted in form as requested without exactly considering his own power of carrying his purpose into execution. The newly conquered kingdom was therefore in a state of horrible confusion: almost all the towns had sent ambassadors on Charles's first arrival submitting themselves to the French, but so little order was observed in the course of that invasion that no French troops were sent to take possession of the places which thus surrendered themselves, and now that the fortunes of the young king appeared in danger by a formidable league, were unwilling to ratify the surrender which they had made. The king however made such appointments to the principal offices of state as the time required. Gilbert of Bourbon, count of Montpensier, afterwards better known for his valour and his misfortunes under the title of the constable, was° created viceroy of Naples with good applause, and the enemy was so completely subdued that Brindisi,° Reggio, and Gallipoli° continued to declare for the unfortunate Ferdinand.[139] Stephen Vesc,° [140] whose intimate acquaintance with the prince's domestic habits had raised him to a private adviser, obtained the government of the finances and was created duke of Nola, and the Scottish lord d'Aubigny obtained the baton° of constable of Sicily: with these new officebearers Charles could not afford to leave above four thousand men, so that while the French were rendered odious by being generally preferred to the natives by having all the important offices conferred upon them, they were deprived of that strength which might have made them dreaded by the inhabitants. Still however the intrinsic terror of the natives prevailed, and even after the great superiority of forces ascertained by the league of Venice they were afraid to attempt the fulfilment° of their scheme by attacking the French army, though now reduced to something under ten thousand men, at the head of whom Charles marched from the south to the north of Italy showing not the least intention of° expecting any opposition from his enemies.[141] The towns of Siena° and Pisa, to which the French proposed restoring their liberty, were the only communities which expressed a friendly interest in the success of Charles. Men, women, and children crowded around the French king in his retreat, lavishing every species of friendship and devotion, and the king himself, moved by the fidelity of these generous communities, quitted° the direct road that he might visit them in the course of his retreat, at the risk of delaying that necessary movement, and with the certainty of diminishing his army by leaving garrisons in these two friendly towns.

Meantime the first serious opposition which was designed against him was now approaching. His enemy Count Alexander had not waited the approach of the retreating army, but it fled from one strong place to another to avoid the vengeance of the king of France. The task of attacking that monarch was committed to the Venetian° general called the marquis de Gonzaga° with an army of nearly forty thousand men. He was so much afraid of giving the French an opportunity of escape that he declined advancing to attack them in the passes of the Appennines,° and preferred waiting for them at the foot of that chain of mountains in the plains which composed the Milanese territory. The duke of Orleans lay beyond these plains occupying Novara, from which he threatened Milan and kept in check the versatile Ludovico° Sforza, who would otherwise have joined forces with Gonzaga and increased that general's army to a preponderant amount. The services of the duke of Orleans attracted the more notice on the occasion because being himself next heir to the crown he exerted himself to the utmost to prevent Charles from falling into the hands of his enemies and extricating him and his army from a situation where his extreme danger threatened the ruin of the king and his army and the great loss of France, but promised nothing save personal advantage to Orleans himself. But the French nobility and princes of the blood were remarkable at this period for their loyal devotion to the cause of the crown, and even the severe measure which the duke of Orleans had received from the Lady of Beaujeu, his confinement for several years, and the manner in which he had been stripped° of his offices, did not prevent his exerting himself to the utmost to assemble at his own expense troops sufficient to cover Charles's precarious retreat.

In the meantime that prince was beset with difficulties. His cannon,° which was the strength of his army, was with difficulty extricated from the mountain passes by a most desperate effort of the Swiss which Gonzaga was too cautious to attempt to interrupt. Thus the French army descended safe into the plains and reached the village of Fornovo,° [142] where Gonzaga had settled he would find room to avail himself of the superior number of his forces.

The vanguard of the French army was led by the maréchal° Gié, who pushed on about thirty miles and came in presence of the enemy, and skirmished with the Estradiots by whom they were roughly handled. The maréchal° Gié sent back to the king pressing him to advance to the relief of his vanguard, and in the meantime posted himself strongly on a mountain near the enemy. Charles accordingly arrived at Fornovo° and rested his army in the vicinity and in front of the enemy. The king arose and arrived° himself early the next morning. He° called repeatedly for Philip de Commynes, to whom he had entrusted some offers of treaty, upon which he communicated with the Venetian° army, but at the same time told the king plainly that he had never seen two such large armies drawn up so near each other which parted without battle. The camp of the Italians was admirably ordered, their army consisted of more than three to one, and their light horse, who, excepting that they did not wear the turban, were dressed and armed like the Turkish cavalry, were reckoned the best troops of the kind which existed in Europe, were° in great numbers and prepared to distinguish themselves. The strength of the French army consisted in a large body of Swiss infantry, who had already acquired that high character which they have since deservedly maintained. On° the morning of the engagement a herald made a species of errand concerning the delivery of a supposed Venetian° prisoner alleged to be in the French camp, but the real purpose of this messenger° was to spy in what part of the army King Charles took his station, for Gonzaga thought that the crown of the victory which he anticipated would be the death or captivity of the French king. To prevent such a calamity a band of nine French knights, who passed by the name of the nine worthies, formed an association for the defence of the king's person and wearing the same dress and fashion of armour that he himself wore.

Charles expressed himself to his troops in a manner to encourage their military enthusiasm. "How say you sirs," he said, "are you not determined to serve me well this day?" He was answered by joyful acclamations. "Do not be afraid, supposing they are ten to one. By° the grace of God I have led you as far as Naples without loss or shame, and have had the victory over every opponent. I have brought you back from Naples to this spot through every obstacle; our quarrel is good. God° will be aiding to every true Frenchman who does his best this day. Trust not in your own strength, but in that of him who has guided you hitherto and can conduct you without difficulty in safety to France." This speech was received with shouts of approbation, and both armies prepared for battle. The Venetian° general Gonzaga proceeded to execute the plan he had long ago formed by charging the French army in the rear. The Estradiots charged the rear of the French army, particularly their baggage, and forced their way amongst them (doing some damage) in towards the place where the king himself was still engaged in making knights. Some men-at-arms of the Venetians° then laid their lances in rest and charged two bodies of the French, to wit the Scottish archers forming one, and some other troops of the king's household making another. These troops met the attack boldly, and had they given way, or broken a single squadron, the cloud of Estradiots would have forced their way with their scimitars,° of which they could make dexterous use, and cut probably the whole of the Frenchmen to pieces. But perceiving that the Italian men-at-arms lost courage and did not come up to the shock of the lance, the Estradiots took to pursue some carts and baggage with the view of finding profit instead of danger, and thus lost the advantage of their numbers. The French, in combatting° at close quarters, showed all the desperate valour which is peculiar to that gallant nation, and notwithstanding the brave conduct of some individual Italian gentlemen the Venetians° in general avoided the close shock of the lance, and having either broken or thrown away that weapon they° in general shunned any encounter with the sword. The actual conflict therefore lasted only about an hour, after which the Italians desisted from an attack which was well conceived indeed, but which would have required more acquaintance with the dangers of actual war than they possessed to have succeeded.

The behaviour of the king himself was such as gave great encouragement to the martial° spirit of the soldiers. Although the person of Charles was° low in point of size, slightly formed, and not possessed of much strength, nothing could be more daring than his whole manner during the action. He was repeatedly engaged hand to hand with the enemy's men-at-arms; one of the nine worthies was made prisoner by his side, and several of his companions killed and wounded. He himself was at° one time overthrown, but his courage, says an eye-witness,[143] seemed to increase in proportion to the blows which he received, and every blow which he dealt and every word which he spoke added fire to the courage of his soldiers. The king is said to have owed his own life to the dexterity and speed of a celebrated horse which he mounted during the action.*

Although thus personally endangered at the battle of Fornovo,° Charles lost only eighty soldiers in this remarkable action, which after all was not rendered available by any improvement excepting a forced march undertaken two days after the battle by which the French succeeded in relieving the duke of Orleans at Novara into which he had thrown himself.

A treaty had been already set on foot[144] between the French and Ludovico Sforza, who was now once more inclined to change his side. The feeble character of Charles seems to have been tired with the casualties, fatigues, and toils of war, and he pushed on to Lyons, where he might once more enjoy the pleasures he was addicted to, and which he pursued so inordinately as to have serious effects upon a constitution naturally weak. Meanwhile, shortlived as he himself was to prove, he seemed destined to survive every beneficial effect of his campaign in Italy. One part of the league of Venice stipulated that Ferdinand of Aragon should assist his namesake, the dethroned king of Naples, with money and troops, the last under the command of Gonsalo de Cordova, so skilful° in military affairs that he was called by the Spaniards the great captain. We do not indeed recognise in the personal character of Gonsalo anything which seems to merit that honourable appellation. The means by which he gained his advantages over the French were rather a faithlessness which had no bounds than any superiority in skill or courage. Nevertheless he was so superior to the French in numbers, and so well acquainted with all the arts of perfidy by which advantage could be gained in such a war, that he possessed himself one by one of the various strong places which the French still occupied as relics of the conquests of Charles.

Ferdinand II had not been wanting to himself while Gonsalo reduced Calabria to his obedience. He had been received with great joy at Messina

---

* Thus mentioned particularly by Philip de Commynes: "I came and found him (the king) armed from head to foot and mounted on the finest horse I have seen in my time named *Savoy*, which was° of the province of Bresse, black, and had only one eye."[145]

and had ventured to Naples itself, where at length Gilbert count° of Montpensier, who acted as viceroy for the king of France, was compelled to yield up himself prisoner with the whole French garrison, and to stipulate that the French troops should evacuate whatever places they° occupied in the Neapolitan territory within the course of a single month. The other French commanders of detached towns and fortresses refused to fulfil terms which they° considered ignominious, and the unfortunate duke of Montpensier and all his garrison were sent to Pozzuoli,° where a malignant disorder cut him off with most of his followers. Ferdinand II during this returning tide of success suddenly died after a few days' illness. His death was greatly lamented. Such were the news with which Charles was supplied after a short residence at Orleans which had been marked by a share of idle attempts at amusements, as balls, processions, tournaments, and the like, and by a family calamity deeply calculated to affect both the king and queen, being the death of their only son Charles the dauphin.

Much hurt by this last blow, the king is said to have relinquished the licentious manner of life in which he had formerly indulged to the great injury of his health; and he also seems to have formed a resolution of renouncing the idea of a second expedition to Italy by which he was at one time occupied, and instead of busying himself with foreign wars and conquests he resolved to attend to the internal tranquillity° of his dominions and to revive several of those useful institutions which had been suffered to fall into neglect during his absence in Italy.

His family distresses had induced the king to retire with his wife to the castle of Amboise upon the Loire, where he proposed to erect a stately palace, and had brought with him excellent Italian artists, tailors° namely and painters, in order to adorn° the apartments.° Neither had he totally laid aside the scheme of reconquering Naples, and promised himself that he would take better care for the preservation of his conquests upon another occasion than upon the last. While these great plans to be executed at home and abroad were agitated in the king's mind the time was° approaching which was to put an end to his earthly labours.

On 7 April 1498 he was engaged in handing the queen to a place from which she might view a game at tennis played in the dry ditch of the castle. The spot to which they were going was a mean, ruinous, and dirty gallery only accidentally used for the present purpose. In entering this singular place the king struck his head against the entry, which was too low, yet not so as to prevent his looking upon the tennis players with some attention. The effects of the blow however, or of some internal complaint of a more important nature, were fatal. About two hours after mid-day he fell backwards, and was only twice or three times heard to speak intelligibly, and finally died in that poor chamber to the great regret of his friends and servants.

Charles VIII was a monarch of a mean appearance in person, except his eyes which were fine. "A little man he was of body," says Commynes, "and no great extent of understanding, but never did there exist a more kindly disposed creature."[146] Some unusual marks of sorrow were shown by those about his person. The queen (Anne of Bretagne) remained abandoned to grief, refusing to stir from a corner of her apartment° or to taste meat for two days. His courtiers were profuse in their lamentations.° No more magnificent obsequies were ever performed for a prince, and it is constantly reported that two members of his household actually died of grief for the loss of their master, a loss the more untimely as he had not attained his twenty-eighth year.

Two sons which he had by his queen Anne of Bretagne had died in infancy. The direct line of Philip Valois° was therefore extinguished in the person of this young king, after having sat on the throne of France during the reign of seven kings, and for the period of one hundred and seventy years. The collateral° branch of Orleans therefore succeeded to the throne in the person of Louis, grandson of the first duke of Orleans assassinated° in the rue Berbette.

Chapter 8

By ancient custom the coronation of each new monarch, which was supposed to be a religious recognition of his right of sovereignty, was dispatched as soon° as possible after his succession had taken place. That of Louis XII took place on 27 May 1498, and certainly the ceremonial was never applied to a prince of whom greater hopes were entertained, and indeed the virtues of the new monarch, his liberality particularly, disinterestedness, and clemency, exceeded what friends and enemies had even been led to expect at his hand. He was in the flower of manhood, being just thirty-six years of age, and trained in the school of adversity, where he had not only learned to value those who had shown themselves his true friends but also the more difficult lesson of forgiving his enemies. If he remembered the sufferings of his youth at all it was only to show that he had pardoned those who were the authors of them. Perhaps it is necessary that I at least should recall to your memory some of the hard measure which he had sustained during youth, that we may judge of the effort which was necessary to forget and to forgive it. In early youth Louis duke of Orleans had been the constant object of jealousy and restraint to his formidable predecessor Louis XI, who could not forget that the young prince was next heir to the kingdom on the failure of his own son Charles, the weakness of whose constitution might have tempted such a man as Louis XI to have laid him out of his way; besides the tyrant compelled his young kinsman to marry his own eldest daughter the princess Joan, amiable and excellent in her disposition, but so plain in her person as to be the object of disgust rather than attachment to the young prince, and so deformed as° not to be supposed capable of bearing children, so that the tyrannical marriage between her and the young duke might be reckoned upon by Louis XI as a sure mode of putting an end to the house of Orleans, of which this present representative was the last in existence. To all the freaks and veracious suspicions of the old tyrant, Louis of Orleans had submitted with patience, and behaved well and kindly even to his wife the princess Joan, although the forcing upon him the acceptance of her hand could be only considered as the most hateful and injurious act of oppression. At the death of Louis XI the duke of Orleans, as we have already mentioned, was naturally and justly disposed to insist upon his own natural right to govern the kingdom during Charles VIII's minority in preference to that of his sister-in-law the Lady of Beaujeu. We have seen how he failed in this struggle, and how in the ambitious claim which he set up for assuring to Anne of Bretagne her free choice of a husband, not doubtless without the hope that his own disagreeable and ill-assorted alliance might be broken by a divorce and he himself allowed a chance of competing for the hand of the witty and accomplished Anne of Bretagne instead of being bound to the unfortunate Joan, who had indeed the disposition of a saint but by whom he had no right to expect any family. Being incautious enough to take arms in the civil war of Bretagne Louis XII was made prisoner in the battle of St Aubin Cormier, in consequence of which he was for several years detained a captive in different state prisons by order of the Lady of Beaujeu.

It is true that after that princess gave up the regency he had no subject of complaint which could be removed by the kindness and confidence of King Charles, whom he served faithfully, and by whom he was rewarded with employment and confidence. But before that period his usage during the reign of Louis XI and the regency of his daughter Anne in the eyes of most men of the period seemed to run up an account° of grievances which his accession to the crown gave the young king the means of visiting upon those who had been the cause of them. But when this was pointed out to him by some of the usual mischief-makers who are found about courts, he answered with a noble sentiment which has almost passed° into a proverb from the sense and wisdom which it contains: "It does not become," he said, "a king of France to remember the quarrels of a duke of Orleans." On this generous maxim he regulated his whole conduct. All the ministers, officers, and magistrates employed under his predecessor were continued under his reign, and the duke and duchess of Bourbon having an only daughter whom they meant to marry with Charles count of Montpensier, whose father Gilbert died in Italy and who afterwards became himself the unfortunate constable of Bourbon, the king aided their views by liberally renouncing his own interest and thereby constituting the bride the heiress of the house of Bourbon.

The frank generosity with which the king served and obliged persons who in former days might have been termed his own personal enemies did not arise from timidity or want of spirit. He carried through several reformations both in the military discipline, in the courts of justice, and in the university; all which showed that when the public interest was concerned defaulters had no reason to hope for lenity from the young prince, who forgot indeed his own injuries but remembered and punished such as had been sustained by the nation. Neither was Louis XII insensible to his own interest when it could be pursued with due attention to that of the kingdom.

It was natural for example that, since the church of Rome allowed parties to be released by a divorce from matrimonial fetters so ill assorted as those which bound him now for nearly twenty years to the princess Joan, he° should be desirous to get rid of an alliance which had no promise either of happiness to himself or of advantage to the country. Accordingly he prosecuted a suit for divorce before the pope Alexander VI, whose desire to oblige the king of France had increased prodigiously since Charles

VIII had shown the power of such a monarch interfering with a strong hand in the affairs of Italy. On the other hand Joan, remarkable for her mildness and patience, made no more obstinate defence than seemed necessary to vindicate the character of her father who had made the match, and a sentence of divorce in all the form was pronounced between the king and queen of France.[147] The queen, now again become the princess Joan, bade adieu to all mortal dignities, and retired into a convent which she herself founded, and where she lived and died in a state more suited to her temper and feelings than that of grandeur and business in which her father desired to maintain her.

The first part of Louis's desire being thus accomplished, he was naturally desirous to confer his liberated hand where the gift might promise happiness to himself and advantage to the kingdom. The queen dowager Anne of Bretagne had since the death of her husband Charles VIII retired to her own patrimonial dominions of Bretagne, and proceeded to exercise the striking of golden money, the granting letters of nobility, and others of the higher rights of sovereignty which some jurists thought above the power even of a great crown vassal. At any rate the practice° intimated that if Anne of Bretagne should form a second marriage out of France she would be as little disposed to hold her coronet as dependant on the crown in these particulars than her father or any of her ancestors. There was therefore a great risk that by any second marriage of this lady all the old quarrels about Bretagne might be revived and that great fief again torn from the kingdom of France, to which in Charles VIII's reign it had been so happily united. To prevent the risk of a calamity which could not but have had its peculiar dangers Louis XII resolved himself to become suitor of the queen dowager. In some degree his doing so was a renewal of an old attachment which had subsisted between them as long as before her first marriage and while she was engaged in war with the regency of France. Louis of Orleans had thrown himself into her army with the spirit of an ancient knight errant, and had he then succeeded in breaking the matrimonial fetters imposed upon him by Louis XI it was thought that the duke, happy in a handsome person and amiable disposition, besides his gallant services as her champion, might very likely have been distinguished by the choice of this great heiress among many suitors who pretended to her hand. On his part the wish to obtain her favour was in every degree natural, for not only would he° have obtained with her hand her inheritance of Bretagne, but also the person of the young lady, unexceptionable in face and form except a slight lameness which was scarce visible when she walked. If there really was so much inclination on both sides to a match it was entirely ended by the battle of St Aubin Cormier, in which the duke of Orleans was made prisoner and continued so for several years, while first Maximilian the archduke married Anne of Bretagne by proxy, and secondly King Charles VIII became actually her husband. This inclination to each other in their younger days was easily revived and formed an

introduction which suited to an union which had points of recommenda-
tion to both parties.°

Immediately on having obtained his divorce Louis set off for Bretagne
and had the art to renew the marriage treaty which had so many years ago
been agitated between them, and shortly after brought back to Paris the
queen dowager, once more converted into the reigning queen, and whose
hereditary territory of Bretagne was now once more united to the kingdom of France.

After the adjustment of this matter, most interesting to him certainly,
both in a domestic capacity and in his political character, Louis had nothing so much at heart as the resuming that invasion of Italy which his predecessor Charles VIII's character and example had shown might be easily
accomplished, although he might have also learned from the same example how easily the fruits of such an adventure might be lost as soon as they
were gained.

When° the king and queen entered into Paris in solemn procession,
Louis XII besides his other titles solemnly laid claim to the two Sicilies
and Jerusalem, with the duchies of Milan and Bretagne. Naples, the Sicilies, and Jerusalem he claimed as heir of the house of Anjou; the duchy
of Milan as representing his own grandmother Valentina; and Bretagne as
husband of the lady whose inheritance it was. Having thus shown his right
to these Italian possessions he made peace, or confirmed it, with all the
powers on the western side of the Alps, and prepared to invade Italy with
an army of twenty thousand men. His principal minister was the cardinal
George d'Amboise, whom the pope appointed legate of France. He had
been long a friend and intimate of the duke of Orleans, and now shared in
his translation from the state of a private subject to that of kingly power.
King Louis in attempting this great conquest had seen the necessity of
employing other forces than his own, and he had formed several alliances
in Italy, a course of policy almost totally neglected by Charles VIII when
he first set out on so dangerous an expedition.

Thus Louis agreed to divide the duchy of Milan, allowing the republic
for their portion the country beyond the river Adda. The pope also entered into the king of France's views, which had been intimated by measures taken on both sides to gratify each other. Thus Pope Alexander's
most earnest desire was the aggrandisement of his favourite natural son,
the celebrated Cæsar Borgia. This fiery-tempered and ambitious young
man his father, having of course the power of promoting him in the
church, had raised with indecent speed to the rank of a cardinal, but Borgia was dissatisfied with this destination and wished to enter into the line
of temporal preferments. In order to accomplish this he became one of
the commissioners° to whom the matter of the king of France's divorce
was entrusted° as a papal delegate. In reward of his services in that affair
the king° created him duke of Valentinois° and gave him the power of personal dignity and temporal wealth.

The pope and Louis XII, being thus bound together by the exchange of mutual good offices, were prepared to second each other's designs; and to narrate briefly a number of events which had too little consequence to AUGUST claim a detailed narration, the king of France made a rapid conquest of 1499 the whole duchy of Milan, into which he made a public entry,[148] and took° the duchy into possession as° the inheritance of his grandmother Valentina.

The usurper Sforza, without means of contending with so large an army, retired into Germany, where he resided at Innsbruck.° But when in the end of the year Louis had returned to France and fixed his court at Lyons, Sforza imagined he saw an opportunity as he conceived of regaining the duchy of Milan. For some time it appeared as if he had been right in his calculation. The places which had been speedily occupied by the French were for a time either through treachery or violence as suddenly recovered by Sforza. This adventurer however had run his race and was now near destruction. The Swiss in his army, finding themselves paid somewhat irregularly, a point upon which they were always very jealous, entered into a formal mutiny, seized upon the person of Sforza disguised as a common soldier,[149] and delivered him up to Robert Stuart lord d'Aubigny, by whom he was sent close prisoner to Louis residing as we have said at Lyons. The opinion as to this man's crimes was so black that the French king was rather applauded for the severity with which he treated him. Louis refused to see a man whose life had been marked with acts of inhumanity, falsehood,° and treachery. He was sent, it was said, to the castle of Loches, one of the state prisons of Louis XI, and was for years the inhabitant of one of the iron cages invented by that singular monarch;[150] and although this severity was at length somewhat mitigated, yet the unfortunate prisoner never obtained his liberty, nor restitution of anything that he had lost.

Meantime while the north of Italy was thus agitated by the French arms they were no less formidable in the southern part of that peninsula. The Neapolitan territory had fallen into the hands of Charles VIII upon his invasion of that country, but had been recovered with no less rapidity by the troops sent thither under Gonsalo de Cordova belonging to the king of Aragon, and by the native insurgents who espoused the cause of the young king Frederick° of Naples. The French, assaulted by the troops of both descriptions, and invaded at the same time by a contagious disorder resembling the pestilence, suffered so much by war and by disease that out of five or six thousand Swiss and Frenchmen left by King Charles for the security of his conquests of Naples and its territories it was not reckoned that fifteen hundred ever again beheld their native country.

In the meantime the downfall of Ludovico° Sforza, his captivity, and that of his brother the cardinal Ascanio, again gave the French through Italy a weight in public opinion which would, it was imagined, soon restore to Louis XII the conquests of his predecessor Charles VIII. The king committed however a very great political error in his mode of prosecuting the Neapolitan campaign.

I have to recall to your recollection that of the lawfully reigning house of Naples three kings had died within a remarkably short space of time. The last of these was King Frederick, who was much praised by the Italian historians who have supposed him capable of gaining back his kingdom from the French as reckoning on the assistance of Gonsalo de Cordova and the Spanish arms which had been sent apparently to his assistance by his relation and ally Ferdinand of Aragon called the Catholic, and well deserving the name of the perfidious if history had devised an epithet for him suitable to his demerits. We have already remarked his ungenerous and treacherous conduct towards his allies of Naples, for whose assistance Gonsalo de Cordova had been sent to the Neapolitan dominions, but whom he lost no opportunity of betraying and plundering. In the beginning of the sixteenth century Ferdinand the Catholic perceived the difficulty, or impossibility, of succeeding in his plans of conquering Naples, if at the same time he had to dispute with the arms of the French, which besides conquering the duchy of Milan were now advancing with a large, and in the general opinion an invincible, army under the command of D'Aubigny° and other experienced commanders, as well as the very flower of the chivalry of France, who thought themselves equal to any conquests, and would certainly have found few tasks to which they were incompetent. The Spanish monarch at least judged it wiser to agree with the French upon the division of the spoil in question than to dispute with him the whole prize. He opened accordingly a negotiation with Louis XII, and while he sent into Sicily six hundred men-at-arms, five thousand infantry, and a naval force to scour the coasts and take the sea-ports of that island, he proposed to the French king a division of the territory between them, to which neither of them, but certainly not Ferdinand at least, had any lawful right. The terms of this treaty[151] bore that the French king should have the city of Naples, the province of Lavoro,° and that of Abruzzi,° in virtue of which possessions he should bear the title of king of Naples and Jerusalem. On the other hand the Spaniard provided° for himself the territories of Apulia and Calabria, with the title of duke of the latter province. Louis XII accepted this treaty certainly without duly estimating his own strength, and moved his army southwards in order to take possession of his share of the Neapolitan territory. In the meantime both the French and Spanish generals assigned as the cause of their joint movements an agreement between Ferdinand the Catholic and Louis of France for an alliance together against the Turks, but in fact they were for the purpose of executing the treaty of division. Frederick° therefore, the young king of Naples, took a strong position at St Germano, to defend the entrance of his kingdom, reckoning it may be supposed on the strength of his ally the great captain, whose treachery he was not then aware of. When the treaty between the French and the Spaniards began to take air, the unfortunate prince, who had been a victim on both sides, renounced the hope of further defence,° and resolved to submit himself to the clemency of Louis, who at least had acted with the candour of an open enemy while Ferdinand the Catholic had displayed the perfidy of a pretended friend. For this purpose Frederick° retreated first to Naples, and there obtained a safe conduct to France, where the king very generously assigned him an honourable retreat together with a pension of thirty thousand crowns a year, the payment of which was continued even after the French were expelled from every part of the Neapolitan territories. The great captain by his military prowess, or political contrivances, speedily took possession of Apulia and Calabria, being his master's portion of the spoil. Otranto° was the last strong place which resisted, in which Frederick° of Naples had deposited the young duke of Calabria his eldest son. The governor of this place, the count de Potenza, to whom the king had given special instructions concerning this boy's safety, found himself compelled to put him into the hands of Gonsalo de Cordova, having first taken that general's oath upon a consecrated host that nothing should be attempted against the prince's personal freedom, notwithstanding of which solemn stipulation the young Ferdinand was sent a close prisoner to the king of Aragon, and though not severely treated or kept a close captive, was never able to attain possession of his liberty. In him became extinct the Aragonese line of Neapolitan kings, the perusal of whose lamentable story is one of the most remarkable with which history makes° us acquainted.

1502[152]

A cause of quarrel was not long in arriving between the French and their allies the Spaniards, respecting their portions of the kingdom of Naples. A small district[153] not° remarkable for the richness of its soil came to be in debate between them as particularly well situated for collecting the duty levied upon corn. After some partial disputes and actions the king of France, regretting that he had ever embarrassed himself with such companions in his Neapolitan spoils, now resolved to get rid of them before that they should have taken root in their new possessions. Gaspar de Coligny° therefore with some other French lords surprised about four hundred Spaniards near the place of Cerignola.° The relics of the skirmish escaped into Canosa, a strong place abundantly supplied with victuals and garrisoned with twelve hundred Spaniards of good reputation. The French nevertheless besieged the place and made a practicable breach which they attempted to storm, and with an appearance of success. But as the Spaniards began to give way before the storming party they were rallied by one of their commanders called Peralta. He rushed with his drawn sword, calling out in a voice like thunder reproaches which° his countrymen were sensible to. "Ah! heretic dogs!" he exclaimed, "well have you made it visible, since your courage has fallen with these walls, that you come of the blood of the Moors and are not descended from the true native Spaniards. Let us make a rampart of our bodies, and these will prove a bulwark which is not liable to be stormed." The repeated efforts of the French against this brave man were in vain; but at length Peralta saw that further resistance would provoke the revenge of the French and cost his gallant comrades their lives. The French commander, being the Scottish man D'Aubigny,° gave hostages for the sure and faithful observance of the articles granted, but Gonsalo, who was of so different a disposition, would willingly have revenged the loss sustained in the defence by putting to death the hostages who had been granted for the preservation of their own countrymen. Other actions took place between the French and Spaniards who combatted° in Italy until the French under the duke of Nemours, the sieur d'Aubigny° and other commanders of eminence, compelled the great captain to retreat into the city of Barletta, where want of ammunition° and money must have forced him to surrender had the siege been pressed by the chief part of the French army. Failing however to observe the advantages within their reach, the duke of Nemours fell into the great mistake of suffering an army large enough to have finished the war at a single blow to be destroyed in detail by distant and petty enterprises. It would be too long to enter into the minute actions upon which the success of the campaign for a time fluctuated and at length turned against the French.

In 1503 the troops of Louis had still the superiority when a new personage entered the field as a negotiator between the kings of France and Spain. This was the archduke Philip, son of the emperor Maximilian, who having married Joanna, the daughter of Ferdinand the Catholic and his wife Isabella, being° desirous of visiting his native dominions of the Low Countries was hospitably permitted to pass through the kingdom of France and treated° with the utmost kindness by Louis XII, who met him at Lyons and gratified him by a most hospitable reception. On this occasion, namely the meeting of the king of France and the archduke Philip in 1503, Philip acting as plenipotentiary for his father-in-law entered into a treaty concerning the affairs of Naples, the object of which seemed to be a perpetual close of the Neapolitan war. The treaty was very brief, and seemingly perfectly intelligible. Both consented to an immediate cessation of arms. Each prince was to have possession generally of such provinces as had been originally destined to him, while such districts as were disputed should for the time be sequestered in the hands of the archduke Philip as a neutral person. The generals on both sides swore solemnly to obey the conditions, on pain of being excommunicated, and both behaved according to the character of their nation. The duke of Nemours immediately offered to fulfil° the treaty as knowing the honour and fidelity of his master; but on the other hand his most Catholic majesty chicaned upon every occasion on the terms of the treaty, and Gonsalo his great captain would not accomplish it while there remained any possible doubt or shadow of a doubt which could be produced in the treaty.

Thus he found no extreme difficulty in availing himself of the frankness of the French, and taking advantage of the retreat of Nemours while he himself refused to comply in abandoning any of the country which he

ought to have ceded, and having spun out the time till he received a large
reinforcement of German troops with which he attacked the enemy defeated the French twice, in the last of which° actions the duke of Nemours
was killed, and made himself master of the city of Naples, which during
this war was so often transferred° from one power to another.

When the archduke Philip heard of the base treachery, for° which he
conceived himself in some degree responsible, he returned back from
Savoy (where the advice found him) again to put himself in the hands of
King Louis as hostage for his father-in-law's good faith. To his generous
proposals Louis answered with the memorable words: "If," said he, "your
father-in-law has been guilty of perfidy I will not resemble him; and I am
infinitely more happy in the loss of a kingdom which I know how to reconquer, than to have stained my honour which I could never retrieve."
With these sentiments, which do his memory the greatest honour, Louis
XII, generously despising any revenge which might light upon an innocent head, confined his efforts to revenging himself as far as possible upon
Ferdinand the Catholic who was really guilty.

Accordingly he exerted himself by assembling all the forces in his
power for the conquest of Italy, a tempting object which seemed always
during the reigns of Charles VIII and himself to float before the eyes and
within the grasp of the French nation, which however had never been
able to attain perfect or secure possession of it.

Considering the strength and military character of the French people,
the prudence also of Louis XII who was rigorous in the wise administration of such funds as he possessed, it required no great wealth to prosecute
the campaign of Italy with every reasonable hope of success. Twenty, or
five-and-twenty, thousand men were adequate to a full conquest of Milan,
Naples, and Calabria. The bands of ordonnance, being regularly trained
and disciplined, could easily supply this bulky part of the infantry. The
Swiss were at all times willing to act in the character of mercenary allies to
any belligerent power, and were in general partial to the French service,
though occasions of disagreement did certainly now and then occur.

The cavalry or men-at-arms were emulously supplied by the French
noblesse, who contended with each other for the glory of serving the king
in the capacity of volunteers. A° force therefore of twenty, or five-and-
twenty, thousand men was easily levied by the king of France, but the difficulty of the conquest lay in contending with the Spanish troops, who
were veterans inured to war, and with their great general Gonsalo de Cordova, who, with a knowledge of military affairs equal in science to any
general who ever lived, was totally emancipated from every obligation of
faith and honour which military men are generally supposed to regard
with peculiar reverence. Accordingly the utmost efforts of Louis XII were
not able to turn the tide of conquest against the Spaniards, while the death
successively of Pope Alexander VI and his successor led to the° accession of
Julius II, greatly to the mortification of the cardinal of Amboise who ex-

pected himself to be raised to the papacy. The character of Julius, though not° so profligate as that of Alexander, was not very consistent with the sacred duties of the pope. He was a bold, ambitious, and courageous man, more suited for a soldier than a priest, and, determined against the French interest, he did all that he could to deprive them of what little power they retained in Italy, and to prevent their regaining it more he secured to the Spanish an ascendance in the council of the petty sovereigns and republics of Italy, which during his whole papacy he kept constantly embroiled. These combinations against France were attended with such a succession of miscarriages on the side of Italy that Louis XII's health became affected by disappointment and mortification. The king became ill[154] to such a degree that his death was apprehended both by his family and his subjects, which led to a circumstance strongly illustrative of the vindictive character of Queen Anne of Bretagne to which we have formerly alluded. Being residing at Blois during the time of the king's illness in 1504, the queen, who beheld the probability of her being again reduced to the situation of a barren dowager, resolved to provide against the evil day by collecting together and removing to Nantes,° the capital of her own principality of Bretagne, such valuables as were at present in her possession. Various rich effects were accordingly embarked in boats upon the river Loire. These were met by the maréchal° de Gié, who took it upon him to stop the further procedure of the embarcation, not thinking it proper that the queen should be permitted to carry wealth out of the kingdom, and risking the very probable chance of offending her rather than permitting such an attempt to be carried into effect. Brantôme has given a curious picture of his own ideas and the queen's when he tells the vengeance which Queen Anne exacted for this affront. The recovery of her husband Louis, who was dotingly fond of her, placed the life of the supposed culprit within her power, but she did not choose° a mode of revenge which would have been so speedily terminated. She prosecuted Gié, notwithstanding the public services by which he had gained the favour of Louis and his predecessors, until she had deprived him of every farthing of money which he had in his possession, reduced him to the extreme of poverty, had him condemned to a rigorous imprisonment, and finally broke his heart. This ill-used gentleman was several years detained a prisoner in the castle of Dreux.[155] He died in 1513 survived by his persecutress only a few months, so well did she know how to concentrate and prolong the effects of her vengeance, and such being her title to such epithets as Brantôme heaps upon her[156] as the real mother of the poor, the comfort of nobility, the refuge of ladies, damsels, and young maidens of good family, the support of men distinguished by learning or by worth, affectionate to her servants, very devout and religious, the foundress of several devotional establishments, not to mention other praises equally inconsistent with her vindictive persecution of the maréchal° Gié, for what could at worst only be termed a disrespectful excess of zeal in his public duty.

Several deaths about this time effected considerable changes in the system of Europe, removing those who had been for a long time active upon the busy scene and introducing other personages who represented the same parts with a total change of principle as well as actors.

One of these princes indeed for some time had little to do upon the painful stage where he had already sustained the most humiliating reverses. This was Frederick° king of Naples, who had been subsisted by the bounty of Louis XII until his death at Tours in autumn 1504, when the last spark of the Neapolitan family of Aragon became extinct in his person. The wife of Ferdinand,° Isabella, who had held the kingdom of Castile in her own right, died soon afterwards, by which event Ferdinand the Catholic was deprived of all concern in the government of the kingdom where his administrator had been so long absolute. The son-in-law of Ferdinand and Isabella, inheritor of both their dominions, was that Archduke Philip whom we have repeatedly mentioned, and who was called for distinction sake Philip the Handsome. Philip was wedded to Joanna, only daughter and indeed only child of Ferdinand and Isabella, a woman of a mind so weak as amounted almost to insanity. She was fond of her handsome husband, but to such an imprudent degree as produced a peevish jealousy rather than affection; and she bore her husband two sons, one of them (the eldest) being that Charles V, who, besides succeeding his grandfather Maximilian in the empire of Germany, came also to the possession of those Spanish dominions which had been the territories of his grandmother Mary of Burgundy, the daughter and heiress of Charles the Bold. The archduke Philip agreed to reside with his wife's parents for some time in order to fit himself in process of time to become king of Castile, Aragon, and those other parts of Spain in which he was one day destined to be a ruler. Being of a gay, pleasure-loving disposition, the young prince soon tired of the grave manners of the Spanish people, the tormenting jealousy of his crazy queen Joanna, and the severe surveillance of his father-in-law° Ferdinand; he therefore, in order to be rid of these domestic annoyances, was resolved to set out for his Flemish dominions, where he hoped to reside more at his ease. In passing through France the archduke Philip formed that alliance in his father-in-law's name which the faithless Ferdinand treated afterwards with such perfidious disregard. The father therefore and son-in-law were upon very indifferent terms, which was rendered still worse by the death of Isabella. This wise princess, respecting the talents, though she must have hated the morals, of her husband Ferdinand, was desirous to secure to him a share in the regency of her kingdom of Castile, of which he had been so long the administrator. On the other hand the natives of Castile were desirous that the old king, who endeavoured to secure the power which he had formerly enjoyed without either gaining popularity or respect, should be excluded from the government. They formed leagues among themselves and began to levy their vassals. The court of Ferdinand was deserted except by two or three noblemen

A.D. 1504 *(margin)*

and statesmen, while the ambassadors who maintained the interest of the archduke Philip were generally patronised and respected. At length the archduke Philip and his wife Joanna were admitted as king and queen of Castile by the Cortes° of the kingdom, a very few months[157] after which Philip himself unexpectedly died. This unexpected event awakened all the parties in the kingdom and all the disputes which had been so lately lulled to rest by the decision adopted. No doubt in most cases there must have been an immediate remedy, for the princess Joanna, through whom her deceased husband had succeeded to the office of king, must have resumed that of queen as her own sole property, it being her just right of inheritance, but her unfortunate weakness of mind had increased so much that she had become absolutely incapable of anything like regal duties. She kept her eyes fixed on the dead body of her husband, in vain expecting that he was to return to life because in some monkish tradition she had heard of a king who did revive, or was to revive, after being in an apparent state of death for fourteen years. This frenzy, which broke forth in a variety of singular instances, rendered the unfortunate patient totally incapable of managing the affairs of a kingdom like Castile, and of course, her eldest son being an infant, the question only remained whether the estates of the kingdom ought to prefer to the management of its affairs Ferdinand, with whose experience they were well acquainted, or Maximilian, who had no knowledge of Spanish affairs, had no disposable quantity of troops or of treasure, and was a stranger to Castile and its laws. The weighty influence of Cardinal Ximenes, at that time archbishop of Toledo, and one of the most able statesmen perhaps that ever lived, determined the Cortes in favour of Ferdinand the Catholic who thus obtained the security of the regency in his person after so many intrigues and so much dispute.

However great his faults as a treacherous and uncertain monarch, he showed himself capable of amending them upon conviction of their being detrimental to his interest. Although therefore he retained that love of power which had long been his principal characteristic, he did not again exercise his authority with rash violence, nor did he attempt by any vindictive courses to call up an impolitic recollection of the debates which had taken place concerning his admission to the regency. The people on the other hand soon repaid the care° of the king for their safety with the attachment which was natural, and the Spaniards at least were as happy during the latter part of this prince's government as when he ruled before in the character of sovereign.

Before matters were thus amicably settled King Ferdinand had formed a new union, hoping that the progeny of such might assist him in gratifying his resentment against his son-in-law the archduke Philip.° The lady whom he married was a French princess, Germaine° de Foix, a daughter of the viscount de Narbonne and of Mary, sister of the ruling king Louis XII. It was this connection which made him willing to enter into the treaty of division of the Neapolitan territories between Louis XII and

A.D. himself. He thought of making a will in which he was to leave Prince
1515 Ferdinand, his grandson, regent° of his Spanish dominions; but the arguments of the archbishop Ximenes prevailed° on him to consider that such
a will would have been in fact a legacy of civil war to the two brothers,
and accordingly he desisted from his purpose.

A.D.   In this year Ferdinand had taken the precaution of naming Ximenes the
1516 regent of Castile. This singular man united in his person the inflexibility of
mind and severity of character peculiar to the monastic profession with
the intrepidity, firmness of resolution, promptness° of decision, and sagacity
proper to those who have merited the title of great statesmen.

      Having thus provided in a most effectual manner for the government of
his dominions Ferdinand the Catholic, remarkable for his total contempt
3 and disregard of the good faith and obligation of treaties, began to break
JANUARY up in health, and died. He was succeeded in his Spanish dominions of
1516 Castile and Aragon by his grandson,° afterwards the well-known Charles V,
who, residing among his Flemish subjects at Brussels, determined even
without waiting the consent of the Cortes to assume the title of king.
Ximenes would° have remonstrated against such an innovation, but receiving orders positively to enforce his commands he took his measures without farther question. When the grandees of the kingdom began to enquire
into the powers by which the cardinal thus dictated the king's will to
them, he led them to a balcony from which they beheld upon the parade
a large body of troops flanked by a strong and well-appointed train of artillery. "These,° my lords, are the powers which I have received from his
Catholic majesty; with these I have governed Castile, and with them I will
govern it until the king, your master and mine, shall come in person to
take possession of his dominions."[158] A speech so bold and decisive brought
the controversy to a crisis. The nobles, unless they had been prepared to go
the length of the most obstinate resistance, were compelled to submission,
which was the course they adopted.

      Meantime ere returning to the wars of Italy we have a few words to say
concerning the character and disposition of Charles V, upon observing
which all useful study of French history must necessarily be formed.

      The education of this highly destined prince, together with the man-
agement of his Flemish dominions, was chiefly entrusted° to William de
Croy, lord of Chièvres, who appears to have discharged the duty entrusted
to him with the greatest industry and talent, and early taught him those
principles upon which his own and other nations had formed their various constitutions. On the other hand Chièvres bred and encouraged° in
his royal pupil a partiality in favour of his countrymen the Flemings,
which was sure to be ungracious to his Spanish subjects as they° differed so
much from those in the Low Countries in manners, in customs, and in
constitution. Charles from habit, and from° familiarity with the Flemish
language and his subjects of that country, was partial to them in every respect, and without intending it raised a general prepossession against himself among the subjects of the two crowns of Castile and Aragon. Chièvres°

was also to blame in this; he was unfortunately a man whose avarice distinguished him as much as his more honourable qualities, and yielding himself to the temptation of making the wealth of his master's Spanish dominions available to his own gratification he was obliged to encourage the other Flemish councillors and favourites in the same practices. Thus every office, preferment, and dignity in Spain became venal, and was disposed of to that person who offered the largest bribe to the Flemish minister who had enough of power to procure the grant. This mode of conducting public business was extremely disgusting to the high-spirited Spaniards, who were at this time accustomed to rest their national government less upon the king than upon the Cortes or national representatives who possessed in many respects the power of controlling them. Prejudices therefore began to exist between Charles V and his Spanish subjects, which the young king was not guilty of deserving, although his ministers of the Low Countries certainly gave occasion° for these discontents, reproaches, and suspicions. Meantime the Reformation suddenly arose owing to the people in general having become completely sensible of the errors and extravagance of the positions concerning the power of the Roman church, which was increased° from age to age as the clergy found new means of extending their exactions. The celebrated Luther arose, a man of a zealous temper and somewhat tinged with a species of fanaticism, but clear-headed, uncompromising, and bold in the extreme, who found no difficulty in expressing himself readily on any subject. His arguments were too well adapted to the popular ear, that (however audacious) they should fall to the ground. The power, the wealth, and the exorbitant claims of churchmen had been long the subject of odium and complaint, and men were long prepared to embrace Luther's opinion, although stated in language which not long since must have been esteemed nearly blasphemous. Besides,° at this moment an art had been discovered of rendering easy the multiplication and dispersion of knowledge by printing. A stream of instruction was thus provided. The public rushed to quench their thirst with an eagerness which could now be amply gratified, and under such circumstances considerable parts of Germany began to assume the new doctrines as a rule of faith which might otherwise have fallen aside as a daring heresy. Another species of reformation began to arise in Switzerland. This did not differ from that of Luther in the religious opinions, but in that of church government. Zwinglius and Calvin rejected the system of hierarchy which Luther had left unassailed while he broke out in invectives against the doctrinal points of the Catholic faith. In poor countries especially, the Calvinistic style of reformation was most popular because the simplicity and poverty of the state was not in such cases insulted by the titles, the exorbitant wealth, and the high rank assumed by the clergy. Such were the new and extraordinary doctrines which arose in the beginning of the sixteenth century and increased so fast within the next quarter of a century that they became ruling principles by which many thousands were willing to lay down their lives in the field of battle or at the stake.

Meantime it appeared that both in religion and politics some great changes were about to take place. In war the invention of gunpowder had at length greatly superseded° not only the use of the bow and arrow but the habit of carrying cumbrous defensive armour, which while it was but an imperfect protection against musket° balls fatigued and jaded both the horses and the rider in those cavalry who yet retained it. New rules were also laid down for the attack and defence of fortified places, and the use of artillery becoming almost general already formed perhaps the principal feature in modern warfare.

But what seemed yet more indicative of some important change in the state of Europe was the existence in the same age of a set of young and fiery sovereigns likely to be influenced by the various changes in religion, politics, or war which occurred° in their time, and to make such the pretences of war among themselves, and conquests at each other's expense. These sovereigns possessed different degrees of power, but that all of them were of the first rank of importance is sufficiently proved by the catalogue. Charles V possessed by far the largest territory of the sovereigns of his time, and if wealth consisted in the quantity of the precious° metals he was also the richest potentate. For the new world discovered under the auspices of Ferdinand and Isabella poured all its immense mass of treasure into the Spanish dominions inherited by their representative. In point of power this mighty sovereign could also dispose of the strength of the German empire, which although unwieldy was equally formidable from its weight and its numbers. The death of Louis of France soon placed that kingdom in the hands of Francis I, a young prince who might be aptly termed the fairest model of the national character, both in its strong and weak points. A gay and fiery temper was joined to a love of the fine arts, and a desire of glory, a love of war, and an ambition of conquest were often indulged by him to the point of ruinous rashness, and we are too often called upon to observe a profligate love of pleasure and an indulgence in self-gratification remarkable for blinding the judgement and hardening the heart of those who subject themselves to its control. About the same time appeared upon the scene the young king of England Henry VIII, remarkable for uniting in his person the rival claims of the houses of York and Lancaster, whose wars had so long laid his kingdom in blood. His dominions, nearly as compact as those of Francis, were not much inferior in riches to the territories of Charles V, if industry be preferable (as is generally allowed) to the tributes of gold and diamond mines. Of these three sovereigns Charles and Francis contended with each other for the good graces of Henry VIII, who, desirous of fame, was not unwilling to mingle in the quarrel which was about to take place betwixt his two neighbours, but had not as yet resolved which side he would adopt. Europe however, it must again be noticed, did not present this singular picture until the death of Louis XII placed Francis I upon the throne of France. Before this period we have some remarkable events to notice.

Chapter 9 ❧

In this year Ferdinand the Catholic visited his Neapolitan territory with the purpose of regulating his affairs, which from the breach of so many treaties had now given him a decided superiority over the power of France. The real purpose of his visit however was to observe more closely the situation and behaviour of the great captain, conceiving it extremely probable that a general who had shown himself very little scrupulous in observing his faith when in his° master's interest was not likely to be nicer when his own interest required him to be negligent of it. Accordingly Ferdinand showed himself as suspicious of the great captain as he would have been of any other person who had been forced upon his confidence by a train of circumstances which on his own part admitted of no choice. He had resolved to remove Gonsalo de Cordova from his power, and, somewhat doubtful whether his commands would be readily obeyed, he chose to be present himself at their execution. In the meantime he held a meeting with Louis XII at Savona near the descent of the Alps, which the French king proposed to raise into consequence as a sort of rival of the republican town of Genoa. It was here that he obtained the accession of the Catholic king to the league which had been formed by most of the Italian states against the republican state of Venice; a league of which the policy hath been very generally questioned, especially considering that their maritime influence afforded the only effectual means of a barrier against the Turk, who at this time endangered all the fragments of the Greek empire besides the frontier of Germany. Without° regard to what appeared to be their common duty the most Christian and most Catholic kings united with Pope Julius, the professed head of the Christian faith, to break down a bulwark which seemed to be an effectual aid to° the defence of Christianity. One desperate blow was dealt by the French king in person and at the head of his own army. Alviano, the Venetian general, fought with the utmost bravery and died shortly after he fell into captivity. The king of France himself began to° be afraid of his own success, and to feel that the victory which he had gained was contrary to his own interest and that of Christendom in general. About eight thousand Venetians were killed in this action, and the clashing interests and separate views of the Italian powers began to produce their natural effects in dissolving this unnatural association. Pope Julius II, whose talents we° have already mentioned, setting his views entirely upon the acquisitions to the power of the pope, made various aggressions° upon the French interest and showed himself particularly hostile to their settlement in Italy. He was emboldened by the passive obedience and religious terrors° of the French monarch, and

although repeatedly provoking him by acts of hostility he trusted to his religious principles° for escaping that chastisement which his conduct had so
often deserved, and which° Louis wanted nothing saving inclination to
have inflicted.

In this year, notwithstanding the dangers he had incurred and narrowly
escaped, Julius II put himself at the head of a new conspiracy against the
French which was called the Holy League. Maximilian and the° Venetian
republic, with Ferdinand of Aragon, engaged in this confederacy, which
had for its object the expulsion of the French from Italy. Its first operations
were successful, and so vindictive was Pope Julius, and so inveterate upon
this Holy League, that a gentleman of Savoy having dropped° an intimation that his master was willing to interfere as a mediator in forming the
terms of a general peace, the pope flew into an extravagant passion, made
the Savoyard a prisoner, and subjected him to examination by torture, so
odious was the very name of peace to the ears of his holiness.

The allies succeeded in taking Brescia and besieged Bologna with good
hopes of success, when their career was stopped° by one of those gifted
men who seem born to turn the fortunes of nations.

Gaston de Foix, duke° of Nemours, was son of John de Foix, count
d'Estampes by Mary of Orleans, sister of the reigning monarch of France;
thus the young nobleman was nephew to his sovereign. His early talent
had fixed upon him not only his uncle's attachment and admiration, but
that of the whole French army, and it was with general applause that the
army beheld him even in his twenty-third year created governor of Milan
and commander of the French army in Italy. He relieved Bologna by
throwing a strong reinforcement into the town during a heavy snowstorm; he forced the enemy to raise the siege. He attacked Baglioni, the
Venetian general, and killed eight thousand of his men.

At length the lieutenant° of France with about twenty thousand men
advanced upon Ravenna, one of the strongest places of Italy.

Emendations to the Base Text

The reading of the present text precedes the bold slash; the MS reading follows. Where the reason for a change is not obvious, in the light of the textual note or an appropriate explanatory note, a brief justification is appended in square brackets.

The following conventions are used:
< ... > deletions
\ ... / insertions
[...] editorial comments
doubtful words are preceded by a question mark.

Scott's hand (as opposed to Laidlaw's) is indicated, in this list only (after the bold slash), by italics. In the main text italics are used in the normal way to interpret underlinings in the manuscript.

Volume I

CHAPTER 1

p. 5   centre / center • Cabochians / Cabochins • difficult to ascertain, but / difficult <to say>*to ascertain*/ [new page] *conjecture*/ but • Charles VI / Charles V • interfere / enterfere • Richard II had / Richard the II. (of England) had • Gascon / Gasco<o>\i/gne • Edward III. It / Edward the third; it • blood. When the / blood when however the

p. 6   Edward III / Edward the IIIs • on the subject. / *on the ?subligion on the subject* • were / was • exorbitant / exhorbitant • therefore to venture on some bold expedient to / therefore by <some sharp> *expedient*/ invention *to venture on some bold expedient*/ to • engross / *ingross* • archbishop / *Bishop* • Salic / Salique • France, and that / France that

p. 7   pretensions / pretentions • Westmorland / westmoreland • exclamation / exclammation • Poitou / poictou • They / The • proposed / *propose* • archbishop / *Bishop* • him, and made / him made • Bourges / Bruges • offered / offering

p. 8   and upbraiding / & <[two letters]> *upbraided* • subjects, and the / *subjects accordingly* [or: *according to*] the • country / *contrary* • fragments / fragment • raise / *raid* • fulfilled / *filld* • negotiation. It / negociation it • adherents / ?*aderents* • success / *such* • Gray / *Grey* • to have had / *to had* • archbishop of Bourges / *Bishop of Bruges* • answered publicly / *answer publickly* • Nicolas / Nicholas

p. 9   welcome / *wellcome* • archbishop of Bourges / *Bishop of Bruges*
• [The following passage appears to be the draft of an alternative version of
the penultimate paragraph of Chapter 1:] *and again asserting his just right to the
Kingdom of France to which the <?li> Bishop of Bruges <made this bold answer>
having first crave the Kings leave Having received the Kings permission and assurance
of safety he <made> made this bold answer "Sir the King of France our Sovereign
Lord is true King of France and over the things to which you say you have a right you
have scarce not one to the Kingdom of England which belongs to the true heirs of the
late King Richard—Nor with you can our sovereign Lord <[?2 letters]> safely ["ly"*
probably hidden in gutter] *treat" For answer Henry commanded the<ir>
ambassadors immediate departure from <?f > England adding in a threatening tone
that he would quickly follow them"* • Cambridge, Lord Scrope / *Cambridge
and Lord Scroope* • accession / *?accssion*

Chapter 2

p. 10   1415 / 1414 • of consequence situated / *on ?consqeuenc situation*
• They dammed / *The damd* • D'Albret / *D'albert* • marshal /
marchall • fugitive. It occurred / \. . . *fugitive./ <?least> <& there embark
with due deliberation> after having <dege> deliberately give the french an opportunity
of battle if then chose to ?exercise it. <This> \it occurd . . ./* • were / *was* •
D'Albret / *D'Albert*

p. 11   D'Albret and Boucicaut / *D'Albert and Boucicault* • fame, until /
fame—?Undil • their own, rendering it / *their <own> \own/ who watched
them closely <and> \?rendering/ it* • [The river of Somme . . . defend
passage.: these lines—designated in the text {. . .}—are a verso insertion, but
there is no indication as to where precisely they are to be inserted.] •
Blanchetaque / *<Blantaque> Blantacque* • St Maxence / *Saint ?Maxenc* •
espy / *?espie* • as / *a* • unable with an enfeebled / *able with an ?enbeeble*
• country / *county* • enemy's / *enemies* • they found all / *they all* •
part of the English forces. At / *part of th At*

p. 12   Daily / *Dailie* • they / *the* • punishing / *punishment* •
ensured / *insured* • heard / *hearing* • Nesle / *Neil* • crook / *?crook*
[or: *nook*] • forward / *?forward* [or: *forwards*] • ford / *forward* • should
be avoided / *?should ?be ?avoided* • scorns / *?scorns* • neglected / *?nlected*
• prevailed / *preference* • experience / *experienced* • fatal mistake like
/ *fatal like* • Shakespeare / *Shakespear*

p. 13   God / *good* • said / *sayd*

Chapter 3

p. 14   they / *the* • as men / *to ?men* • to prevent / *to diminish
considerably to prevent* • D'Albret / *D'Albert* • On 24 October / *On the
22d of October* [Scott follows Holinshed, 3:78; the correct date is in Nicolas,

clxxii note.] • lately passed through / *lately through* • arrangements / *arrenements* • They / *The* • to have been / *to been* • won / *young* • that their generals / *that generals* • marshal / *Marshall* • enemies D'Albret and Boucicaut / *enemy D'Albert & Boucicault*

p. 15 task / *?task* [or: *?toil, ?post*] • cousin / *brothr* [or: *?uncle*] • of Exeter led / *of* [space] *led* • billmen / *billment* • as was his usage, one on / *as ?his usage one of* • tightness / *tight* • knots / \k/*not<es>* • then the fashion / *then fashion* • use. With / *use* *and which were in general six feet long & capable of drawing a cloth-yard shaft to the ear which was <then> the English custom while the archers of ?these countries drew their arrows only to the breast/ \With . . ./* • march. Their / *march that when the archers were placed. Their* • others a sort of headpiece / *others head peices of wicker & others again a sort of head peice* • of them went / *of went* • stuck down / stuck *the stakes/* down • D'Albret / *D'Albert* • Philip / *Charles* • Philip the Good / *Charles the Bold* • John / *Philip* • the counts of Richmond and Eu, and the marshal Boucicaut / *the Earls of Richemont & Eu, the marshal of Bouci<qualt>\cault/* • count / *Earl*

p. 16 with / *which* • bowmen, the / *bowmen. The* • by the nature of / *by its nature <& through a tract of rain> of* • marshal / *Mareschal* • ransom / *ransome* • ransom / *ransome* • averring / *avering* • ransom / *ransome* • the French knights began / *the French Knigh* *the French/* began • counselled / *coucilld* • neglected / *neglecting* • borne / *born* • No doubt if this / *This no doubt <h> if it* *this . . ./* • Brabant / *Bion*

p. 17 moment when the enemy's / *movement when enemies* • discharge, which / *discharge* *in ?that* [or: *?shot*]/ *which* • rendered / *renter* • armour / *armor* • incapable / *capable* • or alertness / *?or* [or: "*at*" for "*and*"] *alertness* • array / *arraye* • D'Albret and Boucicaut / *D'albert & Bouci<cau>\qualt/* • valiant / *valliant*

p. 18 compass / *compas* • constable, James / *Constable Bouciqualt, James* • Dampierre / *Dampier* • de Rambures / *Delamb<ourace>\ures/* • Sir Guichard Dauphin / *Sir Guischard Dolphin* • count / *Earl* • with Marle / *with the Marle* • Vaudémont / *Vaude, Mond<e>* • Roussi, Fauquemberg, Foix / *Roussie, <Fauon> Fauconberg, Tois* • Boucicaut / *Bouciqualt* • Kighley / *Kikely* • Maisoncelles / *Maisoncille* • men-at-arms were left / *men at arms left*

p. 19 25th day of October 1415. [new paragraph] We / *28th day of October 1415. we* [The correct date is in both Holinshed, 3:78, and Nicolas, clxxiii note.] • companions. This / *companions. <Th> [new paragraph] This* • Burgundy. Hitherto / *Burgundy & <who had> hitherto* • route / *rout* • style / *stile* • unlooked-for triumph. / *unlooked for triumph/—*\NL/ <Lewis the Dauphin> upon the receipt of this bad news

Chapter III Upon the recept of this bad news/   •   1394 and made / *1391 made*
•   both French and English / *both and English*

CHAPTER 4

p. 20   Rouen and the / *Rouen <and> the*   •   public service. The /
publick service <was> by means permitted him much liberty of selection. The   •
vassals / *vassalls*   •   vassals / *vassalls*   •   principles / *principals*   •
count / *Earl*   •   entrusting / *entrusted*   •   baton / *batton*   •   than /
that   •   these / *this*   •   were / *was*   •   count / *Earl*   •   temper / *tem*
•   been for his / *been his*   •   hand the resentment of the duke of
Burgundy, that great independent house, when / *hand the grat independent
House of the Duke of Burgundy his resentment when*

p. 21   now at least / now at*ly*/ least [Scott misinterprets "now at" as
"normal."]   •   count / Earl   •   superintendent / superintendant   •
constable executed several / Constable <executed> *selected*/ several [The
Universal History (23:519) has "executed."]   •   the duke's / the *officers filld
by the*/ Dukes   •   modelled / modeled   •   count / *Earl*   •   Jacqueline /
Jacquelline   •   young count of / young <Prince> *Duke*/ of   •   fourth /
third   •   governor / governer   •   quitted / quited   •   Charles / *Henri*
[or: *those*]   •   count / Duke   •   fourth son of Charles VI / *3d son of
Charles VII*/   •   count / Earl   •   time the duke of Burgundy renewed /
time this Prince *(the Duke of Burgundy namely)*/ renewed

p. 22   conspiracy / *cospiracy*   •   stifle / stiffle   •   Cabochians induced
/ Cabochins enduced   •   rabble / rable   •   licence, and he resolved /
license and resolved   •   manner. He / *...mann*/ he   •   scruple / scrupple
•   maître d'hôtel / maitre Hotell   •   revenge with the Armagnac /
revenge *and the Armagnac .../*   •   count / Earl   •   partake in / *...
partake*/ &

p. 23   serving / served   •   country / *county*   •   pieces as / *pieces and
pauning them as*   •   monarch and had / *...monarch*/ had   •   dauphin who
announced to that / Dauphine who <told> *announced*/ that

p. 24   assassination / asasination   •   Armagnac and her / <Armagniac>
armagnac/, her   •   son / *sun*   •   charge / *ch*   •   "Not / "Nor   •
favourites / favorites   •   Isabelle's general / *Isabels generall*   •   unfavourable
effect upon / *unfavour effect up*   •   Isabelle's / *Isabels*

p. 25   count / Earl   •   Armagnac the / Arm\a/g<i>nac that the   •
Clerc / *clerck*   •   Seine / Siene   •   28/29 May / 16 May [The correct
date is in Petitot, 6:336.]   •   Marcoussis / Marcoussi   •   St Paul / *St Pol*
•   wrapped / wrapt   •   wrapped / wraped

p. 26 Charles VI / *Charles V* • of Queen Isabelle / *of the Queen \Queen Isabelle/* • revolution. When . . . success she is said to have expressed herself in / *revolution when . . . success is said to express herselve in* • existed. This / existed this • whom they had in / whom the had made in • Châtelet / chattelet • Châtelet / chattelet • They / *The* • Marle / Marlè

p. 27 attacks / *attempts* • idiocy in which / *idiocy which* • Vincennes / Vencennes • Châtelet / Chattelet • Châtelet / Chattelet • Clerc / clerk • atrocious cruelty / atrocious of cruelty

p. 28 licentious / licencious • their / *the* • principles / principals

<h2 style="text-align:center">CHAPTER 5</h2>

p. 29 cruelties / cruelty • Burgundy. [new paragraph] On / Burgundy. On • dauphin / Duphine • Vignolles / Vignoles • Trémoille, and Barbazan / Tremouille et Barbasan • independence. Thus seconded in his own person, seventeen / independance [new paragraph] Thus seconded \<*in his own person*>/ *in his own person for*/ in himself seventeen • dauphin regent / Dauphine Regent • England . . . In this she was mistaken / England *by which he was to be married with he favour daughter Catherine having the kingdom of France for her dowery. This unnatural mother managed the conferences with Henry himself & to make Henry more eager for the match carried her daughter thither <himself> her that her personal charms which were very remarkable might have their effects in the treaty.*/ <*A treaty \in/ which*> she managed the conferences herself taking with her the Princess Chatharine her daughter whose charms she counted would make an impression upon the English monarch. In this she was not mistaken • by no means / *by means* • such / *to*

p. 30 murder, again / *murder in again* • name / *arm* • aware / *awares* • what / *which* • Isabelle / *Isabel* • have / *hear* • dowry / *dourey* • we will drive / *we drive* • do / *due* • The prince indeed was no less anxious at / \. . . *The prince <might> indeed was no less anxious/* Charles the Dauphin<e> was no less anxious at • death. Whatever / death whatever • 1407 / 1405 • deepest / *deeper* • bred up. Having / *bred up & he retaind the greatest affection to his memory Having*

p. 31 dauphin's / Dauphines • favourite / *favorite* • dauphin's / Dauphines • yet be / yet *it must be/* be • with / *whch* • 1419 / 1418 [The correct date is in Petitot, 6:351.] • ammunition / amunition • state. In / state in • dauphin / Dauphine • centre / center • dauphin / Dauphine • Navailles / Noailles • Foix, endeavoured / Foix who endeavoured • dauphin's suite / Dauphin<s> suit

p. 32 barricades / baricades • impossible. Burgundy's / *impossible Burgundys* • friends / *freinds* • dauphin / Dauphine

CHAPTER 6

p. 33   head, on / head have on   •   entertained sentiments / entertained oposite sentiments   •   grief / greif

p. 34   that in little / that little   •   tenor / tenure   •   France; a / France. A   •   Salic / *Saliques*   •   no legal sense possessed / *no <?sens> a legal possessd*

p. 35   vassals / *vassalls*   •   maréchal de Lisle-Adam / *Marechal de L'Isle Adam*   •   some time / sometime   •   Lisle-Adam for passage of their army, but / Lisle-Adam \for passage of their army/ *to the passage of the Burgundian army*/ but   •   Hal / Hall   •   Montereau / Monter\r/eau   •   Fenin / *Fennian*

p. 36   corpse / corps   •   cerements, and transported / cerements <&> transported   •   Barbazan / Barbasson   •   Barbazan / Barbason   •   Denis / Dennis   •   was / were   •   against him as / against as

p. 37   exchequer in heavy / exchecquer heavy   •   trial / tryal   •   desirous / desireous   •   lieutenancy / Lieutennancy   •   received in / received with   •   queen appeared. / Queen.   •   speak, and / speak in the next chapter &

p. 38   Stewart / Stuart   •   rear the English cavalry pressed / \. . . *rear while the English cavalry*/ <he> \they/ pressed   •   count of Kent / earl of Kent [so *Mémoires de Pierre de Fenin*, ed. Dupont (Paris: Jules Renouard, 1837), 350]   •   balanced / ballanced   •   France. The / France but the   •   harass / harrass

p. 39   earl / Duke   •   *miserere* / <u>meserere</u>   •   31 August / 30 August [Scott is following Petitot, 6:360; the correct date is in Holinshed, 3:133.]   •   Charles VI / Charles V   •   butt / but   •   Denis / Dennis   •   Charles VI / Charles V<II>   •   Charles VI / Charles V

CHAPTER 7

p. 40   English out / English but without the slightest degree of respect <or atte> authority or attattchment *out . . .*/   •   foresaw / forsaw   •   or that / *or of that*   •   interest . . . that of / interest<s> . . . those of   •   brother's / *brothers*   •   side were the / side the   •   Bourbonnais, Auvergne / Bourbonnois, <l>\D/'Auvergne

p. 41   Charles VI / Charles VII   •   Cravant / Crevan   •   Stewart of Darnley / Stuart of Darnly   •   some time / sometime   •   dauphin the / Dauphin to the   •   monarch. Still / monarch *& owing to the influence of all these causes*/ Still   •   Cravant / C<l>\r/evan   •   having / had   •   Cravant / Crevan   •   Dreux / Draux

p. 42   Cravant / Crevan • Ivry / Yvry • Verneuil / Vernoil • Douglas / Douglass • precipitance.The / precipitance, the • losing ranks, station, and breath / losing both breath ranks <&> station \& breath/ • Douglas / Douglass • Marie / or: Mani • wheel and hung / \...wheel/ hung

p. 43   offensive and defensive / offencive & defencive • buried / burried • Cravant and Verneuil / Crevan & Vernoil • situation, answered / \...situation/ he answered • could be, since it was some / could since it is some • livres due / livres France due • persons that / persons nor was it that • slightest regret / slightest resentment *of regret* • if / *which* • readers' / readers

p. 44   Arthur count / Thomas Earl • inclined / *enclined* • peer, and was / \...peer/ been of the English faction & was • baton / batton • Chastel, the dauphin's / Chatel *Dauphins*.../ • also that Louvet / also *Louvet*.../ • John / Arthei • count / Earl • constable and departed / Constable departed • brother's / brothers • Chinon, had stipulated / \...Chinon <receivd> *having stated/* had stipulated

p. 45   him around his / him [caret] <around> his • Beuvron / Buvron • and / had • disastrous / desastrous • maréchal de Boussac / Marechall de <Both> Bossac • compte / *Compt*

p. 46   Trémoille, left / Tremouille *was*/ left • daily / dayly • affronts / afronts • servants. He / servants. <He> *That audacious man Giac<s> or Camus de Beaulieu this new favourite/* shut [Scott's change is puzzling: La Trémoille shut the gates (Petitot, 8:29).] • Penthièvre, the ancient / Panthiever the antient • Montfort / Montefor<d>\t/

CHAPTER 8

p. 47   Jacqueline of / Jacqueline heiress of • pretensions / pretentions • Flanders, a legacy / *Flandres legacy* • Dauphiné, and from / \...*Dauphiny*/ from • Agincourt, any one of / Agincourt; <any one> *either*/ of

p. 48   was / *as* • engines / *enginnes* • streets / streats • storey / story

p. 49   English were now / English now

CHAPTER 9

p. 50   cannon / canon • occasions, either / occasions & either • villagers / *villages* • these / *this* • fairies / Faeries • trifling / triffling

p. 51   gallantry, and was never / gallantry <nor> was *never*/ • the

young / they youg • feminine / femenine • that these suggestions
arose / that <they> *suggestions*/ arose • her visibly and repeatedly / her
visibly/ repeatedly • foretold / fortold

p. 52 upon her / upon him her • similar one upon / similar upon • king
ere my Lent / King <ere> *my*/ lent • maiden, himself / maiden he himself

p. 53 of Metz / of *De*/ Metz • each with / with each • her /
he • messenger / *messengers* • singular person / \. . . *singular persons*/ of
a person • there are men–at–arms / there <are> men at arms • out on
13 / out 13. • which lay / which we have lay • found the / found
that the

p. 54 laic / laick • Catherine de Fierbois / Chatharine de
F<ea>*ie*/bois

p. 55 borne / born

p. 56 fear, and / fear, she • feminine / femenine • resumed to the
combat in / resumed *to the combat*/ the heroine in • levelled / leveled •
sieur / Seiur • passed at Selles / past at Scelles • gave a / gave *me*/ a
• Selles / Scelles • Romorantin / *Romarentin* • three leagues / two
leagues [Scott misreads Petitot, 8:225.] • tied / tyed • folded, and /
folded. and • trifling / triffling

p. 57 medicines / medecines • count / Earl • pretensions /
pretentions • Patay / Paty • one hundred and twenty prisoners /
twelve hundred prisoners [Scott misreads Monstrelet (Buchon, 30:228), who
gives 100 to 120 prisoners.] • The English conceived / The fears of the
English who conceived • literally / litterally

p. 58 beholding him at / beholding [space] at • it. When / it. [new
paragraph] When • passed / past • in / on

p. 59 trifling / triffling • Lagny / Lagniee • been her wish / been
in her <power> *wish . . .*/ • Compiègne / Compeigne • valiant /
valliant • Flavy / *Flavel* • *Holinshed's* / Hollinsheds

p. 60 have / had • upon / up • fancies. To / fancies to •
leader/ *follower*

p. 61 they / the • station would for her have been / *station were have
for her have been* • desirous / desireous

p. 62 accidents which were / accidents were • St Catherine de
Fierbois / St. Katharine de Fearbois • assistance / assistence • which
was hardly / which hard*ly*/ • divine / devine

p. 63   manoeuvres / manuevres • in 1407. / in [space] . • M. Caze's / M. de <Charmettes> \Caze's/ • no / *an* • Shakespeare believed / *Shakspeare beleived* • of this interesting / of interesting • niche / nich

p. 64   Beauvais / Bauvais • principal and only / princpal only • were / was • expression / expressions • In disembarrassing / In this \dis/embarrassing • heretic / *heretick* • they / the

CHAPTER 10

p. 66   indispensable / indispensible • advice / advise • Sorel / Soreille • kingdom, his / Kingdom was his • Sorel / Soreille

p. 67   inconsistent / inconsistant • he / *now* • Montereau / *Montreau* • Marche / March • Francis I / *Francis II* • count / *Earl* • De Montfort / de Montefort • Charles VII / Charles VII's • affairs. During / affairs during • [On the verso facing "his pecuniary distress" there appears in Scott's hand the following insertion, whose intended location in the text is unclear:] "*a prophecy fullfilld which at the first utterance seemd so improbable and with revrence on seeing thir native prince at thir gates.*"

p. 68   at the command of Richmond himself he first / at <the command of> Richmond himself <he> first • vengeance. He / \. . . *vengance*/ he • count / Earl • La Trémoille in the management / la Tremeuille <in the> management • capacity, and invaluable / \. . . *capacity*/ invaluable • duke / Earl • ministry / ministery

p. 69   Montereau / Monterau • aggravated / agravated • St Omer / Saint Omers

p. 70   desire to / desire & to • 1435 / 1434 • Catherine. This / Chatharine this • upbraiding / upraiding

p. 71   St Denis / *Saint Dennis* • 1436 / 1437 • Paris being / Paris & being • Pontoise / Pontois • Montereau / Monterau

p. 72   middle, mounted / \. . . middle mounted/ passed <the bridge in person> \<ditch>/ *the moat*/ mounted • Montereau / Montereaut • metropolis on 12 November / metropolis the 17th September [*Universal History* gives 17 November; the correct date is in Petitot, 9:62.] • bridle / briddle • children: a / Children. A • privileges / preveleges • Eugenius IV / Eugeneus V. • pensions, and exemptions / pensions exemptions • was disposed / *was adverse were disposed* • the pope. These / \. . . *the Pope and with*/ These • present, the / present. The

p. 73   exorbitant / exhorbitant • privileges / priviledges •

friendship / *freindship* • genius / [or: *genial*] • against her by / *against by* • count / *Earl*

p. 74 represented that if / represented <that> if • grace he / grace that he • as giving rise / as <being> *given rise . . ./* • Saône / *Saonne* • acquitted / *achieved* • son / *grandson* • 1418 / *1415* • Comminges / *Comminge* • Poissy / *Possi*

p. 75 panegyrics / Panegerics • his ransom, joined / his ransome *as an expiation of his fathers share in the death of the Duke of Orleans who <wal> was killd in the Paris Bastille These threatening tumults were soon soon put a stop to. Another war with the Swiss who were beginning to make themselves known by their courage was intrusted to the management of the Dauphin rather to keep his horse in exercises and to prevent their <pliu> plundering the country than for any weightier reason. They fought however a battle in the plain of Botteleu from the fury with which the Swiss defended themselves the Dauphin became satisfied that it was better to have the Swiss for friends than enemies an idea which long afterwards he carried into effects by subsidizing a large body troops from that nation At present the war only lasted a short time and was then put an end to.* [new paragraph] *About the middl of august 1445 the death of the Dauphines occasione some enquiry into the manner in which she had been treated by her husband who as we said had never loved her/* These noblemen joined [Scott's insertion, which anticipates events described later in the chapter, cannot easily be fitted into the existing text.] • who welcomed his / who saw in his

p. 76 subsistence—on / subsistence <while on the contrary> France <was> *on . . ./* • burden / burthen • equipped / equiped • *les francs* / le Francs • free archers, a / *. . . free arhers* <wh>/ for a • harassed / harrassed • 1444 / 144<3>\7/ • René / *Reny* • sat / *sate* • the / *this*

p. 77 for / from • René / *Reny* • Montbéliard / Montbelliard • his troops / his <his> \the French/ troops • misbehaviour / misbehavior • fantastic / phantastic

p. 78 it happened / it *state of the* [or: *this*] *army it inevitably/* happened • formed, and the / formed, the • supplies of men and money / supplies or men <or> \&/ money • foreseen / forseen • atone / attone • whom the Englishman returned / whom <he replied> *English returnd . . ./* • Surienne / Suriennes

p. 79 completed / compleated • kyriel / kiriel • serviceable, and were / *. . . sevceable/* were • Formigny / Fourmigny • 15 April 1450 / 5 April 1449 [The correct date is in *Universal History,* 24:31–32.] • completed / compleated • Gascon / Gasco<i>gne • France / Scotland • garrisoned / garisoned • English, rendered / English on the other rendered • be the / be likely the • autumn / spring [Petitot (11.85) is correct; *Universal History* (24:37) is ambiguous.] • overran / overrun • Castillon / Chastillon

p. 80 Castillon / Chatillon • heroes / Heros • Guienne / Guines • Castillon / chattillon • through such a period / through <such> *it had flowd for so long*/ a period • meantime, while the / mean while the

<h2 style="text-align:center">CHAPTER 11</h2>

p. 81 At / *Ye* [for: *Yet*] • cases in / *cases & in* • approbation. It / \. . . approbation Very shortly after this period/ It • obscure, such as / obscure <such> *& so unimportant*/ as • therefore substitute / therefore *flurish on either side*/ substitute • Sorel / Soreille • charms. [new paragraph] Exact / charms. *These exact . . .*/ • tend / *tending* • entrusted / *intrusted* • count of Dammartin. The / *Compte of Dammartin the* • present, and told / *present told*

p. 82 excluded him from / *excluded from* • though this was / *though was* • instead of a / *indeed a* • state a gratuitous / *state gratuitous* • dauphin / *Dauphiny* • father's / *father* • they / *the* • Peter de Brézé / John de <Beze> *Breze*/ • independent / independant • with him besides / *with besides* • personal preference as / *personal as* • king's consent, but / Kings *but . . .*/

p. 83 d'Estouteville / de Esto<i>*u*/teville • Castillon / Chattillon • a / *an* • and / *to* • species / specious • imagine / immagine • part of his own / *part own* • Dauphiné / *Dauphin* • Chabannes / *Chabbannes* • appointments / *accountments*

p. 84 Louis saw / *Louis Louis the Dauphin saw* • Philip the / Phillip *found*/ the • dignified / dignifyed • Genappe / *Geneppes* • opinion his / *opinion of his* • dauphiness / Dauphinè<ss>

p. 85 justified / justifyed • death, which was / death *was . . .*/ • against his life / *against life*

p. 86 country, entered / country, he entered • bringing the / bringing in the • he / so • betray me?" He / *betray* <The> He • trial / tryal • count / Duke • imprisonment. While some / imprisonment <as> *while*/ some • poison. Instead / \. . . *poison*/ instead • avoid the possibility / *avoid possibility* • Mehun-sur-Yèvre / Melun sur <Ivre> Yeuvre

p. 87 this / *these* • borne / born • desirous / desireous • as his / as it was his • occasioned / occationed

CHAPTER 12

p. 88   afraid / affraid   •   count of Charolais / Count Charlerois

p. 89   dependence / dependance   •   pretension / pretention   •
occasioned / occationed   •   gratified / gratifyed

p. 90   removed and the / removed the   •   fulfilment / fullfillment   •
perhaps it could / perhaps could   •   substituting such as were totally /
substituting <such as \who/ of the possest talents> for the offices <or>
\were/ at least totally

p. 91   which Louis / which the king (Louis)   •   thus / *these*   •
economy / *Oeconomy*

p. 92   particular, conceiving / particular conceived   •   marshal /
Marshall   •   falsehood / falshood

p. 93   Chimay / Chemay   •   Chimay / Chemay   •   Croy / Croix   •
had not, it / had <not>, it   •   Luxembourg / Luxemburgh   •   him. He /
him \& *in particularly this stratagem of Rubempré/*. He [It is unclear where Scott
meant this insertion to fit in.]   •   Roussillon / Rousillon   •   apparel /
apperel   •   ridiculed / rediculed   •   coarse frieze / course freeze

p. 94   banished for / banished" said he "for   •   Somme / Soamme   •
Burgundy. In / Burgundy. [new paragraph] In   •   treaty / treatie   •
Croy / *Croye*   •   Hesdin / <Hedein> H'édein   •   Rubempré /
Rubenpré

p. 95   to / should   •   Rubempré / Rubenpré   •   Morvilliers /
Mervilliers   •   archbishop / *Cardinal*   •   others / *other*   •   Charolais for /
Charlerois *in which he took a high tone/* *for . . ./*   •   Marche / March   •
desiring / desire

CHAPTER 13

p. 96   count / Earl   •   baton / batton   •   pretensions / pretentions   •
Morvilliers / Moivilliers

p. 97   Croy / *Croye*

p. 98   upbraided / upraided   •   Croy / *Croye*   •   equipped / equiped
•   public / *Publick*   •   Woodville / *Wood*

p. 99   Chabannes / Chabanne   •   Bastille / Bastile   •   to do in 1418.
/ *to do in [   ]*. [The square brackets are Scott's.]   •   were / *it*   •   Charles
VII / *Charles VIII*   •   Luxembourg / *Luxemburgh*   •   Burgundians /
Burgundia   •   Luxembourg / Luxemburgh

p. 100   time. / time *was in consequence greatly refreshd as we are assurd by Comines who was present & gives us the <eviden> anecdote of his own charger.*/ • skilful / skillfull • if / of

p. 101   similar. The / similar. [new paragraph] The • avoid. In / avoid. [new paragraph] In • other side the / other the • archbishop / Bishope • duke / Count • Somme / Soame

CHAPTER 14

p. 102   Louis, from his knowledge of mankind / Lewis's \from his/ knowledge mankind • from them, either / from *either*/ • irregularly, the / irregularly. <Skir> The • low military / low *a tone of*/ military • Bastille / Bastile

p. 103   they / the • gens d'armes / gens d'arm • defence, and the conflict / defence the confusion the conflict • reconnoitre / reconnoiter • they / the • trifling / triffling • Bouttefeu / Boutefau

p. 104   Bastille / Bastile • transferred / transfered

p. 105   approved / aproved • Bourbon as representing the prince / Berri as *representing*/ Prince • obstinacy and intractability / obstinacy an <the> intactibility • future. As / future as • encampment / incampment • Philip's chamberlain / Phillips <& [followed by some 5 letters]> *the leading of*/ Chamberlain [The correct position of Scott's insertion is unclear.] • Saveuse / Saveuses • opportunely / opertunely • wilfully / willfully • marshal / Marschall

p. 106   marshal / Marshall • marshal / Marshall

p. 107   it. One / it [new paragraph] One • day, 28 October / day [space] Nov. • Charles. Without / Charles without • satirical / satiracal • preferred / prefered

p. 108   complete a / *complete as a* • barrier treaty of France to / barrier <treaty> *of France*/ to

CHAPTER 15

p. 109   foresaw / forsaw

p. 110   the disaffection of / the <insurrection> of

p. 111   native / [or: natural] • Charolais returned / Charlerois <now> (Duke of Burgundy in 1467) returned • utensils / utensels •

acquainted. He / acquainted *and adding insult to violence incensed their violent lord to the most violent degree*/. He   •   canals, which / canals and which   •   St Trond / St Trou   •   of / de   •   and keeping the / & \<keeping\> *maintaining*/ the   •   most effectual for his / most effectual*ly with*/ \<for\> his   •   Balue / Ballue

p. 112   choose / chuse   •   days. If / days, if   •   but you will / but *will …*/   •   St Trond / St. Trou   •   conditions and given / \\… *conditions*/ given   •   lord / Count

p. 113   St Trond / St. Trou   •   Bruestem / *Bruestein*   •   canals / cannals   •   Bruestem / Bruestien   •   Bruestem / *Bruestein*   •   insurgents when the / insurgents *them the …*/   •   St Trond / St Trou   •   But although the submission / But \<although the\> \\?*mplied*/ submission

p. 114   hostages, and imposing / hostages imposing   •   razed. Having / raised having   •   them, he began / them. began   •   treaty / treatie   •   treaty / treatie   •   some measure sanctioned / *some sanctiond*   •   treaty. Thus fortified by / \\… *treaty. Lewis thus fortified*/ thus fortified by   •   francs / franks

p. 115   completely / compleatly   •   completely / compleatly   •   desire for assurance of the / desire \<for\> *assurance for the …*/

p. 116   Balue / *Ball\<ieu\>**ue*/   •   Péronne / Perronne   •   Péronne / Perronne   •   Péronne / Perronne   •   nor were its / nor *was*/ its   •   *rois fainéants* / Rois Feneants   •   Herbert count / Hugh Earl   •   king might / King & might   •   Péronne / Perronne   •   apartments / appartments

p. 117   inhabitants, of whom / inhabitants \<if possible who were\> *whom …*/   •   Bruestem / Bruestein   •   Péronne / Perronne   •   skilful / skillfull   •   enrolling / inrolling   •   John de Wilde / Sir William Wylde   •   Tongres / Tongers   •   attendance on the / \\… *attendance*/ the

p. 118   trifled / triffled   •   inferred / infered   •   was likely / was already likely   •   count / Earl   •   was / were

p. 119   had no / had perhaps no   •   fate. / fate *& thus felt* \<the ex\> *the truth of the proveb by experience that the princes of monarchs are ?neaest to their ?repalations*/. [It has not been possible to decipher this passage fully.]

p. 120   bedchamber: "During / bedchamber. [new paragraph] "During   •   Champagne / Champaigne   •   that he would / that would

p. 121   Commynes's / Commines   •   intended / *ended*

Chapter 16

p. 122   relic / *relique* • such / much • to deal / to do deal •
council / *Counsel* • marshal / Marschal

p. 123   vanguard. Meantime / vanguard meantime • foremost /
formost • suburb / subburb • Wilde / Wyld • suburb / subburb •
Wilde / Wyld • lest / least

p. 125   Wilde / *Wylde* • few that had / few had • They had /
The<y> \wall/ had • borne / born • later / latter • princes, and
put / Princes \put .../ • quarters / *quarter*

p. 126   "Kill" [unlocated insertion on facing verso:] *when they heard the
alarm wa geneal*/ • secrecy / secresy • order and were / *. . . order*/ were
• whose discharge killed / whose <arrows> *discharged*/ killed

p. 127   their neighbours, who / *their neighbour & wh*/ who • hunger,
fatigue, or want / hunger & *fatigue famine or*/ of want • fulfilment /
fullfillment • being / *been* • lowering / *lowring* • tomorrow, it / \. .
. *tomorrow*/ It • desirous / desireous

p. 128   burned / burnt • having, at / having at length *at . . .*/ •
and Brie / & la Bree • and Brie / and la Bree • and Brie / *and La Brie*
• fall to / *fall come to* • because before King / *because King* • fulfil /
fullfill • advantageous a match / *advantageous match* • from the duke /
from Duke • Brie / Bree

p. 129   suborned / subborned • subtlety / subtilty • Balue, bishop
/ Bal\l/ue & the Bishop • Balue / Bal\l/ue • enclosed / inclosed

p. 130   the bishop of Verdun / Cardinal Bal\l/ue • these / this •
devised / devized • barricade / baricade • Charron / Cheron •
Brault / Breuil • centre / center • barricade / baricade • d'Angély
/ *D'Angeli*/ • believe / *beleive* • manner. Louis / \. . . *manner*/ His
cruelty & crime was detected by his own remorse. <The King> *Louis*/ •
Cléry / Clary • soothes / sooths

p. 131   such devotion / such odious devotion • are so characteristic /
is so characteristick

Volume II

Chapter 1

p. 135   Péronne / Perronne • in a train of hostile / in several *train of
hostile*/ hostile • Roye and Montdidier / Roie, & Mondidier •

Monseau / Monsereau   •   monk was / monk who was

p. 136   Tewkesbury / *Tewksburgh*   •   completely / compleatly   •
pretensions / pretentions   •   in both of whose reigns the / in \neither of
whose/ whose reign the   •   also that the / \. . . *also*/ while the

p. 137   dividing / divide   •   Neuss / Nuiz   •   readiness / readyns   •
means, which / *means to the end which*   •   engaged / *ingaged*   •   Neuss /
Nuiz   •   assist / *preve*   •   for / *to*

p. 138   part / *party*   •   rumour / *remote*   •   foresaw / forsaw   •
France, which / france & which   •   intercourse / entercourse   •
interference / enterference   •   subtlety / subtilty   •   Neuss / Nuiz

p. 139   Neuss / Nuiz   •   archers / *archer*   •   suspicion both /
suspicion *than of favour*/ both [Scott misreads "now" as "more."]   •   and to
/ & the to

CHAPTER 2

p. 140   awkward / aukward   •   rank was returned / rank who<se>
\was/ return\ed/   •   skilfully / skillfully   •   chambre / chamber   •   des
Halles / de Halles   •   and upon / and *soon it one instance among many of the
acuteness of Louis's knowlege of mankind who when he had a part to play was*
<lways> *always fitted with the knowlege of a person fitted to represent it*/ upon
[changed to "Upon"]   •   chambre / chamber

p. 141   undertake it upon / undertake <it> *to represent it*/ upon   •   of
/ at   •   borne / born   •   Stanley / Stanly   •   emergency / *emergence*   •
camp / *camps*   •   Lancaster, which had / Lancaster \<as>/ had   •   Ré /
Rhé

p. 142   confidence, which the king / confidence & <he> *the King*/   •
advantageous proposals to / advantage<s>\ous/ to   •   imaginary /
immaginary   •   curious as having / curious hat having   •   country /
county

CHAPTER 3

p. 143   made payment / made present payment   •   Channel / channell
•   principle / principal

p. 144   if it was / *if was*   •   the / *their*   •   country / *county*   •
nobles, Lord Howard and his grand equerry John Cheyne, as / nobles [space]
as [space filled from Holinshed, 2:274]

p. 145   of the towns / *of towns*   •   it / *this*   •   Louis de Sainville /

Leues de Creville • Jean Richer. They were / Jean <?Riher> *Richer*/
were • Sainville / Creville • mimic / mimick • screen / skreen •
apartment / appartment • Sainville / Creville • Sainville / Creville •
ridicule / redicule

p. 146 Sainville / Creville • Louis to seem / *Louis & ?seem* •
came and was / came was • Sainville / Creville • panegyric /
panegeric • ancient / antient • adjusted, and declared / \\... *adjusted*/
declared • of that nation's / of <the> *persons of that nations*/

p. 147 sense / sence • dictated by / dictated <by a sense> *in*/ by •
there / these • Amiens, and / Amiens *for one who left the town*/ and

p. 148 causeway / casway • been sensible / been *in*/sensible •
subtlety / subtilty • palisade / pallisade • nugatory. Louis observed the
/ \\... *nugatory*/ on both sides & Lewis observing the • king, and that of
Louis, not / King <& that of> Lewis, not • head with a fleur-de-lys /
head of which a fleur de lîs • so / to • relic / <relict> *relique*/ •
jest to favour / *jest favour*

p. 149 indebted for the / indebted *the* .../ • lieutenant /
Lieutennant • Paris, which / Paris & which • Picquigny, but on /
Picquigny <but> *on* .../ • friends / *freinds* • palm and his / *palm his*
• he might have a / *he a*

p. 150 remained / remaining • skilful / skillfull • Bretaylle /
Breteilles • coarse / course • Bretaylle / Brete*i*/lle • mischievous
/ mischeivous • tongue / toungue • Gascon / Gascoigne •
Bretaylle / Breteilles • presents which / presents *by means of whch*/ which
• raillery at / raillery <to> the <soldiers> & *at* .../ • desirous /
desireous • subtle / subtile

CHAPTER 4

p. 151 Calais / Callais<e> • Contay / <Conty> *Contey*/ •
equipped / equit • viscount / Duke

p. 152 dropped / dropt • viscount / Duke • and / with •
obstinacy, and suffer / obstinacy, suffer • base, avaricious / base &
avaritious .../ • Burgundy. With / Burgundy *that to retreat into Germany*
or even into England with his treasures. He retrated to Mons in Flanders where was
arrested by Duke Charles of Burgundy who immediatly began to resume a negociciatin
for delivery him up to Louis XI to be tried by the laws of that county Charles was
promised a grant of the greater part of his forefather if he would deliver his late ally to
certain death and ready made this a leading condition of his treaty with the King of
France/. with [This insertion cannot easily be fitted into the dictated text.] •
where he had / where had

p. 153   19 December / Decr 14th [The correct date is in Petitot, 14:23.]
•   character until / character & persevered in untill   •   Ham, and Bohain /
Hain Bohaine   •   found was not / found <was> *were*/ not   •   They /
The   •   men / [or: ?*arms*]   •   Burgundians than / *Burgundian that*

p. 154   relieve / releive   •   surprise / *surprize*   •   wardrobe / ?*wardrope*
•   the duke lost not only his camp / he lost *the Duke lost*/ <not only>
\<*also*> *also*/ his camp   •   22 June / [day hidden in gutter] June   •   battle,
where / Battle & when   •   period, bearing / period and bearing   •
despair / dispair

p. 155   a warm temperament he used / *an warm temperment he use*   •
sorts / *sort*   •   tempered / *tempert*   •   of that element / *of element*   •
Lorraine and who were / Loraine & were   •   extremity / extremety   •
excited / *excitement*   •   prince / ?*prin*   •   yet so / yet historians seem *only
so . . .*/   •   believe / *beleive*   •   him, and historians seem generally / *. . .
him.*/ generally   •   relieve / releive   •   had / having   •   cannon / canon
•   him, resolved / him the Duke resolved   •   dissuade / disuade

p. 156   with an army / *with army*   •   hanging / *hanghing* [or: *haryhing*]
•   5 January / 15 January   •   1477 / 1476   •   Epiphany on the sixth day
of January, the / epiphany <on [space] day of Jan> *on the morning of th*
[space] *of January being that call the Feast of King* ?*r*/ the   •   lie / *ly*   •
distinguished himself by / *distinguishd by*   •   valour Duke Charles was /
valour the Duke was   •   borne / *born*   •   had been round / *had <been ar>
round*   •   that which / that at which   •   prosecuted / *precuting*

p. 157   valour. The historian Duclos says that, instead of being killed by
Campo Basso and his Italian assassins, he / valour *some say instead of being
killd by Campo Basso and his Italian assassins The historian Ducly says that he . . .*/
•   Blomont / *Blemont*   •   Blomont / *Blemont*   •   trod / *trode*   •   grief /
greif   •   believe / *beleive*   •   public / *publick*   •   publicly / *publickly*   •
Portugal / *battle*   •   Arcila / ?*Arbela*   •   Field / *feild*   •   and were fondly
/ *and fondly*

Chapter 5

p. 158   republic / *republick*   •   Franche-Comté / *Franck Compté*   •
Picardy / Picardie   •   these / *this*   •   Emden / *Embden*   •   fabric /
fabrick   •   father, to / father *for*/ to   •   Salic / Salique   •   that he
intended / that <he> *Louis*/ intended   •   twenty-first / twenty seventh   •
better have consulted / better consulted   •   count / Duke   •   state have
formed / *state formed*   •   consummation / *consumation*   •   politic / *politick*

p. 159   count d'Angoulême / duke D'Anguleme   •   province, which /
Province of which   •   that / as   •   between / *towards*   •   de Commynes
/ *des Comines*

p. 160   Dain / D'aim   •   stir / stirr   •   Hugonet / *Hugenet*   •
entreated / intreated   •   servants. Though / servants <yet> \though . . ./   •
Dain / *Daim*   •   of Dain / of Oliver D'aim   •   barber, and whom /
barber whom   •   house, drove / house and therefore drove   •   entrusted /
intrusted   •   justly be considered / justly considered   •   Jacques / Jean   •
Bastille / Bastile

p. 161   Olivier / Oliver   •   1477 / 1467   •   ["Edward IV to" ends a
leaf whose opposing verso bears the unlocated insertion in Scott's hand: "*of the
King of England*".]   •   stifled / stiffled   •   with / by   •   applied / applyed

p. 162   wake into activity. / wake <into> \?*away in*/ activi<ty> ?*pause*
[or: ?*france*]. [It seems likely that Scott misread "wake" as "waste" in revising
Laidlaw's script. The original is restored.]   •   defensive. During all /
defensive <during> \<*In enjoying*>/ all   •   was / were   •   fulfilment /
fulfillment   •   Guinegate / Guingaste   •   ["neither the French" ends a leaf
whose opposing verso bears the unlocated insertion in Scott's hand: "*and the
singular modes which he resorted to in order to parry an inevitable blow*".]   •   them
in / them both in   •   franc / Frank   •   Guinegate / Guingaste   •
Maximilian / Maximillian

p. 163   the king / the Duke King   •   ["\paths/ wh[ich] lead" ends a leaf
whose opposing verso bears the unlocated insertion in Scott's hand: "*He made
signs to open the door and window but they were misunderstood in consequence of
which he deprived those persons of their posts who had <?not> not understood and
executed <?those> his commands*".]   •   chambers, and others / chambers
others

p. 164   his / their   •   constrasted / contrasting   •   group / *groupe*   •
therefore / therefor   •   apartment / appartment

p. 165   supposed to / supposed never to   •   believe / *beleive*   •
Coictier / Coittier   •   medicine / medecine   •   exercised over,
constituted / exercised <over was> *constituted* /   •   a renumeration / an
emuneration

p. 166   brought up very / *brought very*   •   privilege / *privelege*   •   that
/ *which*   •   himself been / himself *to have*/ been   •   Dain / D'aim

p. 167   sense / sence

CHAPTER 6

p. 168   quitted / quited   •   Charles / Lewis   •   marriage state with /
marriage <state the> *with* . . ./   •   Joan / Joan*na*/   •   assassinated /
assasinated   •   Montereau / *Montreau*   •   preferring / prefering   •   that
the Lady / that [caret] *Lady* . . ./

p. 169   The Lady / She *Lady . . ./*   •   emblematical / *embematakal*   •
Dain / Daim   •   exorbitant / *exhorbitant*   •   oppressions, was /
oppression*s/* He was   •   Doyat / Doiac   •   Coictier / Cottier   •
physician / Phisician   •   chief argument / \ . . . *cheif/* the ostensible
argument

p. 170   uniting it to / uniting to   •   had / who   •   nobles, made /
nobles had made   •   that whoever / that if whoever   •   consequences, he
fled / consequences fled   •   Beaugency / Beaujincy   •   maréchal /
Mar*e/*schal   •   is / *it*   •   and at / *and alarmd at*   •   Bretagne, and afraid
/ \. . . *Bretagne/* afraid

p. 171   on the one hand / *on on hand*   •   John of Châlons / *William of
Chillons*   •   endeavoured / *endeavord*   •   dessert / *desert*   •   Orange /
Comye   •   those / *thes*   •   allies was such that / *allies that*   •   had / *have*
•   conspiracy / *conidery*   •   de Commynes / *des Comines*

p. 172   intercessors / *intercessions*   •   founded / *foundng*   •   friends /
freins   •   friends / *freinds*   •   Joan / *Joanna*   •   arrayed / *arraied*   •
entreated / *entreating*   •   pardon, and she hinted / *pardon setting it in view that
the crime of which he was accused and she hinted*   •   and that / *and hinted that*   •
between Maximilian / *between her & <Maxmi> Maximilian*   •   entreaty /
intreaty   •   Orleans, if / *Orleans, that if*   •   suit and make / *suit make*   •
hand. Having / *hand Accordingly offended by a <fw a> few nobles who were
intrusted with his design Having*   •   particular / *particularly*

p. 173   himself, seemed / *himself did seemed*   •   chose / *chosing*

CHAPTER 7

p. 174   welcomed / *wellcomed*   •   united it with / united with   •
Mary / <Margaret> *May/*   •   were / being   •   upon / among   •
[The following insertion in Scott's hand on the verso of (rather than that
opposing) the leaf ending "advance into France" may have been superseded
by his substantial reworking of the end of Chapter 6 and the beginning of
Chapter 7:] *There were several Nobles of Bretagne who thouht they might make
pretensions on the hands of the Dukes daughters and particularly upuon that of the
eldest princess Anne Dunois the son of the <great> celebratd Bastard of Orleans and
Des Buse both Breton nobles expressd their reslution to stand with their life and land
for the independence of their country*   •   such intention / such *real/* intention

p. 175   same time sustained / *same sustaind*   •   separation / *seperation*
•   disposed, without / disposed. Without   •   parliament espoused /
Parliament who espoused   •   tranquillity / tranquility   •   concerned, the
/ concerned, *& ought especially to have consulted the benefit/* the   •   Charles
VIII / *Charles VII*

p. 176   relics / <relicts> *reliques*/ • Appennines / appenines •
independent / independant • laws. Accordingly / laws accordingly •
other; a / other A

p. 177   superseded / superceded • monarch who / monarch and who
• war and was / war was • Ludovico / Lewis • Galeazzo / Galeasso
• Ferdinand I / Ferdinand \II .../ • dissuade / disuade

p. 178   France. His / France his • Aubigny, were personally / Aubigné
& was personally • Montferrat / Montsenate • stopped / stopt •
Asti in Lombardy / Ast *in Lombardie*/ • Galeazzo / Galeasso •
Ludovico / Lewis • inflicting punishment on / inflicting on on • as
Pisa and Siena / as to Pisa & Sienna • had died / had as we have already
mentioned died

p. 179   Alphonso / Alonzo • distant. He / distant he • citizens. He
/ citizens he • Messina / Mesina • operating to restore his / \...
operating for restore/ of his • who were included / who included •
Charles VII's / Charles the seventh • condottiere / Condottier<o>\i/ •
combatants / combattants • other was to make prisoners / other <was to
make> \?*if only to the effect & mking*/ prisoners • philosopher Machiavelli /
phylosopher Machiavel • Castrocaro / Castracaro

p. 180   this unhappy cavalier / this <unhappy> *alarmd*/ cavalier •
condottiere / Condottier<o>\i/ • combatants / combattants • bronze
/ brass [so Petitot, 14:215] • awkwardly / auckwardly

p. 181   Marano / Marrano • Joan / Joanna • offered / offering •
Dell'Ovo / Dell'uovo • contemporary / cotemporary • suites / suits
• Vincennes / Vencennes

p. 182   contemporary / cotemporary • paradise"; / paradise; • Ere
... received Charles / Here ... received. Charles • solemn triumph /
solemn \ceremony/ triumph • arriving / ariving

p. 183   D'Aubusson / D'aubu\i/sson • Bajazet / Bajazot • Bajazet
/ Bajacet • Asti / D'asté • Ludovico / Ludovic • retreat. It /
retreat; <wh> it • Venetians / Venitians • Appennines / Apenines •
Mediterranean / Mediteranean • Champagne / Champaigne •
Picardy / Piccardy • in / on • Charles VIII, determined / Charles VIII
was determined

p. 184   ammunition / amunition • Montpensier, afterwards better
known for his valour and his misfortunes under the title of the constable, was
/ Montpensier <afterwards better known as the Constable of Bourbon> \for
his valour & his misfortunes under the title of the Constable &/ was •

Brindisi / <Beirnbisi> \Brinbisi/ • Gallipoli / Galli Poli • Vesc / Visi
• lord d'Aubigny / Count D'Aubigny • baton / batton • fulfilment
/ fullfillment • least intention of / least <intention> of • Siena /
Sienna • quitted / quited

p. 185   Venetian / Venitian • Gonzaga / Gonzago • Appennines /
Appenines • Ludovico / Ludovix • stripped / stript • cannon /
canon • Fornovo / Forno<ba>\va / • maréchal / Mareschal •
maréchal / Mareschal • Fornovo / Fornova • arrived / arived •
morning. He / morning, he • Venetian / Venician • Europe , were /
Europe \they/ were

p. 186   maintained. On / maintained. The French men at arms & the
archers of His household. on • Venetian / Venecian • messenger /
messanger • they are ten to one. By / the are ten to one by • good.
God / good GOD • Venetian / venecian • Venetians / Venecians •
scimitars / Symetars • combatting / combating • Venetians /
Venecians • they / the

p. 187   martial / marsha • Charles was / Charles who was •
himself was at / himself at • Fornovo / Fornova • skilful / skillfull •
Savoy, which was / <u>Savoy</u> and was

p. 188   count / Duke • they / the • they / the • Pozzuoli /
Puzzoli • tranquillity / tranquility • tailors / Taylors • to adorn /
to decorate adorn • apartments / appartments • the time was / the
close \time/ was

p. 189   apartment / appartment • lamentations . / [The MS has either
"lamentations" or "lamentation."] • Valois / Valoise • collateral /
colateral • assassinated / assasinated

CHAPTER 8

p. 190   dispatched as soon / as soon dispatched • deformed as /
deformed in her person as

p. 191   account / accompt • passed / past • Joan, he / Joan [caret]
that he

p. 192   practice / practise • would he / he would

p. 193   [After "parties." MS has "The Queen was in her temper both
ambitious & vindictive; the latter was proved by the celebrated answer which
she made to a Lady who said to her," followed by a space of three lines for the
speech.] • When / on the 8. Janaury when [Scott misreads *Universal
History,* 24:110; Louis was married in Nantes on 8 January (Petitot, 15:11).]

• commissioners / commisioners   • entrusted / intrusted   • king / Duke   • Valentinois / Valentinoise

p. 194   entry, and took / entry; took   • possession as / possession and as   • Innsbruck / Inspruck   • falsehood / falshood   • Frederick / Frederic   • Ludovico / Ludovic

p. 195   D'Aubigny / D'Aubigné   • Lavoro / Labor   • Abruzzi / Labruzzo   • provided / providing   • Frederick / Frederic

p. 196   defence / defense   • Frederick / Frederic   • spoil. Otranto / spoil Otranto   • Frederick / Frederic   • lamentable story is ... which history makes / lamentable history is ... which [space] makes   • not / neither   • Coligny / Coligne   • Cerignola / Cerignot   • reproaches which / reproaches to which

p. 197   D'Aubigny / D'Aubigné   • combatted / combated   • d'Aubigny / D'Aubigne   • ammunition / amunition   • Isabella, being / Isabella <&> \who/ being   • France and treated / France, treated   • fulfil / fullfill

p. 198   which / the   • transferred / transfered   • for / by   • volunteers. A / volunteers a   • successor led to the / successor & the

p. 199   Julius, though not / Julius so not   • Nantes / Nantz   • maréchal / Mareschall   • choose / chuse   • maréchal / Mareschall

p. 200   Frederick / Frederic   • Ferdinand / Frederic   • father-in-law / grandfather

p. 201   Cortes / Cortez   • care / case   • Philip / Ferdinand   • Germaine / Germain

p. 202   his grandson, regent / his second son Regent   • Ximemes prevailed / Ximines who prevailed   • resolution, promptness / resolution & promptness   • grandson / son   • Ximenes would / Ximines who would   • artillery. "These / artillery [new paragraph] "These   • entrusted / intrusted   • Chièvres bred and encouraged / Chievre bred & incouraged   • they / the   • habit, and from / habit from   • Chièvres / Chievre

p. 203   occasion / occation   • was increased / was \were/ increased   • blasphemous. Besides / blasphemous, besides

p. 204   superseded / superceded   • musket / musquet   • occurred / occurd   • precious / pretious

CHAPTER 9

p. 205   when in his / when his   •   Germany. Without / Germany without   •   effectual aid to / effectual to   •   France himself began to / France began himself began to   •   talents we / talents as we   •   aggressions / agressions   •   religious terrors / religious powers terrors

p. 206   principles / principals   •   deserved, and which / deserved. On which   •   Maximilian and the / Maximilian the   •   dropped / droped   •   stopped / stopt   •   duke / Duc   •   lieutenant / Leiutennant

Explanatory Notes

Brantôme
    Oeuvres complètes du Seigneur de Brantôme. [Edited by L. J. N. Monmarqué.] 8 vols. Paris: Foucault, 1822–1823.

Buchon
    Jean Alexandre Buchon (ed.), *Collection des chroniques nationales françaises, écrites en langue vulgaire, du treizième au seizième siècle.* 47 vols. Paris: Verdière, 1824–1828.

Duclos
    [Charles Pinot] Duclos. *Histoire de Louis XI.* 2 vols. Amsterdam: Aux depens de la compagnie, 1746.

Holinshed
    Holinshed's Chronicles of England, Scotland, and Ireland. 6 vols. London: J. Johnson, 1807–1808.

Nicolas
    Nicholas Harris Nicolas. *The History of the Battle of Agincourt.* London: Johnson, 1827.

Petitot
    Claude Bernard Petitot, *Collection complète des mémoires relatifs à l'histoire de France, depuis le règne de Philippe-Auguste jusqu'au commencement du dix-septième siècle.* 52 vols. Paris: Foucault, 1819–1826.

Tales—Fourth Series
    Tales of a Grandfather; Being Stories Taken from the History of France, Inscribed to Hugh Littlejohn, Esq. 3 vols. Edinburgh: Robert Cadell, 1831.

Universal History
    The Modern Part of an Universal History, from the Earliest Account of Time. 44 vols. London: S. Richardson, 1759–1766.

Wraxall
    Nathaniel Wraxall, *Memoirs of the Kings of France, of the Race of Valois.* 2 vols. London: Edward and Charles Dilly, 1777.

. . .

1. Richard II was born in Bordeaux, and the Gascons particularly resented his murder.

2. Actually in 1414, the second year of Henry V's reign (Holinshed, 3:65).

3. The alleged fundamental law of the French monarchy, by which females were excluded from succession to the crown.

4. See Numbers 27:8.

5. William Bouratier, archbishop 1409–1421 (Holinshed, 3:68).

6. Nicolas (xlix) has "the Harry Crown."

7. Nicolas, vi–xiii, who is inclined to doubt the veracity of the tradition.

8. Harfleur is on the river Lézarde, a tributary of the Seine; the phrasing in Nicolas (xcvii) explains Scott's rather confusing account: "the river Seine . . . enters into the middle of the city, beneath the walls, by a watergate, and two lateral arched tunnels, opening and closing wholly or in part, at the will of the inhabitants."

9. In 1357; see *Tales—Fourth Series,* 3:52–53 (chap. 18).

10. The phrase "they endeavoured to elude" is from *Universal History,* 23:516; Nicolas (cxxvii) has the French agreeing and conforming.

11. For Edward III's situation at Blanchetaque see *Tales—Fourth Series,* 3.12–14 (chap. 17).

12. Scott is following Holinshed (3:75), but Pont-Ste-Maxence is on the Oise, not the Somme.

13. Holinshed has 13,000 (13:76).

14. Scott misreads Holinshed here: "At length thirtie of them agrëed, that the Englishmen should not depart vnfought withall, and fiue were of a contrarie opinion, but the greater number ruled the matter" (3:77).

15. From *Henry V* 3.6.113–19, with small variations.

16. John II of France was captured by the English at the battle of Poitiers in 1356 and taken as a hostage to London; see *Tales—Fourth Series,* 3:89–96 (chap. 19). For Scott's blending of Nicolas and Shakespeare in the following speech see the introduction, xv.

17. Maisoncelles, immediately to the southeast of Agincourt (Nicolas, cccxxx).

18. York was the grandson of Edward III, Gloucester his great grandson.

19. The details are from Holinshed 3:79 and Nicolas ccxvi note (the latter quoting Jean Le Fèvre, lord of St. Rémy's *Histoire de Charles VI Roy de France* [Paris: L. Billaire, 1663]).

20. St Rémy in Nicolas (clxxxix note) says that Vendôme led one wing, and Clugent de Brabant and Louis de Bourbon ('Bourdon' in Holinshed, 3:78) the other; but Vendôme and Bourbon are the same person.

21. Holinshed, 3:80.

22. Nicolas (cxci note, cf. cccxliv) refers to St. Rémy.

23. This and the following sentence are derived from Nicolas (ccvii note), quoting Thomas de Elmham, *Vita et Gesta Henrici Quinti,* ed. Thomas Hearne (Oxford: Sheldonian Theatre, 1727).

24. The expression means "with a line thrown out at right angles to the main body."

25. Nicolas (cccxlvi) is following *The Chronicles of Enguerrand de Monstrelet,* perhaps in the translation by Thomas Johnes, 5 vols. (Hafod, 1809), 2:86: "a knight grown grey with age and honour." The original, in Buchon, 28:340 (bk. 1, chap. 153), reads simply "un chevalier chenu de vieillesse" [a knight hoary with age].

26. Scott misreads Holinshed, 3:83: "Of Englishmen, there died at this battell, Edward duke [of] Yorke, the earle of Suffolke, sir Richard Kikelie, and Dauie Gamme esquier, and of all other not aboue fiue and twentie persons, as some doo report; but other writers of greater credit affirme, that there were slaine aboue fiue or six hundred persons."

27. Nicolas (ccxix) says 200 archers.

28. *Tales—Fourth Series,* 3:340–41 (chap. 26).

29. *Poems Written in English by Charles, Duke of Orleans, during His Captivity in England after the Battle of Azincourt,* ed. George Watson Taylor (London: Shakespeare Press, 1827).

30. Scott is following Petitot, 6:328. The correct date is 6 April.

31. Michel Luillier (Petitot, 6:325).

32. Thomas Rymer, *Fœdera,* 3d ed., ed. G. Holmes, 10 vols. (Hagae Comitis: J. Neaulme, 1739–1745), 4 (1740), pt 3, 190–91: "De Secreto, super Colloquio, cum Duce de Burbon habito, soli Imperatori Communicando" [Concerning the secret meeting and interview with the duke of Bourbon, to be communicated only to the king].

33. Scott is following Petitot's references to Juvénal des Ursins in much of this chapter; this particular reference is at Petitot, 6:343.

34. See *Tales—Fourth Series,* 3:342 (chap. 26).

35. Poilly-le-Fort (Petitot, 6:349).

36. Scott is drawing on Fenin's memoirs from Petitot in this chapter. Petitot highlights the passage referred to in his "Tableau du règne de Charles VI" at 6:357, but the delivering up of the town of Lisle-Adam is in Monstrelet (Buchon, 29:29, bk. 1, chap. 82).

37. Scott is following Holinshed, 3:124; in fact Henry left Paris on 27 December 1420.

38. Correctly, Westminster Abbey.

39. Holinshed (3:128) is Scott's source for the varying estimates of the English army.

40. The *Universal History* (23:531), which Scott is following at this point, says that there were approximately 3,000 English and 1,500 French casualties.

41. On 11 May 1422.

42. Probably dysentry, but Petitot (6:359) says a fistula.

43. Psalm 51.

44. For example, [Nicolas Baudot de Juilly], *Histoire de Charles VII,* 2 vols. (Paris: Didot, 1754), 2:39, writes of "les mépris que les Anglois avoient eus pour elle" [the contempt the English had had for her]; but it was not only the common people but the "plûpart des Seigneurs Anglois" [majority of the English lords] who "prenoient plaisir à l'insulter, & à lui dire en face, que le Roi Charles n'etoit pas fils du feu Roi Charles VI" [took pleasure in insulting her, and in saying to her face that King Charles was not the son of the late king Charles VI].

45. Scott misinterprets the *Universal History* (24:3), which states that Buchan had been created constable and Sir John Stewart of Darnley count d'Aubigny.

46. Petitot, 8:17–18, gives the two points of view.

47. Petitot, 8:19.

48. There has been no previous reference to John VI, who was ten years old on his father's death in 1399.

49. In 1427.

50. Petitot, drawing on "une ancienne chronique" (8:25).

51. Scott is following Petitot, 8:255; the correct date is 23 February.

52. Quoted by Petitot (8:223–28) who dates it c. 1429.

53. See Holinshed, 3:168; the quotation has a number of verbal differences from the original, and is very different in spelling.

54. P[ierre] Caze, *La Vérité sur Jeanne d'Arc, ou Éclaircissemens sur son origine,* 2 vols. (Paris: Rosa, 1819). Caze's argument is outlined by Petitot, 8:325–30.

55. The engagement took place in 1413, when Charles was ten, but the actual marriage was not celebrated until April 1422.

56. "Charles, who without being either a coward or a fool, could submit to necessity with a better grace than ever prince did" (*Universal History,* 24:8).

57. Petitot (6:354–55) makes it clear that although the preliminaries of the treaty (usually known as that of Troyes) were concluded in autumn 1419, it was not finalized until 21 May 1420.

58. In 1431–1437.

59. In 1444.

60. Scott is attempting to follow the *Universal History,* 24:27: "a truce was concluded, to commence the middle of *May* this year [1444], and to end on the first of *April* in the next."

61. "This truce, as the *French* historians say, was a great stroke in politics on the side of the *English* ministers; but in *England* it was considered in a very different light" (*Universal History,* 24:27–28).

62. Scott is following Petitot, 11:42, and the *Universal History,* 24:37, but the correct date is 19 October.

63. In 1444.

64. Petitot (11:185) says not before 28 December 1446; the actual date was 1 January 1447.

65. Both Duclos (1.56) and Petitot (11.186) recognize that different interpretations of the dauphin's conduct are possible.

66. On 30 August 1456.

67. The sieur de Montauban and John de Lescun (*Universal History,* 24:38).

68. On 27 July 1459. In the rest of the sentence Scott follows the *Universal History* (24:43) rather than Petitot (11:213–14).

69. The *Universal History* (24:40) has "in whom can I now put my trust, when the very princes of my own blood conspire against me[?]"

70. The *Universal History* (24:44) has "one of his old servants."

71. So the *Universal History,* 24:47n, citing Monstrelet and others; Jean de Troyes in Petitot (13:258–59) says that there were many mourners.

72. Actually in the *Mémoires de Jacques du Clercq,* printed as a supplement to Monstrelet in Buchon, 39:143, quoted in Petitot, 11:22–27.

73. Petitot (11:229n) has "le procureur-général, un président et un conseiller" [the procurator general, a president and a councillor].

74. Petitot (11:231) says that the citizens were hanged.

75. Petitot (11:247–48n) quotes this observation from the abbé Le Grand's manuscript history.

76. That is, the archbishop (Petitot, 9:12, 11:267).

77. Petitot (11:268) has "le moine" [the monk]; the *Universal History* (24:52) has "a preacher."

78. The word "sister" is here used in the sense of "sister-in-law."

79. Actually, on 18 July.

80. Petitot, 11:371. The battle took place on 16 July 1465 (Commynes has 27 July).

81. Commynes says "cent mille chevaux," or approximately 51,000 men (Petitot, 11:384).

82. Charles the Bold's first wife was Catherine of France, daughter of Charles VII.

83. Commynes has "six vingts" [120] (Petitot, 11:420).

84. Commynes says thirty or forty (Petitot, 11:423).

85. Petitot (11:414n) has "malice" and "frere."

86. The quotation is adapted from Petitot, 11:424.

87. The reference is to *Tales—Fourth Series*, 3:245–54 (chap. 24).

88. Scott misreads Commynes, who has merely "un estant en ce conseil" [one person present in this council] (Petitot, 11:444).

89. The quotation is adapted from Petitot, 11:445.

90. On 28 October 1467.

91. Ferricus de Beauvois, bishop 1457–1473.

92. Petitot, 11:486. The date is 13 October 1468.

93. Commynes says, with Burgundy's officer Nicolas Boisseau (Petitot, 11:491n).

94. Petitot, 11:499.

95. Twelve, according to Commynes (Petitot, 11:504).

96. Commynes has merely "un chevalier" [a knight] (Petitot, 11:510).

97. Scott follows in part the *Universal History* (24:61), which misreads Commynes (Petitot, 12:402) and thus reverses the roles of the two prelates. The correct sense is restored in the present text.

98. Jordanus Fabri (John Fauve Deversois) was abbot of the Benedictine community of St-Jean-d'Angély 1471–1473.

99. Brantôme, 2.23–24 ("Digression sur Louys XI" in *Vies des hommes illustres et grands capitaines françois*). The passage is referred to in Petitot, 12:68n. See vol. 2, chap. 1.

100. The original in Petitot (11:519n) reads: "Maistre Jean Ballue, / A perdu la veue / De ses éveschés: / Monsieur de Verdun / N'en a plus pas un; / Tous sont depeschez."

101. For example, Petitot (12:64–68n).

102. In 1474. Neuss is located across the Rhine from Düsseldorf.

103. For example, Commynes (Petitot, 12:125). Scott repeats the same information at 139 [165].

104. In 1342 John IV of Montfort, who claimed the dukedom of Brittany, did homage to Edward III in return for that king's help against his rival, Charles of Blois.

105. His name was Jacques de Grassay (so Commynes, in Petitot, 12:133, where it is not clear that he was a Breton).

106. The dauphin; see 162 [194] below.

107. For example, Petitot (12:106n, 144n).

108. St. Quentin.

109. In Commynes's account Commynes himself is also behind the screen (Petitot, 12:141–43).

110. Commynes (Petitot 12:151).

111. The phrase was "un tres-mauvais paillard" [a lewd wretch] (Commynes, in Petitot, 12:160).

112. Commynes allots this role to himself (Petitot, 12:167).

113. Pierre d'Oriolle, lord of Loiré, chancellor 1472–1483.

114. On 20 February 1476.

115. Duclos, 2:205, who gives the name as Blomont, which we have adopted. Scott wrote Blemont.

116. The Muslim victory in Morocco, 1578.

117. The closest that Wraxall seems to have come to this statement is on 1:113.

118. In Commynes (Petitot, 12:242) the splendid donations were given to the messengers.

119. The statement has not been located in Commynes.

120. That is, the duchess of Burgundy.

121. Scott misinterprets Commynes (Petitot 12:391): "le corporal, surquoy chantoit monseigneur Sainct-Pierre" [the eucharistic cloth over which St. Peter chanted].

122. Francis of Paola.

123. So the *Universal History* (24:91), indicating John II, prince of Orange 1475–1502.

124. The battle took place on 28 July 1488.

125. Petitot (14:177) has the reverse order.

126. Godfrey of Pompadour, bishop 1486–1514.

127. On 6 December 1490.

128. In the Treaty of Barcelona, 19 January 1493.

129. On 17 November 1494.

130. Scott varies the phrase "without faith, without mercy, and without religion": *Universal History* (24:96), citing André de la Vigne and Dupleix.

131. On 31 December 1494.

132. That is, Naples.

133. Add "at night" (Petitot, 14:214, quoting the abbé Dubos, who also provides the subsequent reference to Machiavelli).

134. The words attributed to Francesco Guicciardini seem to be a paraphrase. Compare his *The History of Italy, from the Year 1490, to 1532,* translated by Austin Parke Goddard, 10 vols. (London: John Towers, 1753), 1:157: 'This manner of fighting was quite new to the *Italians,* and filled them with Amazement and Terror: They had been long accustomed to see their Wars carried on with Pomp and Magnificence; which gave their Armies rather an Appearance of Grandeur, than of Terror and Danger.'

135. See Psalm 127:1.

136. On 22 March 1495.

137. Petitot (14:231) quotes from the journal of André de la Vigne. Scott elaborates the quotation slightly.

138. The Knights Hospitalers, the Order of St. John of Jerusalem, defended Rhodes 1291–1522.

139. Petitot (14:234) includes Otranto in the list.

140. Estienne de Vers, or Etienne de Vesc (Petitot, 13:101, 14:234).

141. Charles left Naples on 25 May.

142. On 5 July (Petitot, 14:238); the battle was on the following day.

143. Quoted anonymously by Petitot, 14:240.

144. On 18 October 1495 (Petitot, 14:241).

145. Adapted from Petitot, 13:130.

146. Quoted by Wraxall (1:143), whom Scott is following here.

147. On 22 December 1498.

148. On 6 October 1499.

149. On 9 April 1500.

150. So Wraxall (1:151), but Petitot (15:39) maintains that he was not caged.

151. Concluded in 1501.

152. The correct date is uncertain, but is thought to be c. 1509.

153. Capitanata (*Universal History,* 28:256).

154. In April 1504.

155. Petitot (15:66) says that Gié enjoyed a comfortable retirement.

156. Brantôme says that she was "tresvertueuse, sage, honneste, bien dis-ante, et de fort gentil et subtil esprit" [very virtuous, wise, honest, well spoken, and of a noble and discerning mind] (*Vie des dames illustres françoises et étrangères,* "Discours premier: Anne de Bretagne, reine de France"), 5:3.

157. Three months.

158. Scott is here drawing on William Robertson, *The History of the Reign of the Emperor Charles V,* 3 vols. (London: W. Strachan, 1769), 2:33.

Index of Persons

Index of Places

This index includes the names of regions, towns, and rivers. It does not include countries, and it does not duplicate the territorial designations of nobles.